LEWIS
HAMILTON
The Biography

LEWIS
HAMILTON
The Biography

*Frank
Worrall*

JOHN BLAKE

Published by John Blake Publishing Ltd,
3 Bramber Court, 2 Bramber Road,
London W14 9PB
England

www.blake.co.uk

First published in hardback in 2007

ISBN 978 1 84454 543 8

British Library Cataloguing-in-Publication Data:

A catalogue record for this book is available from the British Library.

Design by www.envydesign.co.uk

Printed in Great Britain by William Clowes Ltd, Beccles, Suffolk

3 5 7 9 10 8 6 4

Papers used by John Blake Publishing are natural, recyclable products made from wood
grown in sustainable forests. The manufacturing processes conform to the
environmental regulations of the country of origin.

For my father, Frank snr

ACKNOWLEDGEMENTS

My sincere thanks to John Blake, Michelle Signore and Clive Hebard; Lewis and Anthony Hamilton; Davidson and Uelisia Hamilton; Ron Dennis; Angela; Carmen Lockhart; Chris Hockley, the *Sun*; Ash Hussain; Darren Simpson; Dominic Turnbull, Tim Smith, Derek Whitfield, Nic Petkovic, David Michael, Adrian Baker and Andy Bucklow; Alex Butler, the *Sunday Times*; Matthew Syed, *The Times*; Steve Myall; Colin Forshaw; Rory Ross; Gary Younge; Nigel Mansell; Damon Hill; Martin Blundell; Martin Whitmarsh; Emma Lloyd, the BBC; Sam Wostear and Natasha Harding, the *Sun*; Dave Morgan, the *Sun*; Frankie, Jude and Nat; Barbara, Bob, Gill, Lucy and Alex; Stephen; Suzanne and Michael and William; Lee Hassall; Roz Hoskinson; Pravina Patel; Steven Gordon, David and Niki Burgess; Roy Stone, Alan Tovey and Duncan Craig; Tom

Henderson-Smith; Mike O'Brien, the *New York Daily News*; Amir Khan; Adam Spurr; Andrew Benson, the BBC; James Corrigan and the *Independent*; Alan Henry, the *Guardian*; Richard Williams, the *Guardian*; Lee Clayton, the *Daily Mail*; Stuart Winter, the *Daily Express*; Oliver Owen, the *Observer*; Michael Duffy and Paul Henderson, the *Sunday Mirror*; Nick Britten and Tom Leonard, the *Daily Telegraph*; Lawrence Donegan; Robert Matthews, the First Post; Anna Kessel, the *Observer*; Ron Shillingford and Operation Black Vote; Michael Eboda, editor of the *New Nation*; Rodney Hinds, sports editor of the *Voice*.

I also wish to acknowledge the following sources which proved invaluable during the writing of this book:

Williams, Geoffrey, *McLaren: A Racing History*, Crowood Press, 1991

Young, Eoin S., *McLaren: The Man and His Racing Team*, Patrick Stephens, 1995

Younge, Gary, *No Place Like Home: A Black Briton's Journey Through The American South*, Picador, 1999

Leonard Downie jnr, executive editor, the *Washington Post*

movinghere.org.uk website

Grandprix.com website

www.f1complete.com

CONTENTS

INTRODUCTION

Seemingly from nowhere, Lewis Hamilton was suddenly everywhere in the autumn of 2007. The 22-year-old from Stevenage has quite rightly been fêted for giving us what has undoubtedly been the greatest ever debut season in Formula 1 – but his shadow falls just as large in other unexpected areas.

Similar to David Beckham at his peak, Lewis earns standing ovations wherever he goes. He is as much in demand at celebrity bashes as he is at sporting occasions. Indeed, when screen legend Sir Michael Caine picked up a lifetime achievement gong at the *GQ* Man of The Year awards at the beginning of September 2007, it was Lewis who the crowds had really come to see and Lewis who was the big prize for the autograph hunters as he was named Sportsman of the Year. The wonderboy known in motor racing circles as the Stevenage Rocket has made a massive impact not just in sport, but in numerous other areas of British life. Sure, after the retirement of Tim Henman and the flight of Beckham to the United States, Lewis' place as the nation's number one sporting hero is now assured, yet he means much more than that to so many people.

Remarkably for a racing driver, he has made his mark on those who previously would not have given the sport the time of day. Lewis' modesty, his unassuming nature and glowing star quality make him a pin-up for mums, daughters and petrrolheads alike. One thing is clear: this is no drab sportsman. Lewis Hamilton is an icon; a phenomenon who can only go one way – from strength to strength.

This is his story, and an unlikely one at that: from his ancestral roots in Grenada, through his modest start in life on a Hertfordshire council estate and years of dedicated training, steely determination and commitment to the sport he loves in the lower echelons of racing, right up to his glorious debut season in F1. This is the boy who saved F1, a sporting sensation who has established Brand Hamilton as a viable alternative to Brand Beckham. Lewis, it has been a pleasure and a deep privilege to chart your life and witness your greatly deserved success. Long may you reign.

Frank Worrall
London, October 2007

CHAPTER 1

THE REAL
SPECIAL ONE

First up, a humble apology to Lewis Hamilton from myself and Damon Hill: hands up, I was one of the majority who agreed with Damon in January 2007 when he said that Lewis would probably get half a season to prove himself. I also thought maybe he'd find it all too much and be shunted quietly aside, shell-shocked, perhaps back into GP2 until he was really ready for the big-time with a more experienced driver stepping up to bolster Fernando Alonso's assault on a surely inevitable third World Drivers' title. Sorry, Lewis…

It just goes to show you how wrong you can be. Even the great Damon Hill called it incorrectly, and if anybody should know about drivers, it's him. There again, the signs that Lewis was hardly thrown in without any prior training were certainly there. There was the 9-year apprenticeship with

McLaren, the usually infallible judgment of the McLaren team boss, 'Big Ron' Dennis, and Lewis' performances and results the previous season in GP2, when he roared to that Drivers' title. One thing's for certain: Lewis Hamilton is no one-season wonder. The boy is here for the long run. Finally, there's a British hero we can all praise to the ceilings in the secure knowledge that he's always going to be a contender and not just another in the traditional long line of national sporting figures who promise so much only invariably, inevitably, to deliver so little.

Lewis Hamilton is the real thing: he's the Real Special One, comfortably taking the mantle that was once the preserve of Chelsea's big-talking football manager, José Mourinho. The youngster who quickly became known as the 'Stevenage Rocket' on the Formula One circuit soon knocked down the record book skittles as he notched up one achievement after another. The first black Formula One driver, the first rookie to achieve more than two consecutive podium finishes, the first black driver to win a Formula One grand prix, only the second driver to win more than one race in his first Formula One Championship season since its inception, the first driver to achieve consecutive wins from pole position in a debut season, the youngest Briton ever to win a grand prix and the youngest driver to lead the World Championship... and, of course, the first rookie and black driver to be a serious contender for the title in his first season.

As the records show, this was a truly astonishing debut campaign, and one that is only the beginning of many achievements. By the end of the season, Lewis Hamilton was odds-on favourite to lift the coveted BBC Sports Personality of the Year award in December 2007 – in fact, five months earlier in July, bookmaker Paddy Power was refusing to take any more bets on Lewis. Thanks to him, this was also a season that changed the face of Formula One forever, bringing in a larger, more diverse audience. Motorsport was transformed from a rather dull spectator sport into one that had us all, and not just the traditional diehards, gripped with excitement as it hurtled towards a thrilling finale.

Lewis said he was taken aback by his overnight transformation from relative obscurity to worldwide fame. He said: 'It's amazing, I've received letters this week from young kids telling me that all of a sudden they want to be racing drivers. I remember when I was in the same position and now I just try to be a good role model. The fame has come all of a sudden and I'm starting to appreciate the importance of my actions – especially when young kids are looking up to me.'

Formula One expert and *Sun* contributor Chris Hockley was also stunned at the way Lewis had changed the demographic of the sport. He told me it had been an incredibly swift reversal of fortune: 'Yes, his rocket-ship rise to fame has bumped up British TV audiences for grands prix by a whopping 50 per cent. And enthusiasm for Formula One is soaring across the world – even in the stock-car domain of America, they were forced to sit up and take notice when this upstart rookie kid beat off the reigning World Champ to win the US Grand Prix.

'It's a fairytale, you see, enacted across the globe. And all of a sudden everyone, from barmaids to vicars, from paperboys to company directors, has an opinion on Lewis, and asks after his progress. No more is Formula One the preserve of anoraks, petrolheads and techno-junkies who salivate at the prospect of a 0.63 per cent increase in front aerofoil downforce eked out by Ferrari's engineers. Now wives, who decades ago gave up trying to understand their husbands' weird obsession with "watching cars go round in circles" are dallying at the telly and asking: "How's Lewis doing?" Surely it won't be long before traffic cops tell speeding motorists: "Who do you think you are, Lewis Hamilton?"'

Lewis Hamilton was certainly a breath of fresh air during 2007 – some would even argue that he was the very saviour of a Formula One that had lost its way and no longer had the ingredients to thrill. His story could be straight out of an Hollywood script, but its beauty is that it is real and the great thing about Lewis is that, in a sport littered with characters who are usually just the opposite, he is so down-to-earth. In a sport dominated by big money and star names, he is, after just one season, the biggest star of all by virtue of his extraordinary talent, skills and utter lack of pretension. Lewis is a very likeable, no-edges young man. He also seems to have appeared from nowhere, although of course there's a hinterland of many years of slog and determination behind the starry tale of the boy born to be King of Formula One.

I asked one of the McLaren crew if this was why they seemed so behind their new boy. On condition of anonymity, he told me that it was one of the reasons, at the same time giving a hint of the team's thinking on the feud between Lewis and his team-mate Fernando Alonso, ever-present in his debut campaign. 'The thing is there's been all this stuff in the press with Alonso saying we favour Lewis because he is British... but that's rubbish. We're all in this together; we're all McLaren. Big Ron [Ron Dennis] wouldn't have any of that kind of thing in his team – if anything, it was Lewis as the rookie who got the slower car.

'But Lewis is a special talent – he works harder than most seasoned drivers and he's got that touch of magic that most don't have. I watch him in the practice sessions and it reminds me of why I wanted to be part of Formula One in the first place. A lot of the time it seems that Alonso's raging, that he's flat out, trying to cling on to his title, but Lewis was often beating him hands down – looking as if he hasn't broken sweat, always gracious and the crowds love him.

'The thing is, Alonso's a great driver, a great champion and a nice guy underneath it all, but Lewis is something special. Forget all the stuff about being the first black guy and all that – he could be the best driver of his generation irrelevant of all that. It gives me the shivers to be around that to see it happening and, yes, even Big Ron's got a spring in his step these days.'

Indeed, he had. There were even suggestions that, similarly to football manager Sir Alex Ferguson, the rise of a young star within his ranks had re-energised the old man of motor racing and forced him to scrap any plans for premature retirement. When Lewis won his first grand prix, the big man had tears in his eyes, although he would later claim that it was the champagne that was making them sting! It is also true that Dennis' wife Lisa has a soft spot for Lewis. She seemed to cheer loudly when he eclipsed Alonso's lap time for pole in Montreal (1:15.707 against the Spaniard's 1:16.163).

And, in another poignant moment, I am told Big Ron rushed off to a private room after Lewis crashed during practice at the Nürburgring at the end of July 2007. A McLaren backroom boy told me that Ron could be seen holding his head in his hands. He had tears running down his face as Lewis was hurriedly taken away from the circuit to hospital with an oxygen mask over his face, a drip connected to his arm.

The son of a former British Rail worker, Lewis Hamilton is mixed-race. His father Anthony's family originates from the Caribbean island Grenada and he is the first driver of Afro-Caribbean origin to race in Formula One. Anthony scrimped and saved, at one point taking on three jobs to give his son a chance in the racing world. He has become a hugely supportive influence. Lewis later paid tribute to him, saying: 'I have been incredibly fortunate having my father's support, because I don't recall any of the other competitors [in the early karting days] coming from the same background as us – they all had wealthy parents. I know there will be setbacks during my career but I have the attitude that if it was easy to win championships everybody would be doing it.

'I guess that approach springs from the fact that, ever

since I was 9 or 10, I have spent every weekend at a race-track, so I wasn't hanging out and doing stuff with my friends. I was with Dad, and was best friends with him. If you want to fit in and mix with the grown-ups you have to learn at a faster pace than other youngsters. And although I suppose I missed out on doing the silly things at school, I quickly realised I can have all the toys I want if I keep working and winning at McLaren.'

It was that brand of tunnel vision determination that put Lewis on the road to success from the age of 6, when he first excelled at karting. That talent, in turn, was to earn him a life-changing spin-off: with his now legendary meeting with Ron Dennis, as a starry-eyed youngster in 1995. With no doubts about his own talent and no hesitation, he asked for his future employer's autograph while the other boys at the event nervously stood by. 'He looked me square in the face and informed me where he was going in his life,' Dennis recalls. 'Without breaking eye contact, he told me how he was going to go about his career. It impressed the hell out of me.'

Dennis started following his career and a few years later signed him up to McLaren's Driver Development Programme, investing £5million in him over nine years. During that time, Lewis learned the ropes under the master; his natural talent honed with one ultimate aim: to make him World Champion. He would become the best, but never got carried away as his success snowballed over the years. 'Confidence is often coupled with arrogance,' Dennis said, 'but there isn't an ounce of arrogance about Lewis.'

Lewis later admitted that was correct; he put his success down to hard work and his faith. From a devout Catholic family, he would say 'My faith is very important to me. I'm a true believer. I really believe that my talent is God-given and that I've been truly blessed. I guess every driver is talented but some of us are prepared to work harder to make the most of our talent. Some don't possess the talent of someone like Kimi Raikkonen [Ferrari's number one driver and, after Alonso, Lewis' main rival], but they've worked harder to become better than him. I don't know if I have more talent than Fernando Alonso, but I do know I've worked very hard.'

His impact on Formula One was both instant and remarkable, drawing comparisons to Tiger Woods and his success in the world of golf. Like Woods, Lewis was articulate, good-looking and possessed a similar talent. He had this to say on the Tiger comparisons: 'It's obviously nice to be compared to somebody like Tiger Woods but you just have to remember I'm not Tiger Woods, I'm Lewis Hamilton and this is Formula One – it is not golf. Whether or not it can have a similar impact, I'm not sure. It will be good for the sport if it can. I hope my purpose here serves its place.'

Top Formula One journalist Rory Ross maintained Lewis had made a much bigger impact worldwide than he or anyone else had imagined: 'His popularity has spread like morning sunlight. In Brazil, he has eclipsed Felipe Massa, the Brazilian Ferrari driver, especially in the Favelas, where they see in Hamilton one of their own doing well. In Spain, he is more popular than Fernando Alonso, much to the irritation of the Spanish champion.'

And Kevin Eason of *The Times* commented: 'Bernie Ecclestone is rubbing his hands with glee. Formula One's ringmaster was stuck with a show that was losing fans in increasing numbers. Schumacher was a serial winner, but outside Germany and Italy, home of the retired former champion's Ferrari team, he was a turn-off for millions. Hamilton is pure box office… and the interest is coming from all over the world, with camera crews from places as far afield as Colombia and Russia queuing for interviews.'

Unlike Tiger Woods, Lewis Hamilton has had to rise above a much more talented playing field of rivals. Woods' ascent came at a time of relative mediocrity in golf, but Lewis had to overcome drivers of immeasurable quality and defiance, opponents and team-mates alike. It was a measure of his ability and maturity that he had the double World Champion almost in tears, certainly tears of fury at times during the season.

The duel between the two was another reason why the masses tuned into Formula One in 2007; to see if the young lamb could stave off the aggressive tactics of his older, seemingly less wise team-mate. Alonso had transferred from Renault to McLaren, believing it to be a dream move: he had always wanted a car like the McLaren-Mercedes MP4-22. He believed it his destiny to show just how good he was in that new car, that he was a champion truly worthy of creating his own era after the dominant years of Michael Schumacher.

Alonso niggled at Lewis as the season – and Lewis' remarkable results – unfolded. He claimed he had never been 'completely comfortable' and added that he believed Lewis was unfairly favoured by McLaren because he was a British driver and they were a British team. He said: 'We knew all the support and help would go his way.' The Spaniard was playing the victim. Later he would try to unnerve Lewis and undermine his confidence by saying his team-mate was 'lucky'.

Ron Dennis has continually refuted Alonso's claims, saying: 'There is a healthy competition between the teams working on each car but I can categorically state that both drivers have equal equipment, support and opportunity to win.' It seemed he was determined not to appear biased towards his protégé in much the same way as the father who employs his son in the family firm and deliberately gives him a harder time than the rest of the staff to prove there is no favouritism. At times, it appeared Lewis was getting a rough deal from the man known in the pit lane as his surrogate father.

To an extent, you could see Big Ron's dilemma. He was paying the World Champion £10 million a year and Lewis a basic £340,000. In Alonso he had made a major investment and was therefore keen to see him happy. I don't doubt that in an ideal world Dennis always wanted to see Alonso champion again and Lewis second.

But the script did not run to type in the first nine races. After Silverstone Alonso was 12 points behind Lewis and constantly moaning to the Spanish press about how bad a deal he was getting. He had come to McLaren expecting to be treated as an incoming hero and had thought Lewis would be a willing No. 2 to his own garlanded, victorious warrior. He was a young pup to offer the occasional scrap of advice, a boy he could teach to drive almost as majestically as himself. But for a World Champion with five years' more experience of Formula One than Lewis, Alonso sometimes came across as incredibly insensitive, too earnest and grim. It was hard for the public to take a shine to him and he seemed to allow the young whippersnapper to get under his skin. He lost the all-important psychological battle with a boy on his debut campaign and his behaviour was at best immature, but at times ungracious and somewhat unbecoming of a double World Champion.

As the season went on, Lewis appeared perturbed and puzzled by the Spaniard's attitude towards him. In comparison, he was always friendly and approachable, and made time for the people who matter the most – the fans. One Formula One fan, Allison Foster, said 'The way that Hamilton treats his fans separates him from most other drivers. It's great to see a driver who acknowledges the fans' support, and I hope he keeps it up.' She gave the name of one British driver who was supposedly far less personable: 'In his home Grand Prix, with 20 people who just wanted an autograph, he refused to even acknowledge that the crowd was there and left without a word to these people who had been up since 3am to support him. I guess the difference is that Lewis remembers what is was like to be a fan, trying to give the driver you support a bit of encouragement.'

Already the legends of Formula One were queuing up to pay tribute to the young man who could be the greatest driver ever to grace the sport. When Lewis scored a sensational victory in the GP2 race at Silverstone in 2006, Sir Stirling Moss was impressed. His wife Suzy sought to drag him off to an important appointment, but Moss hesitated. 'Just a moment, darling. I must congratulate Lewis.' David Coulthard – who initially urged caution in believing Lewis could achieve much so early on – would then say: 'How good is Lewis? Undoubtedly, the guy is very special. I'd say he is a combination of Senna and Prost. We had Senna and Prost, Mansell and Piquet, then Michael Schumacher. We have now just entered the Lewis Hamilton era.' And three-times World Champion Niki Lauda admitted he had been 'stunned' by Lewis' achievements.

The legendary Formula One commentator Murray Walker also pitched in with his own tribute, saying Lewis would easily live up to the ever-growing hype: 'It's my considered opinion that Lewis Hamilton will go on to be one of the greatest drivers of all time...There aren't enough superlatives for what Lewis Hamilton is doing, race after race... It is unprecedented in the history of Formula One. I've been watching Formula One since it began and I have never seen anything like this in my life; it is quite incredible. It's more than feasible that he could win the Championship this year, which would be incredible.'

Inevitably, there were dissenters, and, perhaps not surprisingly, they were from those who had once been heroes themselves, men who now maybe looked on with a glint of disbelief at the young man who made it all seem so easy. Nigel Mansell was one of the first – although to be fair, later in the season he paid tribute to Lewis. The 1992 champion said, 'We had to win races and challenge for championships before we got the rewards. Now you seem to get the rewards before you achieve… They [McLaren] have been way overdue for success. Timing is everything. When a driver can arrive with a team and an engine coming right, it makes a difference. No disrespect to him… I think it was ordained, my story was a lot harder.'

Eddie Jordan was also a bit of a party pooper, questioning whether Lewis had the required ruthlessness to rule Formula One: 'Lewis is fortunate to have a well-grounded team with a structure he probably wouldn't have got anywhere else. But if he needed to do what Schumacher did to Villeneuve or Hill, would he do that? You need to do that to win. Winning is in the mind, and you have to do it at all costs. Anyone who tells you different is either lying or hasn't achieved what they're capable of. There has to be a steely aspect that we haven't seen, otherwise Hamilton will be swamped. He needs to have that arrogance otherwise he will not succeed. Does Alex Ferguson have it? Yes. Does José Mourinho? Yes. Winners generally are not nice people. They try to be, but they are immensely selfish, immensely arrogant and have a total belief in their own ability. Nothing else matters to them when they are at work.'

When told of the comments Lewis simply shrugged. He was that kind of guy: cool, easy-going, but hard-nosed when necessary. But Jordan's mention of the great Schumacher was interesting. His name and that of Ayrton Senna were to come up again and again when the talk turned to Lewis' style of driving, and Lewis himself would later admit they were his Formula One idols. He admired the German for his coolness and as a boy he had cried when he heard of Senna's tragic death.

Schumacher remained a sort of 'Phantom of The Opera' figure in Formula One during the 2007 season, his name and face haunting the pit lane even after his retirement – a result no doubt of his astonishing years of success and dominance. And it seemed to me that, yes, Lewis' driving had elements of both him and Senna: the cool, measured approach of Schuey mixed in with the heady aggression and risk-taking of the Brazilian. Psychologically; Lewis approached races with Schumacher's deadly intent, aware half the battle was indeed in the head, but he was also not averse to pushing himself to the limit and taking a calculated gamble in the style of Senna if that was required to secure victory.

I asked Formula One insider Darren Simpson about that assessment. He told me: 'Yes, Lewis is calm, consistent and hard-working but also has an edge about him. For example, the way he chooses to drive so close to the wall, allowing him to maintain incredible speed coming out of corners. And the kind of tactics that he used in the US Grand Prix against his team-mate, Alonso, when he used a centre-to-right and then slight right-back-to-centre defensive overtaking manoeuvre that just about avoided punishment.

'Driving so close to the wall is a breathtaking tactic while it pays off, but we must pray he will not one day end up in the wall like Senna. Only once was the wall a problem for Schumacher, when he broke his leg in 1999 at Silverstone. The rest of the time Schumacher's ruthless "win at any cost" mentality, which on occasions resulted in Formula One driving becoming a contact sport, was the problem. Ask Damon Hill!

'There is an inescapable fact: Hamilton drives like a karter. He loves the edge of the track and takes a late turn in to the hairpin and clips a late apex. In fact, his driving does reflect that of Schuey's early in the German's career. Lots of sharp turn-ins, lots of brake lock-ups.'

Asked which driver from the past he would like to face, Hamilton replied: 'The likes of Juan Manuel Fangio, Alain Prost, Ayrton Senna and Michael Schumacher because I have always wanted to race against him.' He then joked: 'The year I get here, he bales out – I don't know if I had something to do with that!'

By October 2007 there was talk that the German superstar might even come out of retirement – such was the pull and presence of the new kid on the block, who had so comfortably taken on his role as the superstar of Formula One. Lewis' world had changed dramatically: he was now indeed a superstar, but the normal lad remained underneath his elevation to celebrity status. His dad Anthony said: 'Lewis is a feet-on-the-ground kid and as long as I've got anything to do with him, he'll remain that way.' But after his son's first podium finish in Australia he said that he was not naïve enough to think Lewis could still lead a normal life, that he could walk down the street without being recognised. Anthony understood their lives would never be the same: 'The emotions are incredible – it's taken us 10 years to get here. I don't want Lewis to lose focus. We're ordinary people but, yes, we know things are going to change.'

There was another factor keeping Lewis' feet on the ground – the smiling face of his 15-year-old half-brother Nicolas, who suffers from cerebral palsy, but who, along with their father Anthony, accompanies Lewis to every race. The boys are extremely close and Lewis said 'Nicolas is my greatest inspiration. I look at him and that puts my life into perspective. He comes to all my races we are very close – I race for him. He's what keeps me up there and keeps me motivated. I always wanted a brother and I remember when my parents [as he always refers to his father and stepmother Linda] first told me they were going to have a boy, I was well excited. It's quite a cool feeling to watch someone grow up, to see the difficulties and troubles he's had, the experience he's had. To go through them with him and see how he pulls out of them. I think he's just an amazing lad and I really love to do things for him. For instance, we love to race remote-control cars. I bought him a new one, then I bought one as well so we can race together. I've been a couple of times to the site where they race them and I get hassled a little bit now.

'Nicolas loves a challenge and he's got a lot steeper challenges ahead of him. He is seven years younger than me and he's a great character. He might have cerebral palsy, but he definitely wants to do something special with his life

– maybe in the wheelchair Olympics or even something around Formula One. I wouldn't put it past him trying to be a commentator. We hang around together a lot and he gives me real perspective. He's the one member of my family who'll keep my feet on the ground, especially in Formula One.'

Keeping those feet on the ground includes regular routines such as a family Chinese takeaway after race meetings and chats with family and close friends in the build-up to races. Lewis says: 'I'm not into all those lucky charms or voodoo routines before a race. I just talk to my family and get into the dressing room, focus and get out there. I'm lucky to have my family and a few good friends supporting me. I can count my friends on one hand and I keep those closest to me. Trust needs to be earned.'

He would certainly need to stay grounded and take heed of what his family and friends told him. By the time of the US Grand Prix, world famous celebrities were queuing up to meet the boy who had taken racing by storm. Yet even the stars of showbiz who had so easily fallen under his spell – including the singer Beyoncé, who was said to have been 'very taken' with Lewis when they were introduced – spoke of his charm and endearing normality.

American rapper Pharrell Williams appeared trackside on several occasions to support Lewis. At the US Grand Prix, he said 'He's a good kid – he represents a lot of humility for all his achievements. It sounds like gibberish but that's what brought us here. It's not in the pocket, but in the heart and the mind.'

He was also being described as a trailblazer, one that would open up Formula One to children who previously would not have presumed they could enter the sport because of its predominantly rich, middle-class, white background. Ash Hussain of the *Mail on Sunday* newspaper, himself a man who had battled to break down barriers in journalism to reach the top, believed Lewis would indeed have a beneficial effect. Himself a Formula One fanatic, Ash told me: 'I strongly believe Lewis will inspire kids from ethnic backgrounds into motor racing. I think what he has already achieved in the last few months has already encouraged a whole generation of young ethnic drivers to compete in motor racing. Certainly I have met many thinking that way, which is in itself a revolutionary change from the past.'

He also admires the way Lewis has no desire to distance himself from the fans and his determination not to play the big star. He believes this endears him to the youth of today, and encourages them to be part of its tomorrows: 'He's just a great guy, absolutely fantastic. At the Goodwood Festival of Speed last summer, for instance, he came out and signed autographs in driving rain. He could have gone off home but he spent the whole day there. That is the difference between him and other drivers – he is such a terrific ambassador for the sport, and the ethnic minorities.

'In many ways, he reminds me of Amir Khan and how he has brought boxing into the young Asian community. They are both decent, down-to-earth young guys despite their talents and fame. I am proud of Lewis and Amir and what they have achieved, and the great things they will no doubt achieve in the future. They are both true heroes and great role models.'

A role model and a worldwide star... this was certainly a long way from where it all began, back in Stevenage in 1985 when Lewis was born, and even humbler surroundings before that when his paternal grandfather emigrated from Grenada to England. Years of hard work, from his first outings in karts at the age of 6 through his apprenticeship with McLaren and F3 and GP2, years of dedication had now finally paid off.

So how exactly did Lewis Hamilton become the biggest name in Formula One? Let's first examine the origins of the boy who was to become an idol for a whole new generation, one who would resurrect an ailing Formula One and, at the same time, be hailed its new king...

CHAPTER 2

ROOTS, ROCK, REGGAE

The pretty Caribbean island of Grenada has more spices per square mile than any other in the region and is hence known as The Spice Isle. Indeed, sales of cinnamon, cloves, ginger, mace and, in particular, nutmeg – 20 per cent of the world's supply of nutmeg – are vital exports and, along with tourism, play a key role in the nation's economy.

Now the island is fast becoming as famous for its links to Lewis Hamilton – and his larger-than-life granddad, Davidson Hamilton. Take the tour bus to Grand Roy, time it right – either just before secondary school starts, or just after it finishes for the day – and you can't miss him. He's the guy driving the kids to and from school in the shiny new minibus, the one who will automatically give you a big wave of the hand and a beaming smile if you catch his eye. Failing that, just ask where Lewis Hamilton's grandfather lives and you'll immediately be pointed in the right direction. His grandson's overnight fame has turned Davidson Augustin Hamilton into a celebrity and the old guy just loves it.

A sprightly 77-year-old, he is a man who likes to keep active. 'Busy brain and busy body makes for a longer life,' he says. 'I like to be doing things – I'm not one for sitting around getting old.' Likeable and popular, Davidson is a trusted figure in his local community and that's why, despite his advancing years, they allow him to drive the kids to and from school in his pride-and-joy minibus.

On the back window is a sign that proclaims the belief and moral dictum by which this proud man has lived his life: To God Be Glory. It's a slogan from which his grandson Lewis also operates and he is the first to admit that he believes the good lord is behind his astonishing feats.

The sign also provides a link with his son – and Lewis' father – Anthony. It was Anthony who insisted on upgrading the battered old Mitsubishi his dad used to drive around the island, replacing it with the new £20,000 minibus. That way, he also provided a small income for Davidson, who had previously refused gifts for gifts' sake. When Anthony explained the motive behind the minibus – that it would provide the old man with a few pounds to help out in his retirement years and would also be safer to ferry around the kids – Davidson finally accepted his kind offer.

Of course that's after checking first with his wife Uelisia. He explained what Anthony had told him and how the money would come in handy, little though it was (with him charging just 20p a trip the venture would not make them millionaires), and she had finally given her blessing.

A matron at a nearby retirement home, Uelisia is also a person of high morals and a strong belief 'in living the right way – God's way'. She is a member of the Seventh-day Adventist church in Grenada – in fact, she is on the executive committee of the Grenadian Conference, the organising body for the island's Adventists set up in 1983. Her role within the organisation perhaps goes some way to explaining the work ethic so common in the family as a whole. The Seventh-day Adventists is an evangelical movement which believes strongly in passing on the message via missionaries and recognises the Sabbath as Saturday rather than Sunday.

A spokesman for the movement said: 'The emphasis in our church is on making the most of the gifts that God gives us. We believe in clean healthy living, the importance of the family, hard work and developing our God-given talents for the benefit of our families and the wider community. We believe that the Sabbath is a time to come together as families and as a community to pray together and eat together, but we also believe that we should try to live up to our ideals every day, not just on the Sabbath.'

Lewis' grandparents enjoy a quiet life and Davidson admits he 'gets a great deal of joy and satisfaction' at putting something back into the community in which they live by taking the kids on their daily 15-minute journey from Grand Roy to the nearby St John's Christian Secondary School.

It's all a far cry from the hedonistic world of Formula One, but Davidson says he is proud of his grandson and the impact he has had on motor racing. Indeed, he admits he would not have minded being a racer himself – and gave a hint that racing at high speeds has not just arrived with Lewis... that it has run in the family for generations. He said, 'I used to be a bit of a speed king myself in my younger days! When I was 18 I passed my test and bought a motorbike. I used to tear up and down the roads but I never had an accident. People would say: "Watch out, Davidson's about."' Davidson then got an Austin A40 car and got stopped for speeding – at 40mph in a 30mph limit. 'That was when I learnt my lesson and decided to take things a little slower. Now I just drive the minibus, but I'm a slowcoach now – I only do 15mph!'

To the locals he will always be known as 'Uncle Dave' in reverence to his kindness and warmth. I am told he is renowned for always having the time for people, and if he hasn't got the time, he invariably makes it later. Elvis Glean, a court bailiff and friend, told the *Daily Telegraph*: 'Uncle Dave's' speeding was legendary when he was younger among the 600 residents of Grand Roy. He once rode from Grand Roy to the police station in Gouyave – the next town along the coast, about three miles away – in not much more than five minutes. I think he was riding one of those huge BSA bikes. He rode like the wind and we sometimes worried he would end up dead, but I don't think he even ever had an accident: he is a true survivor.'

Proud Davidson joined up with his famous grandson at Silverstone in July 2007 to watch him in a Formula One grand prix for the first time. It was several years since he had seen him in a race. Lewis was delighted that he had been able to fly over for 'the big one', saying: 'Grandad was at a karting race years and years ago, but he's never been to a grand prix. He's coming over to meet the family, and it's just convenient it is at the same time as this grand prix.

'But a lot of my family have not seen a grand prix – and I've a very big family. You can't always get passes so I'm sure it will take quite a few years for them all to come and see me. I'm just glad Granddad has been able to make it now – it's great to see him again.'

Davidson watched from the paddock with a big smile as his grandson finished third and returned to Grenada and his daily routine the following week a happy man. He admitted the occasion had brought a tear to his eyes. 'He is such a fine young man and a very talented driver,' he said. 'I pray that his good fortune continues and he becomes World Champion. Lewis may live far away from us in England, but we are a close-knit family. He is a very nice young man, who is respectful and thoughtful when it comes to the welfare of others as well as being a competitor.

Talking to the *Sunday Mirror*, Davidson was the picture of a doting grandfather: 'He is a regular guy. He loves to joke, listen to reggae music and go to the beach when he comes here on holiday and he sometimes joins us at church. His father has been so careful about his upbringing that the money won't change him. He will remain kind-hearted and down-to-earth because that is how we are in this family.'

When Davidson was 25, people were more interested in

getting off the island – which is the second-smallest independent country in the Western Hemisphere (after Saint Kitts and Nevis) – than visiting it. He was part of the 1955 exodus to Britain, one of many hoping for a new and better life than the one back home, where poverty and natural disaster were rife. It would be almost another 25 years before he returned to his homeland and his roots.

He decided to make the move after struggling to earn a living in Grenada. In 1955, British Transport were actively encouraging immigrants from the Caribbean. Bosses even visited some of the islands to discuss with interested locals what was on offer in the UK. Davidson was one of those who were keen to try their luck elsewhere. For him, the last straw had been the devastation caused in the year of his departure by Hurricane Janet. Being on the southern edge of the hurricane belt, Grenada has suffered only three hurricanes in the last 60 years. But Hurricane Janet passed over the island in September 1955 with winds of 115 mph, causing severe damage.

While it spelled the end for Davidson, his brother Fleet stayed on in Grenada and became a major success. Nigel Forrester, a teacher in Grenada and Lewis' second cousin, said that Davidson's brother saw an opportunity to thrive after the hurricane destroyed most of the island's nutmeg trees: 'My grandfather – Davidson's brother – replanted, seizing the opportunity to buy the land from people who wanted to sell. He did very well out of it. There's a determination and perseverance in the Hamilton family. They're always trying get to a higher level.'

But Davidson remained convinced that that 'higher level' would not come in Grenada. At about 15 per cent, the island had one of the highest unemployment rates in the Caribbean. Unemployment was particularly high among young people so he clambered aboard the ship that would take him to England, setting in motion a whole train of events.

The immigrants were among the second wave from the Caribbean islands in the twentieth century. The first arrived after the beginning of World War I, working in the war industries and the Merchant Navy. They established themselves in the seaports and major cities and initially they were welcomed as they contributed to the war effort. But as men returned home from the war and the country plunged into depression, resentment grew because the immigrants were seen to be taking 'native' jobs. Ultimately, this sparked off race riots in the years immediately following the war. Despite the trouble, many immigrants considered themselves British nationals and refused to return home. Together they formed the nucleus of Caribbean communities in cities such as Cardiff, Liverpool and London.

The final phase of settlement, which would include Davidson Hamilton, happened after World War II. By that time Britain's labour market was depleted and a quarter of a million Caribbeans settled permanently in Britain between 1955 and 1962. After alighting from boat trains at London stations such as Paddington, Victoria and Waterloo, many dispersed to industrial centres like Liverpool, Manchester

27

and Birmingham. The majority, however, stayed in London – Davidson among them. He settled in west London and worked for the London Underground, initially laying track.

But the new immigrants were not welcomed with open arms by many Britons. Rather than being seen as essential workers – as they had been at the start of World War I – the fresh intake were viewed with suspicion and suggestions that they would be a social problem. It was feared they might take jobs from the locals and put pressure on housing, and that caused resentment within local communities which was later to be fired up by the likes of right-wing agitator Oswald Mosley. Davidson told a family friend: 'It was not the easiest of times. I had just arrived in a new country and some people would point at us newcomers aggressively on the street and shout obscenities. Of course, there were others who were nice to us, but it was difficult to feel at ease.'

A year after his arrival, the tense atmosphere led to the British Caribbean Welfare Service (BCWS) being established to look those who were finding it difficult to integrate. Housing was in short supply as wartime bombing had decimated stock and Davidson and others were met with signs and notices in windows stating 'No Blacks' and 'No Coloureds'. Many migrants ended up in areas where compatriots and friends were already settled and housing was more available. Trinidadians tended to go to Notting Hill and Davidson, who had made friends with some of them on the boat over, also ended up in west London. Historically, Grenadians had friends from Trinidad, their closest neighbour in the Caribbean, and so it was perhaps inevitable that he would follow the trail already mapped out in London.

The west of the capital did not provide an immediate vision of heaven, for some landlords exploited the housing shortage by expelling long-term residents and packing their properties with migrants paying exorbitant rents. Despite all this, Davidson would eventually settle in the area in a small, cramped flat with his sweetheart, Agnes Mitchell, at 12a Broughton Road, Fulham. The couple were married by Catholic priest Maurice Beckett at the nearby Church of Our Lady in Stephendale Road on 26 May 1956. Davidson was 25 and now working as a railway guard, his bride was 23 and unemployed. A couple of years later, they moved a few miles further west to 82 Avenue Road in Acton, and their son Anthony Carl Arthur was born on 31 May 1960 in Hammersmith Hospital.

Anthony had a tough childhood in west London, with his father constantly worried his boy would end up with the wrong crowd. By the time Davidson returned to Grenada in the late seventies, Anthony had moved out to Stevenage, 30 miles north of the capital, with a then population of around 40,000. In 2007 Lewis said Anthony had 'had it tough' because his mother (Agnes) died when Anthony was young. But the family did not wish to talk further about how her death affected the family.

Stevenage seemed an unusual choice of location for a young black man – it was a predominantly white town and had hardly been a magnet for ethnic minorities in previous years. Stevenage became the first of the post-war new towns specifically built to take the overspill from London. By 1961 the UK census showed that a total of 172,877 people moved to Britain from the Caribbean in the previous decade. Antagonism and racism against the newcomers remained rife for another two decades, however, with reports of petty yet persistent incidents well into the mid-1980s.

The situation had calmed down slightly when Anthony Hamilton settled in Stevenage after marrying young, but it was still a testing time for the boy with Grenadian ancestry – particularly when he married a white girl, Carmen Larbalestier, who was five years his senior – at the start of the eighties.

A couple of excellent newspaper articles highlighted the 'loneliness' and 'resentment' blacks like Anthony Hamilton had to overcome when settling in overspill towns such as Stevenage. The influential American journalist Leonard Downie jnr of the *Washington Post* travelled to Britain to report on the country's new towns and how they compared with America. He was keen to learn whether the urban problems experienced in the States were mirrored in Britain. While accepting that the new towns had indeed relieved the pressure on housing, his findings occasionally made grim reading, revealing how immigrants had found 'proper jobs' difficult to come by and how they suffered in 'ghetto-like' conditions.

He wrote: 'The British have successfully used some of their new towns to relieve overcrowded conditions in working-class neighborhoods of the big cities and provide many of their residents with better homes. Planners arrange for the combined transfer of willing businesses and their employees from London to Harlow or Stevenage, for instance... In some places the move of people and industry to the new town was so well co-ordinated that as high as 85 percent of the new town residents – in Harlow, for instance – worked at jobs inside the new town itself and continue to enjoy some of the shared interests and friendships of the old big city neighborhoods from which they came. However, this very success in matching workers and jobs has made many of Britain's new towns single-class communities. To move into most of them, a prospective resident must be assured a job by one of the new town's largely technological or clerical employers; thus the population of each project is disproportionately dominated by white collar and skilled workers. There are few non-skilled workers, non-whites or immigrants of any kind, low-income families, or, at the other end of the spectrum, upper income people. Although this is not particularly disturbing to the British, who readily segregate themselves by social and economic class, the sameness of everyone and everything in each new town bores and disconcerts the visitor, reminding him too much of the economic stratification, and resulting sterility, of too many American suburbs.

'The lack of opportunities for unskilled and lower income workers does leave real problems back in the central cities. In London, for example, from where skilled, middle income, white workers were attracted to new towns like Harlow and Stevenage, mostly low income and jobless

Pakistani, Indian and black immigrants remain today, many trapped in ever worsening, ghetto-like conditions. In this respect, just like U.S. suburbs and new town projects, the British new towns have exacerbated rather than eased a critical urban problem' wrote Downie jnr.

Anthony Davidson was one of those lower income workers, surviving on the meagre wages he earned with British Rail. It was a depressing scenario, but here was a man with a lion's heart and a determination to make something of his life. Just as his father had taken a huge gamble in leaving Grenada for Britain, he too was convinced his destiny lay in another field. Little did he know it would involve nurturing and supporting a brilliant son with a God-given talent.

Anthony would tell friends: 'No, it was not easy. At first it seemed as if I had moved from one nightmare [London] to another. But there was no way I was going to run away – I had had enough, I wanted some stability.' This was to eventually come when Lewis was born in 1985.

In 1999 another fine journalist, Gary Younge, whose hometown is Stevenage and who writes for the *Guardian*, published an outstanding book about his travels through the American south. This also provides insight into the sort of problems that Anthony, and later Lewis, would have had to overcome.

Younge wrote: 'There were three types of reactions a black family could expect in a place like Stevenage. There were those who welcomed us. There were those who tolerated us. And there were those who positively despised us... The despisers, like the Norrises, a scrawny white family who used to stand at the top of the road and shout "Woggy, woggy" at us. Once, when the Norrises had gone too far, she [mum] called the police. The policeman said he wouldn't ask them to stop: "I'm afraid that you are an ethnic minority in this area and you are going to have to put up with that kind of thing from time to time," he said.'

It was powerful stuff. Anthony himself refused to be intimidated and he stood his ground, as did Lewis in later years. Both made it clear to anyone who tried to bully or taunt them that they were there to stay. Lewis even took up karate to look after himself better. First Davidson and then his son Anthony showed a determination and staunch belief that they should be allowed to live and bring up a family in England. It was another example of that fierce Hamilton pride in action. Rooted in strong Catholic faith, throughout time the Hamiltons would always stand their ground and stand up for what they believed in. Yes, the die had been cast for the Hamilton generation and the Lewis Hamilton era. Even now, Stevenage – which one local described to me as 'slightly soulless and nondescript' – only has a 1 per cent black element to its 80,000 population. But, as Gary Younge wrote in the *Guardian* in June 2007, 'Right now, black Stevenage represents 100 per cent of the town's most famous sons.' Yes, that's Lewis Hamilton – and Ashley Young, the promising England football international, who was in the same secondary school class as the Formula One whizzkid. And there was also Albert Campbell, who became the town's first black mayor in 1987.

The hardships his grandfather went through in coming to Britain and staying there in such racially prejudiced times are indelibly carved on the heart of Lewis Hamilton: he knows he owes much to the courage of Davidson Hamilton. He, along with his father Anthony, is the rock on which he has built his success... a rock that originated in the Caribbean.

Nowadays, when Lewis goes to visit his relatives in Grand Roy, he can share a laugh, enjoy some local cuisine cooked up by Uelisia and relax with a cool drink. He also likes listening to some of Bob Marley's tunes on his iPod, as well as some by the reggae legend's sons Ziggy and Damian on the beach. But he will never forget what his family went through to ensure that he and his father had a good start in life; one they would never have enjoyed, had Davidson not taken a gamble by moving to England to start a new life.

Success and fame have their consolations, for in addition to the new minibus Davidson drives around Grand Roy, the Grenadian government has now placed on record its personal pride in its most famous son. After Lewis' fabulous debut grand prix victory in Montreal on 19 June 2007, Edwin Frank, of The Grenada Board of Tourism and the Ministry of Tourism, said: 'We would like to congratulate Mr Lewis Hamilton for the success that he has been achieving as a participant in his first season in Formula One racing. The GBT notes that as a young British driver of Grenadian roots (his grandfather is from Concord in St John), he has placed among the top three in all of the six races that he has participated in for the season. As a member of the McLaren Mercedes team, he has shown and demonstrated to the Formula One racing fraternity that he could indeed become the next big sensation of the sport.

'His recent victory in his first grand prix race in Montreal on Sunday 10 June 2007 has made Grenadians very proud. His achievement has served as an inspiration to the young people of Grenada, who consider him a genuine living example of what hard work and determination can bring to focused individuals.

'The Government and people of Grenada join in applauding his achievements and celebrate the fact that through his excellent performance, people around the world have learnt of his Grenadian ancestry. He is a demonstration of the Grenadian spirit.'

And indeed he is... Let's move on now to fill in some more gaps by taking a look at Lewis' early years.

CHAPTER 3

BOY RACER

Even in the eighties in some quarters, the sight of a black man with a white woman was still met with raised eyebrows by a prejudiced society, which can hardly have helped the union of Anthony Hamilton and Carmen Larbalestier. To be fair, London was much more advanced and liberal in its views, perhaps inevitably given the large black population in districts such as Brixton and Notting Hill.

It was all the more difficult to understand, therefore, why Anthony and Carmen would decide not to base their lives in the capital, instead plumbing for Stevenage, a town which, as we have already noted, even in 2007 has only a small black population. Yet the couple settled in an end-of-terrace at 57 Peartree Way on the Shephall council estate. The couple had married at Stevenage's St Hilda's Catholic

Church on 5 May 1979 when Anthony was 18 and Carmen 23. Anthony was still working for the railways and money was tight; Carmen, who was born miles away in Birmingham and whose father Maurice was a draughtsman, had been working on an assembly line in a factory. It was into this humble, struggling background that Lewis Carl Davidson Hamilton was born on 7 January 1985 in Stevenage's Lister Hospital. That Christmas before the boy's birth had not been easy – a shortage of money, a poorly Carmen and a stressed Anthony made sure of that. But that cold winter's day the couple put their problems aside as they stared at their beautiful son. They had waited long enough to bring him into the world, on some occasions wondering if they were to be denied the child they so wanted. Carmen admitted: 'Lewis is very special for me because we tried for a long time to have him. I didn't think he was ever going to come along.' He was her third child – Lewis has two older half-sisters, Nicola and Samantha.

It was Anthony's idea to name their precious son after US Olympic gold medal winning athlete Carl Lewis. He was something of a hero to him following his remarkable showing at the previous summer's Olympic Games in Los Angeles. Carl Lewis had won an amazing four gold medals – in the 100 metres, the 200 metres, the long jump and the 4 x 100 metres relay. Anthony also added the name Davidson at the last minute, in tribute to his own father. Yet Carmen would also have a say, insisting that her newborn son's Christian names should be turned around so that he was called Lewis Carl. It was the last time the word reverse would be used when talking about Lewis Carl Hamilton – from now on, it was always fast forward...

Carmen admitted to the *Daily Express* that from the very start her son was a motor racing natural: 'Lewis had a love for speed as soon as he cut his first teeth. On his first birthday, he was given a toy steering wheel for his baby buggy. It was a big plastic one you could stick on the buggy and drive it along. He's had his hands on a steering wheel since that day.'

But the couple's joy was short-lived. Within months it was clear their marriage no longer worked and when Lewis was 2, Anthony and Carmen separated. Anthony moved out of the house in Peartree Way and Carmen's new boyfriend, Raymond Lockhart, moved in. Carmen would later wed Raymond and they remain happily married to this day. Back then, Lewis was happy enough to be living with his mother and the man who had become his stepfather. He was a good boy, who spent much of his time reading and playing football on the streets of the council estate with his friends. Easy to get on with and always with a smile on his face, he was well liked in Shephall.

His first school was just 200 yards from home and he fitted in easily at the Peartree Infants School despite the fact that he was the only black boy in his class. The school's deputy head, Carol Hopkins, confirmed he was a popular boy, but said that at that time he had not yet shown any of the competitiveness that would eventually mark him out as a possible racing great: 'I remember him for his bright, smiley face and lovely manners. He enjoyed school to the full, certainly, but in those early years you would not have seen him as a competitive little chap, just very happy. Bright little button, but normal, very normal.'

Naturally enough, he is now a hero at the school. The young pupils set up their own 'Lewis Hamilton Corner' during the 2007 season, where they put up his cuttings and marked off his race wins. 'He is somebody for them to look up to,' says Carol Hopkins. 'He is their hero.'

By the age of 5 Lewis had already shown an interest in cars – Carmen said he spent hours playing with the array of toy cars littered across his bedroom floor and would, inevitably, end up racing them against each other with lavish victory ceremonies for the winners. He also began driving on Dodgems at amusement arcades, and it was then that his father Anthony – now his manager – recognised the remarkable hand-eye coordination his son possessed.

At 6 it was not only his mother who had noted his love of cars: friends and neighbours shook their heads and smiled as he played excitedly in the street with the radio-controlled car he got for Christmas while other boys kicked their footballs about. His first driving victory came, also aged 6, when he raced his radio-controlled car against other youngsters in a competition on the children's TV show *Blue Peter*.

Anthony, by now a motor racing fanatic, would visit regularly and also noted his son's fascination with everything automotive. By the time Lewis progressed to junior school, he decided to take his ever-growing hobby a step further: on some of his visits he would go karting with him.

Lewis had his first drive in a go-kart while on a childhood holiday in Spain. Shortly afterwards, Anthony managed to scrape together £1,000 to buy him his own. Carmen says: 'When his dad bought him a go-kart for Christmas before his eighth birthday, I thought, good grief! He bought him all the kit – the suit, helmet – and popped him in it. Down the street, and he was off. He went from model cars to go-karts, to Formula One.'

She said that by the age of 8 Lewis had started to get interested in Formula One. His hero was Ayrton Senna, who would die tragically in 1994 when his young fan was 9. Carmen, now says: 'He was kart-racing the weekend Ayrton Senna died. The news came through and he was really upset, bless him, but Senna's death didn't sway him. I knew early on that his passion was so big that nothing would stop him.'

Lewis remembers that weekend and admits the death of Senna had a major impact on him: 'Yes, I was 9 when Ayrton Senna died, and he was my hero. I remember racing that weekend in Hoddesdon. My dad had a small Vauxhall Cavalier and a trailer at the back. We'd sit in the Cavalier and wait for my turn to race. And that day I was told Senna had just died. It hit me hard, but I never liked to show emotion in front of my dad. So I went behind the trailer and cried. That was the turning point of my life: because when you're so young, you believe people like Senna are invincible. And then you realise that they're also mortal. It made me understand I need to make the most of my talent.'

When Lewis was 10, his life and that of his father

changed forever after Anthony took him to the Rye House kart track, a few miles south of Stevenage. Lewis had already lapped his father when they raced in karts at other circuits and now he told him that he wanted to be a professional racer. Tony Delahunty was at Rye House on the same day with his son, Andrew, who was a couple of years older than Lewis. Delahunty, a commentator on karting for British Eurosport, said: 'Anthony told me that before this Lewis had been an expert in model-car racing – you know, that remote control stuff – and that Lewis had been winning everything, but that most of the people he was competing against were adults. So they were looking for something more apt for a youngster.' Delahunty was mighty impressed by the young Lewis – so much so, in fact, that within a year, 'I was doing press releases for him.'

Anthony too knew his son meant business and *was* the business. He himself was a strong, determined man, who had made advances in his own life since splitting from Carmen eight years previously, becoming computer savvy and moving up to the job of IT manager. Despite this, he now decided to take a gamble, putting everything he earned on his son's future. He took redundancy from his job so that he could be with Lewis as he advanced, taking on casual work, and at one stage he was doing three jobs at a time to make ends meet, including putting up estate agents' signs. According to Lewis: 'I don't think he ever went into debt but he had quite a few jobs on the go. He had his main job, but I also remember him putting up "For Sale" signs – he'd get £15 a sign.'

This was quite a remarkable show of faith and commitment. Anthony Hamilton was such a winner that eventually the computer firm he set up while dedicating his life to his son also become big-time, employing 20 staff in 2007, but the 47-year-old stressed that his first loyalty remained with his son, who he now manages. Back then, he would also drive Lewis to races all over the country and overseas as part of his duties.

Anthony explained he had done a deal with Lewis over their new commitment. He would only keep to his side if Lewis continued to try his best to achieve academic success at school and dedicated himself to racing: 'From the start I also tried to ensure that Lewis looked after himself and was never in any danger of going off the rails with too much partying and late nights, all the temptations that young kids like to get up to. To be frank, I think that honesty and trust played a big, big role in our relationship as Lewis was climbing up the ladder.

'I think we've always tried to bring Lewis up to do things right and to understand that positive consequences flow from taking an honest approach to things, whether we were talking about his kart racing or his school work. I told him that if he had any doubts then he shouldn't do it. But I was also confident that if he took my advice and listened to what I was telling him, then a few years down the road it would all work out for him the way he wanted.

'I suppose you could say it was tempting to apply the carrot-and-stick approach to Lewis for getting behind with his school work by saying "Right, you're not going to the next race", but in truth Lewis was too good to be penalised in such a way.'

The decision to push Lewis onwards also meant a change of living arrangements. After eight years with his mother, the 10-year-old now moved in with Anthony, his stepmother, Linda, and stepbrother, Nicolas. Carmen and stepfather Raymond also opted for a change of direction, announcing they were to marry and had chosen to settle down in London.

Understandably, Carmen was sad that she would now be apart from the boy she had loved and nurtured, but she still felt it was for the best given that Anthony would do anything within his power to ensure their son reached the very top. Looking back on the initial split from Anthony when Lewis was 2, she said 'It didn't damage Lewis. He is probably better for it than if we had stuck together in an unhappy marriage. Tony wanted to be somebody and he has achieved that. I wanted the quiet life and that put a barrier between us. I couldn't see myself in that busy, hectic lifestyle, but I didn't stop him making sure Lewis got what he wanted.'

And speaking of the time when Lewis left her at the age of 10 she also said, with typical honesty and pride, paying her former husband considerable compliments: 'It was heart-breaking... but I had to let him go and live with his dad for him to be a star. His dad has worked very hard to raise the money for Lewis' career. Without his dad's constant, constant work, he would not have been able to continue, as it's a very expensive sport. It takes millions and a lot of kids have millionaire parents. The parents can't understand quite why their sons are not winning when Lewis is. It's not all about money, it's about talent.'

There have been suggestions Carmen has not been happy at being portrayed in the press as someone Lewis left behind, and she herself has publicly refuted further suggestions that she feels as if 'she has missed the boat' as her son's star rises inexorably upwards. She now lives in a terraced house in Letchworth Garden City, Hertfordshire with her husband Raymond. They bought the property in June 2006 for £197,000. The area is described as one of 'Blue collar enterprise – White van culture' by Experian's neighbourhood classification system, Mosaic.

Lewis, Anthony, Linda and his brother Nicolas, meanwhile, reside in a £1 million-plus detached mansion in Tewin Wood, Hertfordshire. Lewis also has his own luxury £250,000 apartment, near the McLaren HQ in Woking, Surrey. The extent of Anthony's own success with his computer firm is shown by the fact that he paid a cool £630,000 for the house back in March 2001, way before Lewis' success in Formula One. The area is deemed highly sought after and populated by corporate chieftains, usually very wealthy people who have rewarding careers rather than jobs, and who own expensive cars and indulge in the most exotic leisure pursuits.

At the start of the Formula One season in 2007 it was revealed that Carmen Lockhart had entered a TV competition to win a trip to Sydney to see Lewis make his debut in the Australian Grand Prix in Melbourne. The implication being, of course, that she could not afford the trip and that her son had not invited her to Oz, nor offered to pay for her.

A family friend tried to put the whole situation into perspective for me with these words: 'When Lewis went to live with his dad at 10, Carmen really missed him but knew she couldn't have the same input into his karting career as Tony. It has been hard, but both sides have worked hard to maintain family ties. However, there are times Carmen feels left out and, I think, a little jealous – [and] who wouldn't? – of his closeness with Tony.

'It's only natural and like any mum in this type of situation she is a bit wary of the press and their implying she wasn't there for him because he lived with his dad. The truth is in fact it was because she loved him she let him go to become the champion he is. It was actually an act of true selflessness.'

To me, this seems a fair take on the situation and I am assured by others who know the family that it is along the right lines. Both Carmen and Anthony were in attendance when Lewis signed his Formula One contract with McLaren at a London nightclub. And, as the 2007 Formula One season progressed, his parents were hardly at loggerheads, but seemed to be good friends, attending races together. There was even talk of them going away on holiday with their new partners. Lewis himself also admitted he loved it when he and Carmen went on their regular ten-pin bowling trips – they would go at least once a month and 'have great fun, even though she usually beats me!'

Carmen confirmed everything had settled down and that she now enjoyed quality time with Lewis: 'I am his biggest fan. I am so proud of him – how could I not be proud of him? Lewis has got such a magnetism about him. His personality is outstanding and he just makes people get on. Everyone in racing thinks we're an unusual bunch. They're quite amazed when they see us come down the pit lane.

'Lewis now has his racing life with his dad and his normal life when he comes over to my house. Everything Lewis has got, he's worked really hard for. He wasn't born with a silver spoon in his mouth. Lewis has got everything – he has the personality, the looks, the physique and charisma to become a massive, absolutely massive star. I'd like people to see beyond the colour. The fact that he's the first black driver is going to be the cherry on the cake.'

Like any concerned mother, she admits she keeps a wary eye out for gold-digging women near her boy. She had thought he would stick with his college sweetheart Jodia Ma, 21, saying: 'She is the kind of girl that will help him keep his feet on the ground. She is not after the high life. I think he'd rather hang on to somebody he knows than have all these dolly birds in Formula One. You never know what they're after. Jenson Button had a lovely girlfriend and all that finished. Maybe now he wished he had hung onto her.' It turned out that Carmen was wrong on this one: by September 2007, Lewis and Jodia Ma had split up.

Lewis soon settled down into his new life, living with his father, and he and Anthony made a fine team as they pushed for glory in the karting world. It was the first step on the road to their joint ambition: to be the best in Formula One. Lewis proved an immediate sensation. Wearing black plates as a novice kart racer, he was at once competing with the fastest. His obvious talent soon brought attention from enthusiasts. Martin Hines was one such early fan. His kart manufacturing company, Zipkart, was based near to the Rye House track and he approached father and son with an offer of help.

Martin recalled in the *Guardian*: 'I would go round to watch the kart racing. If you are a novice racer you have to wear a black numberplate for your first six races. Normally, that means all the novices are at the back of the grid because they don't have enough experience to get through the field. But one day I saw Lewis Hamilton, with his black plate, and he was battling it out at the front. Someone off the street wouldn't have noticed the difference, but I knew straight away – he stuck out as something a bit special.

'I introduced myself to Lewis and his father, and offered to supply them with kart chassis. It's usually the case in motorsport that you can only go as fast as the amount of money you have. The Hamiltons weren't rich, I wanted to help.'

This would be the start of a 5-year association. Martin is glad to have helped out at such a vital time in Lewis' burgeoning career, but also to have him and Anthony as friends. Lewis, in turn, has never forgotten the faith shown in him. Anthony remains grateful to this day, saying: 'In those early days we were very lucky in finding some very gentlemanly personalities in karting, who really helped us when money was tight early in his career. We had Martin Hines helping us out with the chassis, John Davies and John Button [Jenson's father] helping us out with the engine and an old friend Martin Howells supplying us with tyres. If it wasn't for guys like that, I don't think Lewis would have got off the lowest rung of the karting ladder.'

Bill Sisley, boss of the Buckmore Park circuit, near Chatham in Kent, where Lewis was to dominate races from the start of his karting career and would later admit to it being his favourite track, could also see the genius: 'I have talent-spotted for over 35 years. I always say I can tell within two laps whether a young driver has what it takes, but the sort of raw talent enough to take them all the way to Formula One is rare. In fact, there are only one or two in a generation that good. Lewis was certainly one of them and it showed; his talent shouted out.

Sisley recalled how Lewis just did everything right. The youngster was quick, braked at the right times, overtook at the right times, instinctively took the right line into the corners and, importantly, he didn't crash. Even at that young age, his desire to win was obvious. There have been other drivers as naturally talented, but lacking that aggression and passion to get to the flag first.'

Anthony had taken Lewis to the track, knowing Bill was a famed talent spotter. Bill was quickly bowled over: 'Lewis was a once-in-a-generation talent and very few, if any, will match his achievements, but the interest he has created in a short time is fantastic. He had the three key ingredients that made up the perfect package for a great racing driver: he was packed with natural talent, he subsequently had the financial backing of the McLaren organisation and he had the professionalism and determination.

'He also had a very nice, supportive family, and when you add that to the mix you get the extremely likeable and totally focused young man that Lewis Hamilton is.'

Former Radio 1 DJ David 'Kid' Jensen was covering the kart racing at Buckmore Park for Channel 4 in 1997 when Lewis rode the circuit for the final time. He thought he would be a great, saying 'Even at 11 he was a pleasure to interview, really interesting and amenable. Lewis just had a natural way about him that was always appealing, never arrogant. He was the star of the show. He is a credit to his father.'

Jensen was full of admiration for the way in which Lewis and his father operated, their tremendous sense of respect for each other shining through: 'I saw some awful things. It would be a normal sight where a 6ft-plus guy would be bending over a 3ft-nothing little kid, bellowing insults at the top of his voice.' Anthony was an exception to this type of behaviour, someone the commentator never saw losing it. 'He was one of the ones not living out his own frustrations or vicariously trying to make up for their own failures through his child.

'In fact, the pair were a great father-son combination, which was even more commendable when you discovered that Lewis' parents had split up.'

Looking back, Lewis recalls those karting days with affection. He admits that it was the hard work in practice and testing that kept him from falling by the wayside: 'If I didn't love it, I'm sure I wouldn't be as good as I am today because I'd have put half the effort in and just have done the races. I think you find drivers who just rely on their racing ability and don't do the hard yards. When you're young you don't really understand that philosophy: work hard and see the result. You think, I can't be bothered to work hard now, and when you get there you struggle and complain. But if you really put the effort in, you see the result. Even if you don't do well, you know you've done the work, so next time you can improve on it.'

His headmaster at his junior school, Peartree, John Seal, also feels it is down to Lewis' focus and determination back then that he is the brilliant Formula One driver he is today: 'He stood out at school, and not just because he was winning all these karting trophies. He was popular, he was composed when it came to speaking in public, and he was focused – exceptionally so for someone so young. More than anything, I remember just how much support he got from his father. They were just an ordinary family from a hard-working background, that's why it's so good to see that things have turned out the way they have.'

Lewis was soon crowned Britain's youngest cadet kart champion (aged 10) and it was at the subsequent Autosport Awards ceremony in London that his legendary meeting with McLaren boss Ron Dennis took place. He asked Big Ron for his autograph. The Formula One supremo duly obliged – telling Lewis to 'try me in nine years' when the youngster said he also wanted Ron to let him drive for

McLaren. But it was to be a mere three years down the road when they would meet again. Lewis remembers that first encounter fondly: 'We couldn't afford a suit and so I'd borrowed a dark green silky suit off this guy who had won the same karting championship the year before – I even got his shoes. I went up to Ron and told him I wanted to drive for McLaren and become World Champion. He wrote in my autograph book: "Try me in nine years". But two or three years later he called me.'

Lewis moved up to secondary school, becoming a pupil at the John Henry Newman Roman Catholic School in Stevenage, where he proved himself good at other physical activities. The football he had years previously tossed aside to concentrate on his remote-control car re-emerged as he starred at John Henry Newman with a boy who would go on to become an England under-21 player. He also found the karate he had taken up a couple of years before was a more than adequate deterrent against the unwelcome attentions of another pupil.

One journalist reported: 'He took up karate after he caught the eye of the school bully. By the age of 12, he was a Black Belt. He was also a more-than-useful footballer at John Henry Newman… and played in the same team there as Ashley Young, the midfielder who joined Aston Villa from Watford in January for £9.65 million.'

Lewis told him: 'I was quicker than Ashley Young, stronger than him – so I had that with me. But he was very skilled and very neat, and would dribble the ball round people very nicely. I was very powerful in the team, I was always a midfielder and in my team I was the fittest by far because of my racing and the training I did. I'd run up and down, and up and down, and if someone tackled me I'd get them back. I'd always get them back because I never gave up, whereas a lot of people would get tackled then just leave it for the next stage of the game. I'd never let that happen.'

Meanwhile, his career in karting was to bring more honours. In 1996 he won the Champions of the Future, Sky TV KartMasters and Five Nations karting series and, a year later, moved up to junior Yamaha and won the Champions of the Future series and Super One series. Former Jaguar Racing team boss Tony Purnell was another of his sponsors, via Tony's Pi Research Company. He too was convinced he had seen the future of motor racing, saying Lewis' talent particularly shone through when McLaren took him under their wings. 'Admittedly, ever since he was 12 when I stopped sponsoring him, he's had the very best equipment. That's because he had that most important of assets, an infinitely wealthy "father figure" – McLaren's Ron Dennis. But it's one thing to have the best tools; it's quite another to be gifted enough to use them.

'Perhaps it helps to note that Lewis has always comprehensively blown away his team-mates. Consider his team-mate in Formula A [the top Euro karting class]: one Nico Rosberg. I saw Lewis race a handful of times during this period, and he was fantastic. Nico? Well, ordinary, I'd say. In short, Lewis races like... Michael Schumacher. The boy's a winner.'

At this point it's useful to note the origins of Lewis' now-famous yellow helmet.

The reason why he wears it goes back to the days when he was racing karts. His father Anthony insisted Lewis wore a yellow helmet because it would make him stand out from the crowd; also he would know instantly if his son was involved in a crash if he did not spot the helmet.

It was in 1998 that Lewis signed up with Dennis for the McLaren and Mercedes-Benz Young Drivers Programme. He was 13, still at John Henry Newman, and now he was the youngest driver ever to be contracted to a Formula One team. His father and Big Ron agreed that as he was spending such a large amount of time testing and racing, McLaren should pay for a private tutor to supplement his education. Both were keen for him not to fall behind with his schoolwork. The records were already being broken and Lewis continued his rapid rise by dominating every level in the karting world in the three years that followed. Competing in the junior Intercontinental A section, he was second in McLaren Mercedes Champions of the Future event in 1998 and fourth at the Italian Open. In 1999 he won the Italian 'Industrials' champion at Intercontinental A level, was Vice European champion and lifted the Trophy de Pomposa. He was also fourth at the Italian Open Championship at junior-Intercontinental level. As the new millennium dawned, Lewis won all four rounds in Formula A to become European Champion and also won the World Cup and the Masters at Bercy. It was the icing on the cake after another fabulous season when he was named British

Racing Drivers' Club's 'Rising Star'. Six years had passed since he and Anthony had made their pact to take him to the top of the racing world. He had experienced ups and downs in his home life and had ended up moving away from his mother to live with his father. Along the way, he had also had to sacrifice many things normal kids take for granted in their teens: 'Kids at school would say, "What you doing this weekend?" and I'd say, "Oh, I'm going karting." They'd say, "I might see you up the road then" at the local karting track. I would just nod because I wanted to keep the real extent of my racing quiet. It helped make school feel like an escape if no one knew what I was achieving in racing.

'School was my time to mess about and have a kid's life, to be normal. But at weekends I never had a chance to go to any of those under-18 clubs or parties. And that affects you because your friendships are not so strong. When you say, "I can't go out because I'm racing this weekend" your friends think you're just blowing them off. Even when, near the end, I'd tell people at school I was going to Japan for a week to race, they'd look at me blankly. It just didn't click.'

His time at secondary school passed largely without incident – he was well liked by fellow pupils and teachers. One rather bizarre incident deserves a mention, however. It revolves around him being wrongly expelled in a mix-up in his final year when he was 16, after another boy was attacked and needed hospital treatment.

Lewis was one of six teenage boys excluded in 2001 when 15-year-old classmate Sebastian Webber was attacked in the toilets, suffering two fractured fingers, bruising and an injured arm. But when Anthony Hamilton protested his son's innocence, Lewis was cleared of any wrongdoing and reinstated two months later by a local authority appeals panel. The inquiry concluded that he had been wrongly identified and he received an apology from the education authority. Vincent Hayward, Lewis' form teacher at the time, recalled 'It happened during the lunch hour. Some of them took this lad to the toilets and gave him a bit of a going over.'

Former pupil Michelle Vooght said: 'I remember the incident and it was other boys, not Lewis. He was a nice boy, friends with everyone and genuine. He was self-confident, but he'd never brag about his racing. He'd get dropped off at school in a Mercedes with "Lewis Hamilton" down the side!' Another ex-pupil, Sean Beahan, agreed: 'A lot of people had their names dragged into the attack incident and it was later found that Lewis and a few others had done nothing wrong.'

Hertfordshire County Council spokesman John Ryan said: 'Lewis was cleared of all involvement after an independent review. He was originally accused by one of the teachers. It was basically an administrative cock-up that led to the accusation and it boils down to mistaken identity.'

Perhaps inevitably, Lewis' best friend during those teen years was another racing fanatic: Nico Rosberg, who would go on to race for Williams in 2007. Lewis said: 'We were karting team-mates in Italy for two seasons and were racing to see who would become the youngest ever driver in Formula One. Nico got there first because he had a season in GP2 while I was in Formula Three. GP2 is vital because the set-up of the car is very similar to Formula One and on some tracks we hit the same speed at the end of a straight.

'He's the most competitive person I've ever met and he was really tough – but I won the European Championship and he came second. But we shared the same hotel room and always spoke of how fantastic it would be to compete against each other for the Formula One World Championship.'

Lewis had now won everything there was to win in karting. He had secured his deal with McLaren, winning a place on their prestigious training programme and he was ready to move up another gear. From karts to cars... the next stage of his quest for world domination was about to take shape.

CHAPTER 4

A WINNING FORMULA

The next move on the road to the top came in 2001 when Lewis Hamilton finally stepped into a racing car and, in his debut season, finished fifth overall in the Renault Winter Series. His career was being mapped out and engineered by Ron Dennis and McLaren. Lewis was now 16 and, although he did not know it at the time, just six years away from Formula One.

He was undoubtedly a quick learner and by the end of the following season he finished third in the British Formula Renault series – along the way notching up three wins, three fastest laps and three pole positions. Not only this but he was also fifth in the Formula Renault EuroCup Championship with one win and three podiums after competing in four rounds out of nine.

His learning period in the series was over, and he soon

roared to the 2003 British Formula Renault Championship with 10 victories and 11 pole positions. His 419 points compared dramatically with the 377 points (including just two wins) of his nearest rival, Alex Lloyd. Victory had come in double quick time during the season – he had lifted the title with two rounds to spare – and that comfort zone meant Lewis could debut in the British F3 season, taking part in the last two races of the Championship.

The team boss of Manor Motorsport, John Booth, was the man who guided him during his Formula Renault years after McLaren decided he was ready to move up from karts. John has helped a number of promising drivers in his successful team, and was glad to have been there at the second stage of the Lewis Hamilton racing career story. The wonderboy would race for him in Formula Renault and then in his early F3 days. John told the *Guardian*: 'McLaren asked us to give Lewis a test in our Formula Renault car. He had never driven a racing car before, not even a road car because he was only 16, and he crashed after a couple of laps.' This was hardly surprising, but what really impressed Booth was once the car had been put back together, Lewis went back out and immediately picked up the pace. The accident hadn't fazed him at all.

'He did the 2001 Renault Winter Series with us – and the full UK Championship in 2002 and 2003. There were a few mistakes, what do you expect from a 17-year-old?' What indeed... always a great deal in the case of Hamilton, perhaps too much at times. Stepping away from the racing circuit for a moment, Lewis was also doing well at college, especially considering his other commitments. He had moved on to the Cambridge College of Arts and Science – which, despite its name is located in Stevenage – to study for his A-levels after completing GCSEs at John Henry Newman. The college could offer him a flexible timetable, allowing him to fit his studies around his commitments as a Formula 3 driver.

A college newsletter, produced while he was studying there, revealed a little more about their star pupil: 'Lewis came to CATS after a recommendation from a friend, when he was looking for a place where his studies could be better fitted around his racing schedule. Lewis still finds it hard to concentrate on studies when his mind turns to the weekend's racing, but his studies have gone well.' Written in 2002, the report predicted big things: 'Lewis now races in the UK Formula Renault Single-Seater Championship and plans to become a full-time racing driver and graduate to Formula One when he finishes his studies.'

It was at Cambridge that he met girlfriend, Jodia Ma. Although Lewis refuses to speak publicly about their relationship, it is known that she lived in London for a spell after finishing her studies before moving back to Hong Kong in January 2007. She and Lewis remained an item for five years, with him splashing out £10,000 on a diamond bracelet for her 21st birthday. In stark comparison to his council house upbringing, she comes from a wealthy background. Her parents own a massive house in a gated community in Hong Kong's Clearwater Bay, a seaside village populated by wealthy professionals.

Jodia flew back from Hong Kong to London to be with

Lewis on her 22nd birthday on 28 July 2007. She has admitted to friends that she moved back home six months previously as she had been unsure whether they would remain together – because of Lewis' race commitments and her own uncertainty about what the future held for her. But Lewis refused to give up on her. In March of that year, he went to Hong Kong to see her, and from there, they went on holiday to Bali. Then in July she flew in to the UK to be with him, confirming they were still going steady despite the 6,000 miles between them. Jodia said: 'I think the world of him. I am just so proud of him. He is a lovely, amazing guy and so talented. He is a national hero and I can understand why people are so interested in him.'

A few weeks later she travelled to Hungary to see Lewis in action at the grand prix in Budapest – the first time she had watched him race. A friend of the couple said they had talked about the possibility of Jodia moving to London full-time to be with Lewis, and how she could perhaps develop her career in events management in the UK. But her hopes of a lasting relationship with Lewis would be dashed when they separated during the summer of 2007.

Jodia was only Lewis' second serious girlfriend. His first was Rachel Butterfield, whom he dated a year previous to meeting Jodia, while at secondary school. Rachel, of Biggleswade, in Befordshire, later did a 'kiss and tell', selling the story of their time together to the *News of the World*.

In between college studies and racing commitments, Lewis did a succession of small jobs. When he moved to Tewin, he served at the White Horse gastro pub in Burnham Green and also worked for a car valet firm. It was around this time that he passed his driving test – at the first attempt and after just six hours of lessons – though he had to be cautioned to slow down on the bends. His driving instructor, Stephen Sivell, said he knew at once that the 17-year-old had a special talent, but added: 'I had to warn him to slow down at corners and stop revving the engine of my Nissan Micra so hard.'

Now 53, Stephen's business records show that he was first contacted by Lewis' father Anthony on 10 April 2002 to inquire about driving lessons for his son. And initially the instructor was apprehensive after noting the unusual clothing Lewis wore for his first session: 'He was dressed all in white when I collected him from his home and was wearing Oakley designer sunglasses. He looked stylish, but I thought to myself: we've got a right boy racer here.'

Stephen was also concerned about the skills his learner driver had picked up in karting. He added: 'I had to point out that while he took the racing line, that wasn't what the examiner was going to be looking for when it came to his test. He would swing out to the right before turning left, which might have been acceptable for an advanced test, but not for the basic one.

'And he was taking the bends a bit fast on the country lanes – he was going into a bend so fast it was making me flinch. I think he saw that it was making me a bit nervy and he seemed to be enjoying it in a mischievous sort of way. I told him he could come out of a bend more quickly than he went in, but he had to go into them more slowly. He listened, and he learned very quickly.'

Stephen's old, silver Nissan Micra had never known anything like it: 'At one point I had to say "If you rev any harder, you will propel the engine into orbit!" But he added that Lewis was also tremendously focused. 'He took everything on board very quickly.'

After four 90-minute lessons in little more than a week, at a cost of £18 each, Stephen advised his young client that he was ready to sit his test. He passed with flying colours. Stephen said 'I know he passed first time because he phoned me to tell me. I believe he only had a very few minor faults, but that superb control that he had always had saw him through.' The driving instructor also witnessed Lewis' delight when his father presented him with his first car, a Mini coupé with a checkered flag on the roof. He recalled, 'We got back to his home at the end of one of our last lessons to find that Lewis' father, Anthony, had bought him the car. Lewis was thrilled, and I reckon he deserved it.'

Stephen remembers Lewis talking about racial taunts and snobbery he had encountered on his way to the top: 'I think it was difficult for him because some people weren't being over-pleasant to him at that time. Some parents were throwing everything they had got financially behind their children, getting them all the best equipment, but they were less talented than Lewis, and I think that caused jealousy.

'But Lewis was more talented than the others, and he was still winning. The odd remark, such as "Blacky", was chucked in from time to time. I would love to see him again. I'd just give him a big hug and say "Well done!"'

So, by the time of his second season with Yorkshire-based

Manor Motorsport in 2002, Lewis had passed his 'normal' driving test and was expected to pass the next test in his racing career: he was clear favorite to win the Formula Renault title. 'We'd been quickest in the pre-season test,' recalls John Booth. 'But things went awry at the first race – he got taken off by a backmarker. He went for three races without winning, which was a surprise to us, to say the least.'

Then came the big breakthrough: Lewis' first win in a racing car, at Silverstone. John says, 'He was lying fifth, on slicks, and it rained. He came through and won quite comfortably. That was it. He just clicked, his confidence was up and I don't think he was beaten again for the rest of that season.'

Lewis' debut in F3 at Brands Hatch was a nightmare. In the first race of the day he was forced out with a puncture and in the second he crashed out and was taken to hospital after a collision with team-mate Tor Graves.

Stella-Maria Thomas and Lynne Waite of Motorsport.com reported wryly on his F3 debut on 13 October 2003: 'At the back, life was proving interesting for Lewis Hamilton (Manor Motorsport). Having made his debut in the category in the morning's race, he started this one from the back after making a mistake in qualifying and failing to set anything that vaguely resembled a time...

'Trying to pass his teammate, Tor Graves, the two of them made contact, and the resulting off saw Graves' car almost destroyed, while the driver escaped with a suspected broken thumb. Hamilton wasn't quite so lucky. He was trapped in the car for a while, complaining of back pain. Naturally the marshals at the scene weren't about to take any chances and his extraction would clearly take some time.

'Finally Hamilton was extracted, his neck in a collar, and was taken away in the ambulance to the medical unit and later to hospital. He was declared fit but the doctors wanted to keep him in overnight for observation. He's not likely to forget his F3 debut weekend in a hurry.'

Lewis and Manor then made their debut in the 2004 Formula Three Euroseries. They won just one race and Lewis finished fifth in the Championship. But he did win the Bahrain F3 Superprix. John Booth admitted the problem lay with the car and not the driver: 'When we moved into F3, we didn't have the most competitive car. Lewis won a couple of races, but it was quite difficult for him being in a car that wasn't the best because he has this amazing desire to win. But even when the going is difficult, he didn't have a spat or a tantrum.

Booth admired the natural way Lewis had even then that gets everyone on side, in marked contrast to Ayrton Senna. 'He would have the same aim, but be manipulative. When we were racing together, Ayrton was a very pleasant young man but he'd be quite cold about it. He would say, "I will do this, and I will get the mechanics on my side." But, with Lewis, you would regularly see him bouncing about with a smile on his face. That's the way he's always been.'

By the end of 2004 the writing was on the wall for the link-up between Lewis and Manor – and in mid-December of that year it was announced that he had completed his first test drive for McLaren at Silverstone on 1 December.

There was even speculation he might jump two levels and become their third F1 man. One report said: 'Team McLaren-Mercedes have confirmed that Alexander Wurz will not test the new 2005 car, the MP4-20, in January, as he is too tall to fit into it. Although the team added that the car may be modified to accommodate the Austrian, it is thought this may take some time, and as such Pedro de la Rosa has effectively been promoted to "third driver".

'Jamie Green, Lewis Hamilton and Alex Lloyd are also all rumoured to be in the frame, after testing the MP4-19 recently at Silverstone, and despite McLaren's statement on Monday, that Mika Hakkinen will concentrate solely on the DTM [the Deutsche Tourenwagen Masters] in 2005, he may also be given the opportunity.'

It was not to be, but at least Lewis was in the frame. A good two years before Ron Dennis would make him his new chosen one, he was out testing with more established names. As he entered the second year of the F3 Euroseries, he was given another helping hand by McLaren when they engineered his move to rival team ASM. Yet he would not forget the part John Booth had played in his career. Before the French Formula One Grand Prix at Magny-Cours in 2007 he searched him out to see how he was doing. John, who was that day preparing for action with his Manor Motorsport Formula Three team, was touched by the gesture: 'That was so typical of Lewis. There he was, facing a big weekend, leading the Formula One Championship, and he took time to come and have a chat.'

At the end of the 2004 season there was also talk in the

pit lane that the test drive in the Formula One car at Silverstone may have gone to Lewis' head, that he and Anthony did not agree with Ron Dennis' decision to keep him in F3 for another season. Also, that Lewis and his father wanted to move into GP2 racing straightaway. Sources claimed there was a falling-out, which led Lewis to compete in the Macau F3 Grand Prix without McLaren's backing and that the Hamiltons sought another sponsor to race in GP2.

It is claimed they failed to attract enough support and 'had to go back to Dennis cap in hand'. Lewis, his father and McLaren all refuse to confirm or deny the allegations, but if it was correct then it was a salutary lesson for the young man. Dennis proved to be spot-on – when Lewis moved to ASM in 2005 success was to come easily and quickly, and it enabled him to eventually step up to F2 with even more confidence.

Backed by ASM's plentiful resources, Lewis' second season in F3 began with an emphatic victory at Hockenheim and he went on to become a brilliant champion. His Roll of Honour included 15 wins, 10 fastest laps, 13 pole positions and securing the title with four races remaining. At the same time, he also won the F3 Masters at Zandvoort, notching pole position and the lap record, and triumphed at the Monaco F3 Grand Prix and the Pau F3 Grand Prix in France.

By the time he wrapped up the title with four races to go in August 2005, Formula 3 paid personal tribute, acclaiming Lewis the best-ever driver in F3: 'Lewis Hamilton (ASM F3, Dallara-Mercedes) was regarded as one of the big favourites already at the beginning of the 2005 season – and the 20-year old succeeded in dominating the Formula 3 Euro Series like no other driver in the series' history. In the 16 rounds of the season contested so far, the young Briton has clinched 11 wins, gained 11 poles and set seven fastest race laps, thus securing the title with still four more rounds to go.

'Lewis Hamilton is clearly dominating the 2005 season. He makes nearly no mistakes and is always extremely quick. Hence, his title triumph was the logical consequence.

'When not sitting behind the wheel of his car, Lewis Hamilton is a calm and polite man, whose second passion apart from motor racing is to play guitar.'

It was a nice tribute from F3's bosses, and it would not go unnoticed at McLaren that his feats that season equalled the early achievements of driving legends Jackie Stewart and Alain Prost.

ASM team boss Frederic Vasseur was also full of praise for his driver, admitting it felt like something of a coup when McLaren asked him to take Lewis under his wing: 'My first encounter with Lewis was in the Formula Renault Eurocup at Assen in 2003. ASM won the second race there, with Simon Pagenaud, and Lewis finished second. He had the look of a very good driver, and graduated with Manor to the F3 Euroseries against us in 2004. It was a difficult situation for him, as both he and the team were new to the series, and the Kumho control tyres have particular characteristics that needed to be learned. There was also strong competition in Jamie Green, Nico Rosenberg and

Alexandre Premat. By the end of it, I was very interested in signing Lewis for 2005, but before I got the chance to speak with him, Martin Whitmarsh [the McLaren CEO] phoned me, saying he wanted Lewis to drive for us!'

Lewis' relationship with Vasseur was to continue beyond F3. When McLaren decided the time was right for him to move up to F2 in 2006, he stepped up a level with ASM's sister team, ART Grand Prix. But first he would take a well-earned rest at the end of that successful F3 season in 2005: 'I spent time with my family, my girlfriend and my friends just catching up; I did a bit of travelling. I started off by going to New York with my girlfriend and we went sightseeing. We went to the top of the Empire State Building, on the boat to the Statue of Liberty, and of course we couldn't go to New York without doing some shopping! Then I moved on to Bermuda with some friends for a week – it was their winter, but it was still nice and warm. It is a really beautiful place and very relaxing, which is just what I needed before the start of the season.'

He would move easily and comfortably from being champion in F3 to champion in GP2. As he stormed to the title, his Roll of Honour read like this: five wins, six fastest laps; first double win at the Nürburgring; pole position and winner of Monaco GP2 race; second double win at Silverstone in home race; seven second place and two third place podiums.

Frederic Vasseur remembers with fondness Lewis' domination of F2, not to mention the devotion and professionalism of Lewis' approach to work: 'It was obvious that he was a natural, but also very dedicated. All drivers say that their ambition is to be World Champion but very few actually focus on doing it. Lewis is one of the few. He is able to motivate the team because he is friendly with everyone. And he is completely honest with himself. If he qualified badly, he would say, "I did a poor job. The car is fine. Don't change it, it's my fault."' This was a key attribute of the youngster, because it ensured the most efficient use of the engineers' and technicians' time – you can waste so much time changing the car when in fact it is the driver who is at fault.

Vasseur recalls numerous impressive drives: 'I remember particularly a few from GP2. Silverstone [when Lewis overtook two cars with a single move] was a fantastic moment for me. And in Turkey, when he had spun to the back of the field, his comeback was incredible. And yet he did not take any big risks. Usually when a driver is coming back from something like that, he passes everyone – and then crashes. Lewis was using his brain, thinking of the Championship and picking off the other drivers one by one. At the Nürburgring, when it started raining and everyone was on slicks, Lewis was 2 to 3 seconds a lap faster than the others. I got on the radio and said, "Calm down." He replied, "OK, it's not a problem." It just came so easy to him. At the pit wall during a race, I was never nervous about him.'

Significantly, he was having a great fight with his team-mate, Alexandre Premat, in Barcelona: 'Premat hit Hamilton and sent his car into a spin on the last lap and yet he congratulated Alex on the podium. "Alex is not the problem," he said. "The problem was my start." Meaning that if he had made a better start, the problem would not have arisen. That's Lewis, an incredible guy.'

Nicolas Todt, co-boss of ART Grand Prix with Vasseur, was also delighted Lewis had taken them to a second consecutive GP2 Championship: 'I am very, very happy. Winning the title last year [with Nico Rosberg] was a really good achievement because it was a new series. Winning it again proved that it wasn't a stroke of luck last year. It proves that we really deserved it. Lewis was astonishing. He was very fast and very determined. It was a pleasure to work with a guy like him. The combination of Lewis and Alex Premat, who was with us last year as well, was the best that we could have.'

Lewis paid tribute to Todt and Vasseur and their team for helping him to get to Formula One more quickly than many had expected. 'Yes, I had a great couple of years with both of them. I think I learned a lot from my engineers there because they run a fantastic two teams in F3 and GP2. They really gave me a good understanding technically, because when you get into Formula One you really have to have a great knowledge of the car to be able to communicate with your team. That's what I learned from those teams.'

His GP2 triumphs at Silverstone in June 2006 are considered by many to have been the moment when Ron Dennis decided he could no longer hold back his protégé; this was when he gave the nod for Lewis to become part of the McLaren F1 set-up. Certainly the team's own official comments on that day seem to back up that theory: 'Lewis Hamilton's dazzling victories in the two GP2 races [at Silverstone] supporting the 2006 British Grand Prix stole the spotlight from many of the drivers in the senior race.

'After winning the first race on Saturday, GP2 rules dictated that he start last on the grid for the Sunday morning sprint race. Lewis dodged past both Clivio Piccioni and Nelson Piquet jnr in a brilliant three-abreast lunge through Maggotts and into Becketts. This mind-boggling manoeuvre vaulted him up to second place, after which he worked hard to displace Felix Porteiro and set the seal on his second win in less than 24 hours. Many predicted that the drive would earn him a Formula One ride for 2007.'

On Saturday 9 September 2006, the momentum for him to be given a McLaren drive increased after confirmation of his GP2 title win at Monza. Renowned Formula One blogger Oliver White set the scene in this way: 'Although Hamilton only finished third in the race, winner Giorgio Pantano had his fastest lap taken away from him as it was set under yellow flags. This gave Lewis an extra point and this means he has beaten his rival, Nelson Piquet jnr. Ron Dennis – team director of McLaren F1 – refused to be led into questions on his driver line-up next year but did have praise for his 21-year-old protégé: "The manner of his many outstanding performances this year, such as those at Silverstone and Turkey, has been phenomenal and he is a deserving champion. Lewis has an exceptional talent, which has been demonstrated this year, and his overall performance during the season gives you a definite sense of pride and satisfaction. In due course the team's and Lewis' plans for 2007 will be announced."

'Hamilton is said to be pleased that the season-long battle with Nelson Piquet jnr was finally over, and is jubilant at his success. With Kimi Raikkonen expected to be at Ferrari next year, Ron Dennis has a tough decision to make for his 2007 drivers. McLaren currently have Fernando Alonso, Pedro De La Rosa, Lewis Hamilton and Gary Paffett available for next year, and while it is possible for Kimi to remain at the Woking squad, it is unlikely.

'Ron would do very little wrong in keeping Pedro in the car. The Spaniard has done well since taking over from the departing Juan Pablo Montoya, and has shown the team that he is a safe pair of hands. But the temptation to put a young, motivated charger in the second seat must be strong.'

Indeed it was, and in the end temptation proved too strong. After nine years, Big Ron decided the time was right for Lewis to come out to play with the big boys. On Saturday 30 September 2006, just before the Chinese Grand Prix, he was invited to his house. Lewis himself takes up the story: 'We sat there and he said, "We have decided you are going to be our driver next year." I had to put a professional front on and I had a small smile on me, but inside it was overwhelming.' In taking him into the big-time, Big Ron was also gambling against his own ground rules. He had gone against his normal recruitment demand, that he would only employ drivers already established in Formula One.

Days of learning through the ranks were finally over and Lewis Hamilton had achieved his lifetime ambition. Starting in Melbourne, six months down the road, he would be a Formula One driver. But learning how to be one was just beginning and long, hard days of testing, practice and training were to follow. This would involve much time in the McLaren Technology Centre at Woking, a location Lewis already knew intimately. It was where his motor racing training and education had been evolving since being first signed to McLaren by Dennis.

Let's take a little look at the training programme that helped turn Lewis from a karting hopeful into a Formula One winner in his nine-year McLaren apprenticeship. Commenting in 2007 as the countdown to his F1 start continued, Lewis said 'I am in the McLaren Technology Centre every day. I have relocated to Woking to be close to the team and the facility. I train every day in the gym, meet team members for training and development sessions, and generally get to know the team and watch closely the progress of the new car. It also gives me the chance to work closely with my new engineers and for us to get to know each other like the back of our hands!'

Joseph Dunn of the *Sunday Times* described Lewis' training in this way: 'The intensity of it is astonishing. High-tech telemetric read-outs enable the driver and engineers to refine lap times down by fractions of a second, while racing simulators and 3-D virtual reality cars mean drivers can know a circuit off by heart without having driven it for real. Some reports have claimed Hamilton has spent thousands of hours in such a simulator at the McLaren base in Woking, although Hamilton downplays its influence.'

Rory Ross developed that theme in the *Daily Telegraph* magazine: 'He is 5ft 10in, 10st 10lb, and has a 16.5in neck, broad shoulders and a superbly developed upper body. His forearms are streaked with pulsating veins like brown thunderbolts...

'For six months before the start of the season, Hamilton was groomed for his Formula One debut. Every day, including weekends, he submitted himself to two 3-hour training sessions: he swam 2 kilometres, cycled 50 miles and spent two hours in the gym. "It's all about endurance," he says. "There is nothing worse than getting to mid-race and starting to fatigue, because your mind needs to work doubly hard to give energy to the rest of your body, and then you lose focus and you can crash. It is about your mind being at ease that you are fit enough."'

The *Guardian*'s Richard Williams talked about the word 'robotic' being used in describing how Lewis had been brought up by McLaren and of a 'training period that included thousands of hours in the McLaren team's unique and highly secret simulator' and 'some of the specific training techniques brought to bear on astronauts and fighter pilots.'

He went on: '[Ron] Dennis put at Hamilton's disposal the greatest learning tool that any driver has ever been given. McLaren's simulator, developed over the past eight years at a cost estimated to be above £20m, has been Hamilton's schoolroom, where he sits in a full-size Formula One car, minus wheels and a functioning engine, in a darkened room in front of a large, curved plasma screen. The chassis is suspended on a multi-point hydraulic rig that moves in response to his touches on the steering wheel and pedals as he watches a circuit unfold on the screen, with appropriate sound effects.

'Everything in this grown-up video game is programmed via the simulator's software: the minutest details of the circuit, the response of the engine under different conditions, the type and wear-rate of the tyres, as well as the noise of the engine.'

It was certainly true that Lewis had undergone a nine-year training period, the like of which no other Formula One driver had ever been subjected to. He was, in that sense, the prototype of the new breed of driver; developed from an early age to be a champion although, as Williams also points out, skill and talent are also essential.

Lewis was happy enough to admit before the British Grand Prix in 2007 that he probably could not have got to where he was so quickly without the £5 million training programme: 'I don't think you get to this position without working hard, as they've said. I was given an opportunity. I remember Ron said "You have the opportunity, but I want you to be the fittest guy out there" and so I had to make sure, even in my own self-confidence and self-belief, I wanted to be the fittest out there. Whether I am or not, who knows?

'I had an opportunity to have a training programme, [to] learn as much as I could about the car, so that I got to the first race and I had no problems. And we didn't look back and say "I wish we had done this differently" or "I wish we had worked an extra day." We took every day as it came and really maximised every day. This is what I've been working for so many years so when you get the opportunity, you don't just let it pass by, you get as much out of it as you can.'

He also admitted before the British Grand Prix that the training programme instilled in him the need to continue learning and ploughing through data, books and videos to reach the absolute top: 'I have had my head buried in books for the past nine months. When I'm not looking at books, I am watching DVDs or talking to the McLaren team about the car. The cars have so much software these days – it's not just mechanical. You don't just get into a car and drive it around a track; you have to learn about the aerodynamics. I've been studying from September to March to make sure that I have it in my head. Then I have to study each individual track. The advice I would give to other drivers is never to give up, even if you spin off. I think once I spun off and I got back on and focused, and ended up coming second.'

'You just can't afford to lose focus. When I am driving at 200mph, if I lost focus then I could die, so it kind of puts it into perspective.'

David Coulthard also backed the McLaren way of doing things, conceding that his training with them had been enormously helpful in his own career. At a press conference before the British Grand Prix in July 2007, he was also at pains to add that Lewis' natural skills completed the winning package: 'Having been part of the McLaren system,

I know some of the facilities that they had up to the point that I left, and I would be surprised if any grand prix team has quite as complete a package in simulation devices that the drivers can use. It's obviously a state-of-the-art facility, more modern probably than anyone else's out there.

'But Lewis has had to prove himself, otherwise he wouldn't be sitting here. It's not charity work that McLaren are doing. They invested because they saw the talent and they've helped him develop that over the time. As Lewis inevitably moves offshore and grows into his life, he will inevitably spend less time at the factory because there just won't be the time. He will need energy, recovery time, to maintain the level that he's achieved already over the next 10–15 years.'

There was a suggestion by some pundits that Dennis played Frankenstein to Lewis, that he was merely his Formula One creation. This theory was backed up, they claimed, by the fact that Big Ron had hired Dr Kerry Spackman, a New Zealand-born neuroscientist, apparently to turn the boy into a race-winning machine. Spackman's research had shown that while in Formula One some cars are faster than others, it was ultimately the driver who is the key to better speed.

One writer, Robert Matthews in the online news magazine thefirstpost.co.uk, spoke of the scientific approach in this way: 'A major part of Spackman's approach is the intensive use of computer simulators, which expose Hamilton to every twist, turn and eventuality of a race until dealing with them is utterly instinctive.' It was the same approach NAS had to astronaut training more than 40 years previously. Spackman, however, goes much further, applying insights from Neuroscience and Psychology to create a more comprehensive picture of Hamilton's technique and mindset, and bring his foibles under control. 'The result is a driver who combines the standard skill-set of focus and controlled aggression with relentless consistency.'

Guardian columnist Richard Williams pointed out that it was more the case that Dr Spackman's work complemented the skills of the wonderboy: 'Spackman's use of virtual-reality techniques has enabled Hamilton to exploit his natural talent even further by expanding his mental capacity. In a way, it is like adding an extra litre to his Mercedes engine.'

Ron Dennis himself was keen to play down the idea that Lewis was simply a factory-manufactured Formula One driver: 'First of all, we've done it for several young kartists. We constructed a karting team for both Lewis and Nico Rosberg. Obviously they've both done a great job and Nico – though really more because of his age than anything and the way the licensing system works – I think he just stepped ahead as regards getting into Formula One a little earlier.

'But I was always keen for Lewis to dominate every category in which he raced because that gives you a certain mind-set and obviously we wanted him to follow the right path into Formula One. But it's important to remember, no matter who gives opportunity to young drivers, ultimately it's their own abilities, their commitment, their own dedication and sacrifices, that determines the result. I will never, ever claim to be the reason that Lewis is the great success he is.

'That is his own effort and his own commitment. Yes, he's had opportunity; yes, he hasn't had to worry about money, but the most difficult thing is actually to deliver, given those opportunities, and that's all down to him and obviously the support of his family.' It was a fine tribute to the boy he had treated as a son for almost a decade. Clearly the bond was deep between them.

But before we move on to the start of Lewis' Formula One career, it's time to take a look at the man he described as his ultimate hero – Ayrton Senna – and McLaren, the team he had always wanted to be a part of. Let's find out exactly how McLaren, with the help of the late, great Senna, developed into the legendary motor racing giant it had become by the time it was ready to welcome Lewis Hamilton aboard.

CHAPTER 5

IN SENNA'S FOOTSTEPS

Asked what had been the biggest dream come true of his life before entering the fray in Formula One, Lewis Hamilton answered without hesitation: Joining McLaren. Without that welcome act of faith from Ron Dennis, back in 1998 when he was 13, there would have been none of the glitz he now laps up. His father Anthony summed it up like this: 'McLaren were the catalyst. Lewis' objective is to stay with McLaren.'

Indeed, McLaren and Lewis Hamilton appear the perfect team. The fastest motor racing outfit on the planet – and the fastest and best driver. The car in which Lewis performed so dazzlingly in his remarkable debut season, the Vodafone McLaren Mercedes Mp4-22, went like the proverbial rocket with eight cylinders powering its enormous 95kg Mercedes-Benz FO 108T engine.

It was mooted the car had been specifically designed for the arrival of double champion Alonso at the start of the 2007 campaign but it would be Lewis who felt most at ease with it. Before the first race, he warned: 'Just wait and see, this car will blow the socks off anyone who even looks at it!' And he wasn't far wrong. Alonso had voiced his fears after McLaren's under-performance, even with the superfast Kimi Raikkonen at the wheel the previous year, and is said to have asked for pledges before he left Renault that the new car would be supercompetitive. It certainly was that.

What Alonso had not expected, however, was that he would be upstaged by his young No. 2, whom he had assumed would be playing a supporting role and learning the game from him, the supposedly superior worldly-wise No. 1.

Lewis is a deep thinker and a man who spends whatever time it takes to get things right. That respect for planning and preparation also helps to explain why he wanted to join McLaren in the first place. This was, after all, no run-of-the-mill outfit – along with Ferrari it is the most legendary of the racing set-ups, with a history to match. It had not escaped his attention that not only would he be testing himself against Alonso, but that he would also be compared with the ghosts of McLaren's own glittering past. To some commentators McLaren is known as the 'jinx team'. Three of its greatest drivers died in their prime: founder Bruce McLaren, the Brazilian genius Ayrton Senna (although not in a McLaren car) and Britain's own marvellous maverick, the great James Hunt. Lewis would say of Senna: 'He's my icon. I used to watch the way he diced around the track and

Above left: Lewis's biggest supporter, his father Anthony Hamilton. © *Getty Images*

Above right: With his half-brother, Nicolas, who takes special pride in watching his older brother race. © *Getty Images*

Below: The first home Lewis shared with father Anthony and mother Carmen in Peartree Way on the Shephall council estate, Stevenage, Hertfordshire.

© *Rex Features*

A proud Lewis aged 8, showing off a trophy after winning his first ever race with a letter of congratulation from former F1 driver and current ITV commentator Mark Blundell.

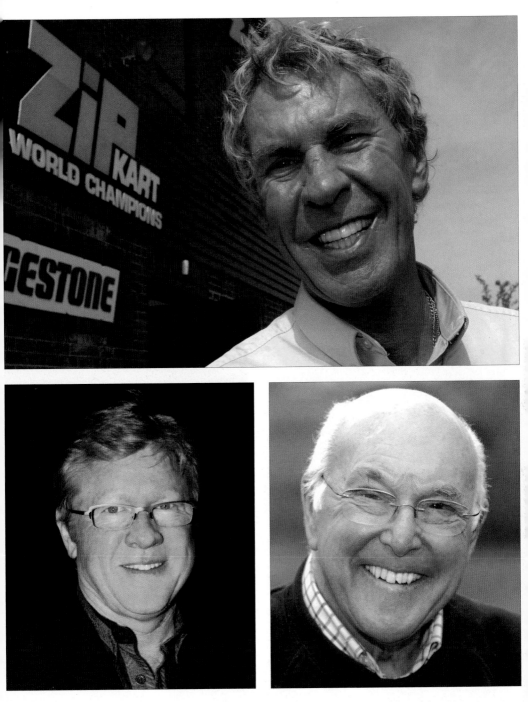

Above: Martin Hines, who played a large part in the development of Lewis' career as a Zipkart racing driver, in Hoddesdon, Hertfordshire.
© *Rex Features*

Below left: Former Radio 1 DJ David 'Kid' Jensen was full of admiration for Lewis while commentating on his kart racing at Buckmore Park for Channel 4 in 1997 when Lewis rode the circuit for the final time.
© *Rex Features*

Below right: The legendary voice of F1, Murray Walker. He was tempted out of retirement to commentate on the European Grand Prix by Lewis' incredible start to the 2007 season.
© *Rex Features*

Above: Posing with his go-kart, overalls and distinctive yellow helmet, 1997.

© *Rex Features*

Below left: Lewis aged 12, holding his trophy after winning the McLaren Mercedes Champions of the Future series.

© *Rex Features*

Below right: Aged 13 with Page 3 Girl Katie Richmond, Ron Dennis and fellow go-karter Wesley Graves in 1998. It was in this year that Lewis was signed by McLaren and Mercedes-Benz for the Young Driver Support Programme.

© *Clevamedia*

Above left: Already proving to be great marketing material. Lewis jumps in the air at Earls Court in a shoot promoting Joe Bloggs clothing, September 1997.   © *Rex Features*

Above right: With his father Anthony after winning the Industrial Championship for Karting in Parma, Italy, October 1999.   © *Rex Features*

Below: Prince Charles with a 14-year-old Lewis at the McLaren headquarters in Woking, March 1999.   © *Rex Features*

Above left: Lewis' best friend during his teens and karting team mate, Nico Rosberg.

© *Rex Features*

Above right: Alex Lloyd, Lewis' closest rival in the 2003 British Formula Renault championship. Lewis had ten victories and eleven pole positions that year, winning with 419 points, 42 points clear of second-place man Lloyd.

© *PA Photos*

Below: The White Horse pub at Burnham Green near Tewin, Hertfordshire, where Lewis worked while studying and fulfilling his early racing commitments.

© *Rex Features*

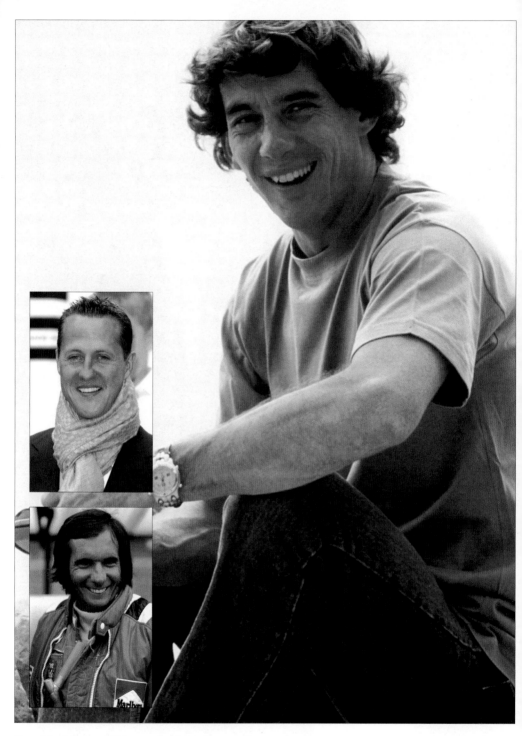

Lewis' ultimate F1 hero, the late Aryton Senna.

Inset above left: Lewis' driving skills have been compared to seven-time F1 champion Michael Schumacher.

Inset below left: In 1974, Brazilian Emerson Fittipaldi became McLaren's first world champion. Fittipaldi believes that Lewis is opening up a new exciting era in motor racing.

overtook the other drivers. I studied his books and videos, and I hope I learned something from him. I am so very proud to be racing for McLaren because that's who Senna raced for. It feels I am continuing his legacy in a way.'

The McLaren Formula One team was formed in 1963 by New Zealander Bruce McLaren. Bruce McLaren Motor Racing Limited, as it was known then, set about building a Formula One car, and three years later the team made its debut at the 1966 Monaco Grand Prix. In many ways, McLaren was like Lewis: he would not take the short cut to success. A devotee to detail, his motto could also have been that of Lewis: 'Success depends on the highest standards.' McLaren, too, was a brilliant driver but it was his vision beyond the grand prix races, again similarly to that of Lewis, which propelled him to greatness.

From an early age Lewis Hamilton would visit the garages and learn about the mechanics and specs of his karts and cars. This gave him an inside knowledge and an edge to his racing skills, as well as the nous to know how to treat the car almost as if he were riding a horse and nurturing it to victory. Bruce McLaren agreed with all that; he would surely have nodded sagely and smiled at Hamilton's insistence on ensuring all was right before he pulled on his helmet.

As founder, McLaren also took seriously his role as inventor, constructor and tester. By July 2007, the team he founded was well on the way to becoming the greatest in history, having won 152 races since its formation. True, Ferrari had won 195 but they had been racing since 1950 –

16 years more than McLaren, and the gap was ever closing with the exploits of Lewis and Alonso. The team has also dominated CamAm events (56 wins between 1967 and 1972) and taken three Indianapolis 500 races.

In his book *McLaren: A Racing History*, Geoffrey Williams writes: 'Just as Jackie Stewart came to personify the increasing professionalism, commercialism and safety consciousness of grand prix racing in the 1970s and similarly so with Ayrton Senna as the dedicated professional of the 1990s, Bruce McLaren typified the happy, often comradely spirit of earlier times. The most universally liked driver of his era, Bruce's background suggested he may have something out of the ordinary to offer the sport.'

Williams was spot-on with his analysis of Bruce McLaren – the founder who, like Lewis, was always destined for motor racing greatness. Born on 30 August 1937, Bruce had a happy upbringing, with fate decreeing he would spend his formative days in the perfect atmosphere: his father's garage. His parents, Ruth and Les, owned a service station and, more often than not, Bruce would be found in the workshop. Les had raced motorcycles before World War II, but after the hostilities ended, he switched his attentions to car racing. His son Bruce was equally fascinated by cars and what made them tick, and how, exactly, to get the best out of them.

We have already noted how Lewis had to battle against certain obstacles as a youngster to ensure his dream kept on track; it was no different for young Bruce. At the age of 9, he was struck down by Perthes Disease, a debilitating hip condition. The illness affects the top of the thighbone, softening and breaking it down. It usually occurs in children and causes a limp and other symptoms, but the one positive aspect of all this is that the affected bone gradually reforms as the child grows.

Only one in 10,000 children are hit by the disease: Bruce McLaren was one of the unlucky ones and for two years he was severely restricted in his movements. This was an unhappy time for the boy who loved to roam and learn around his father's garage. He was forced to live away in traction – at the Wilson Home for Crippled Children in Auckland, New Zealand – his body strapped up with a so-called Bradshaw Frame to help repair his hip. For months on end, he lay there, immobile. Later, he was allowed a wheelchair but at one time there were fears he would never walk again. But like Lewis, this was a boy who would not be beaten. When his father visited they would talk about cars and what was happening back at the garage.

When he returned home, Bruce had a permanent limp – his left leg was 1½ inches shorter than his right – but an even fiercer determination to make up for those lost 24 months. He spent his time helping his father in the garage and learned to drive in the quarter acre of land they owned at the back. The big breakthrough came when, at the age of 13, he and Les put back together an Austin 7 Ulster. It was then that Bruce knew for sure where his destiny lay. He had caught the car bug for ever and would later describe it in this way: 'With a truck full of boxes of spare parts and towing the Austin Ulster arriving at 8 Upland Road, my motor racing career had started. How Mum put up with Dad and me with her kitchen table covered in bits and pieces of the engine during meals I will never know. She used to say, "If I gave them dry bread and water they wouldn't have noticed."'

By the age of 14, he had persuaded his father to let him race the aging Austin 7 Ulster, which they had now fully restored in his first event, a hillclimb – a competition in which drivers compete against the clock to complete an uphill course. Two years later he took part in his first real race and performed well. He moved up from the Austin to a Ford 10 special and an Austin-Healey, then on to a F2 Cooper-Climax sports. The latter was his opening to the big time. Working on it all hours to improve its performance, he did such a good job that by 1957 he finished runner-up in the New Zealand Championship series.

His plucky displays that season brought him to the attention of motor racing legend Jack Brabham, conjuring up a similarity to Lewis Hamilton. Just as Lewis would profit from the mentoring provided by Ron Dennis, so McLaren himself got his big break courtesy of Brabham. Bruce's performances in the domestic campaign earned him an entry into that season's New Zealand Grand Prix and although he did not win the main race, his skills caught the eye of the big Aussie, who would one day invite Bruce to drive for him.

Ironically and tragically, given that this book is about a new British hero, another would die that day at the Grand Prix at Ardmore: Smethwick-born driver Ken Wharton. He was no Lewis Hamilton – his best result ever was a fourth place finish in Berne, Switzerland, in 1952 – but having been captivated by the same motor racing bug since childhood, his hopes and dreams had been the same.

Brabham encouraged the New Zealand International Grand Prix organisation to select Bruce McLaren for the 'Driver in Europe' scheme. Its aim was to provide a promising Kiwi driver with a year's experience at one of the best teams in the world. In 1958 McLaren was the first recipient. As Ron Dennis and McLaren would later take Lewis Hamilton under their wing from an even earlier age as an apprentice, so Bruce McLaren ended up learning his trade at the sharp end with the Cooper team in the UK. He made a name for himself in F2, but the big time arrived when he took part in the 1958 German Grand Prix at the Nürburgring. Featuring drivers from Formula One and F2, Bruce only earned a starting place from the reserve list, but showed his mettle, finishing fifth overall and first in the F2 lot.

The days of scrapping around and begging for a chance were over. He was promoted to Cooper's Formula One team for the 1959 season, with Brabham as his team-mate. Bruce would enjoy a fine 6-year spell with Cooper, that first season winning the final grand prix of the year at Sebring. At 22 this made him the youngest ever winner of a grand prix, and to ice the cake, Brabham won the World Championship. Bruce's record would stand until the 2003 Hungarian Grand Prix when Fernando Alonso superseded him as the youngest driver ever to win a grand prix at the age of 22 years, 26 days.

By 1960 Cooper was the top team: Jack Brabham finished the year as the world's No. 1, Bruce McLaren was No. 2 and Sterling Moss, also with the Cooper team, came third. That year Bruce won the Argentinian Grand Prix and he would remain in the top 10 drivers in the world for the next 10 years. It was a remarkable rise to fame for the boy from Auckland, and typical of the fierce winning mentality of the McLaren team and the determined character trait of McLaren himself and all those who would follow in his legendary footsteps.

By 1963 he had become disillusioned with the Cooper team and formed his own outfit. But he did not believe their cars were progressing enough technically and registered the name Bruce McLaren Motor Racing Ltd. Until 1966, he continued to race for Cooper, designing and developing his own car in his spare time until the day he was convinced it was finally ready for action. In 1966 he announced his own grand prix racing team, with co-driver and fellow Kiwi Chris Amon. That year they won the 24-hour race at Le Mans in a Ford GT40. A year later Amon was to leave to drive for Ferrari. By 1968, McLaren designer Robin Herd had introduced the Ford Cosworth engine to their car and Bruce signed up fellow New Zealander, World Champion Denny Hulme, as his co-driver. Hulme had won the world title in 1967, in a Brabham. For the developing team, these were heady, exciting times.

Bruce won his first grand prix in his own McLaren car at Spa in 1968, while Hulme won twice in the McLaren-Ford. In tribute to his homeland, McLaren's cars always featured the 'speedy Kiwi' logo. Bruce actually won in Belgium without knowing it. He admitted: 'It's about the nicest thing I've ever been told! Jackie [Stewart] had stopped at the pits for fuel, starting the last lap and I hadn't seen him as he went by. I had won without realising it...'

Yet all the glory would be forgotten when the tears fell on 2 June 1970 at 12.22pm, the day when Bruce McLaren was killed at Goodwood in England. He was just 32. His mother Ruth, in bed in Auckland, later told how she awoke suddenly at the very moment of the crash, sensing her adored boy was dead. Bruce died when his own CanAm car crashed during testing. He had been putting his new M8D through its paces when the rear bodywork came adrift at speed. The loss of aerodynamic downforce destabilised the car, which spun, left the track and hit a concrete bunker used as a flag station. He was killed instantly.

In *McLaren: The Man and His Racing Team*, Eoin S. Young summed up the sense of loss felt after the tragedy: 'In the dark days that followed it was realized that Bruce, the complete man, had virtually penned his own epitaph in the closing paragraph of his book, *From the Cockpit*, written in 1964. He had put down on paper the grief he felt at the death of his teammate Timmy Mayer, killed in a practice crash in Tasmania, but he had also recorded his justification for going racing and those last few sentences in his book are a fitting beginning for this one:

'"The news that he had died instantly was a terrible shock to all of us, but who is to say that he had not seen more, done more and learned more in his few years than many people do in a lifetime? To do something well is so worthwhile that to die trying to do it better cannot be foolhardy. It would be a waste of life to do nothing with one's ability, for I feel that life is measured in achievement, not in years alone.'"

In 1991 Bruce McLaren was inducted into the International Motorsports Hall of Fame, and into the Motorsports Hall of Fame of America in 1995. In the latter, his entry is commemorated with perceptive words that go some way towards defining the man who founded the McLaren legend. They say he was 'universally well liked and remarkably self-effacing. He never claimed to be the world's fastest driver and often smilingly discounted his own engineering ability. "Make it simple enough so even I can understand it," he'd tell his team. But his own work at the drawing board and in the cockpit resulted in racing machines that vanquished all comers.'

By the time of his death McLaren had won four of the 101 grands prix he had started, scoring a total of 196.5 points. But his legacy is much richer than those figures alone, for it extends to the massive enterprise of McLaren International today. Located in Woking, England, with a 325-strong team of designers, engineers and skilled staff, complemented by advanced computer-aided design and manufacturing facilities, it represents everything stunning about modern-day motor racing.

And the team continues to carry the name McLaren as Lewis Hamilton leads it into a new generation of glory, just as it did back in 1974 when Brazilian Emerson Fittipaldi became McLaren's first World Champion. Fittipaldi, once

Formula One's youngest champion, took his second crown with the team in 1974 after a first with Lotus as a 25-year-old in 1972. Then in June 2007 the first Brazilian world champion, and the youngest until Alonso won with Renault in 2005 at the age of 24, showed his loyalties remain with his old team when he spoke of his excitement at the development of Lewis Hamilton: 'For the Championship I would go for Lewis now, for sure. When you are so young and suddenly you are leading and winning, it is a tremendous pressure and he [Hamilton] is taking the pressure in a positive way.'

Likening Lewis to golf's Tiger Woods or football's Pelé for his ability to take the sport to a broader public, Fittipaldi outlined his belief that Lewis was opening up an exciting new era: 'I see we are going to reach beyond the borders of motor racing with Lewis Hamilton like we never have before. If you look at all the World Champions before, even the best that we had never reached the public that Lewis can reach.'

Fittipaldi was in Montreal for Lewis' first grand prix victory in May 2007 and was struck by how relaxed the youngster appeared off the track and how in control he was behind the wheel in comparison to his team-mate Alonso: 'Lewis talks to the car and the car talks to him. They understand each other very well, and Fernando, I think, was screaming to the car. He was not having a conversation.'

Fittipaldi will always be a McLaren idol for bringing the world title to Britain. But he will never own the same place in the hearts of the fans as Ayrton Senna or James Hunt, who would also die young. Like Bruce McLaren they too were also fast and furious at the wheel. Two years after Fittipaldi's triumph, James Hunt won the title for McLaren. 'Flamboyant' and 'Privileged' are terms often associated with Hunt... and some also dub him 'lucky'. Let me explain... James Simon Wallis Hunt was born on 29 August 1947, in Belmont, Surrey. He did not have to struggle to make it through life – far from it, in fact. He was the son of a successful stockbroker and educated at Wellington College, Berkshire. In his early teens his ambition was to become a doctor. But at 18 he went to see his first motor race and instantly caught the bug, so much so that he abandoned plans of becoming a medical GP, instead turning to the prospect of racing GPs for his salvation. Moving up quickly through the ranks of Formula Ford and Formula 3, he was landed with the nickname of 'Hunt the Shunt' after he was involved in a series of crashes.

He built up a reputation for wild driving but his big break came at the grand old age of 26, when his rich friend Lord Alexander Hesketh hired him as a driver with his fledgling Hesketh team in Formula One in 1973. His first win came in 1975 in the Dutch Grand Prix at Zandvoort. The following year Hesketh ran out of money, his team folded and Hunt joined the McLaren team for the 1976 season. It was a debut season that ended in glory as he roared to the world title, winning six races. But, for some that achievement was not enough. Certain pundits would belittle him, saying he had only triumphed because of his main rival Niki Lauda's near fatal accident at the Nürburgring on 1 August 1976.

The Austrian-born driver became trapped inside his Ferrari after it swerved off the track before bouncing back into the path of the oncoming cars and catching fire. Eventually the 27-year-old – who had been leading the Drivers' Championship since the beginning of the season – was pulled from his vehicle. Within six weeks of the accident Lauda was back, but Hunt pipped him to the title by just one point. My view is that, yes, Lauda had been well on course to win the crown, but Hunt still had much to do after the accident, and kept his nerve, driving with confidence and style. I do not think he earned the plaudits that should have gone his way. Nonetheless, the title win made him a hero in the eyes of those who really mattered in the sport... British Formula One fans.

That year proved to be the peak of Hunt's career. In 1977 he only won three grands prix races and the following year he scored hardly any points. In his personal life, he was rapidly heading for skid row too. Stories abound of him turning up at black tie events in shorts and a filthy T-shirt, and his drinking and womanising were legendary. One female journalist seduced him and wrote about his performance in a Dutch magazine. In 1979, he turned out for the Wolf team in what was to be his final season in Formula One. He then set about establishing a career in the commentary box as back-up to the great Murray Walker. It started badly when he arrived late and drunk to his first commentating job at Monaco. Barefoot, with a cast on his left leg from a skiing injury (also incurred while drunk), he plonked his leg on Murray

Walker's lap and began his commentary, pausing only to open a bottle of wine.

But the partnership between the two developed and prospered, thanks in no part to Murray's desire to see James get well. Ultimately, his life was tragically cut short just when he seemed to be getting it back on track after years of abuse and financial mismanagement left him close to broke. Yet it was not the hard-living and playboy lifestyle that did for him when he died of a heart attack, aged 45 in 1993. No, this was simply a congenital defect. Just hours before his death he had asked his girlfriend Helen, who was half his age, to be his third wife – and she had accepted his proposal.

He had remained friends with Niki Lauda right up until his death, and one of the most telling quotes about the real James Hunt would come from the Austrian when he was told he was dead: 'Shit. James was one of the really great guys.'

McLaren had to wait until 1984 for their next world title, courtesy of Lauda. In 1980, Marlboro brokered a merger between McLaren and Project Four headed by Ron Dennis. This revitalised McLaren, leading to Lauda's triumph by a half point from team-mate Alain Prost. The Frenchman then lifted the crown from Lauda, winning in 1985, 1986 and 1989, but now there was a new face in the team, and arguably the most legendary of all.

Ayrton Senna da Silva is still believed by many to be the greatest talent ever to grace a Formula One car. He joined McLaren in 1988 and his rivalry with Prost became legendary. The duo was total opposites: Prost, a reflective, measured operator, while Senna was an instinctively brilliant but uncompromising driver who verged on the dangerous. Their duels, as they battled for supremacy and the prize of the world title, would never be forgotten and their rivalry grew into the most bitter the sport has ever seen. Both won three crowns for McLaren (Senna's coming in 1988, 1990 and 1991), but Senna would edge Prost in terms of grands prix wins: 35 to 30.

Andrew Benson, the BBC's motorsport editor, summed up Senna's mastery of the sport like this: 'Michael Schumacher may statistically be the greatest grand prix driver who ever lived, but to many who watched Ayrton Senna's career no one can equal the brilliant Brazilian. Senna's greatness does not lie in statistics, impressive though his career record is. It is embodied in the irresistible force with which he dominated an era of Formula One.'

The Brazilian's potential, like that of Lewis Hamilton, was apparent even before he made it to Formula One. Born on 21 March 1960, he was the second child of Milton da Silva, a successful businessman and landowner. Ayrton was brought up in the middle-class area of Santana in São Paulo. He first drove a kart – a gift from his father – at the age of 4 and by 8 he was driving the family car. As soon as he turned 13 he was racing competitively. His drive to Formula One had ringing similarities to Lewis' progress. Just as he graduated from karts, so too, in 1977, Senna would win the South American Kart Championship.

He was invited to Europe for speed trials and swiftly

adopted his mother's maiden name, Senna, as da Silva was a very common Brazilian name. Senna went on to win the Formula Ford and Formula 3 Championships. In 1983, the Williams' team gave the then up-and-coming F3 driver a test in their grand prix car, and within 40 laps he had taken it around Donington Park faster than its regular drivers, including reigning World Champion Keke Rosberg. Inexplicably, Williams did not sign him; instead Senna was picked up by Formula One minnow Toleman.

In 1984, his debut year, Senna should have won at Monaco. In driving rain he overtook Prost's McLaren to lead on Lap 31 but the race was red-flagged a lap later. Prost triumphed under the rule that should a race be stopped, the classification would go back to two laps previous, but the boy from Brazil had laid down a marker. Senna had secretly been negotiating with Lotus and joined the former greats in 1985, winning his first grand prix in more treacherous conditions at Estoril. Five more wins followed in three years at Lotus, but Senna slowly realised this was not the dream team he had imagined. No longer the Lotus of Jim Clark, it was an outfit in decline. In 1988, he jumped ship. His time had finally come... at McLaren.

They were the team he had always been looking for, the one that would finally give him a car worthy of his talent and ambitions. In his first season he was welcomed by Prost, but the warmth did not last long. This could have been the prototype of the frosty way Alonso treated Hamilton after Lewis won his first grand prix. Senna won eight races as he took his co-driver's world title away from him. The following campaign the duo's battles became increasingly bitter as Prost regained the title with Senna runner-up. The Brazilian had lost the Championship to Prost after the pair collided at the final race in Suzuka. Prost blamed Senna and it was effectively the end of their relationship.

The BBC's Andrew Benson remarked: 'Senna did sometimes appear to be putting his ambition ahead of his instinct for survival, most notably at the Japanese Grand Prix in 1990, when Senna secured the second of his three titles by driving into the back of Prost's Ferrari at 160mph, taking them both out of the race.'

Senna, for all his outward propensity to shock, was an inwardly deep, religious man, who thought long and hard about his role in racing and life itself. He admitted his fears that he would not always be on top of the game, revealing how that edge to be the best kept him going: 'You are doing something that nobody else is able to do. [But] the same moment that you are seen as the best, the fastest and somebody that cannot be touched, you are enormously fragile because in a split second it's gone. These two extremes are feelings that you don't get every day. These are all things that contribute to, how can I say, knowing yourself deeper and deeper. These are the things that keep me going.'

With those motivational sentiments in mind, in 1994 Senna joined Williams for a new challenge: to prove himself all over again at a new team. Williams had dominated the sport in 1992 and 1993, and it was anticipated Senna would easily win back the Championship he had last won (for the third time) at McLaren in 1991. But it did not work out that way. The Williams' car had a serious design flaw and by the time of the San Marino GP at Imola on 1 May 1994, Senna was struggling to keep up with Michael Schumacher (in the superior Benetton) in the title race. Yet as he headed into the Tamburello corner at 192mph, he was a second ahead of the German when the Williams' FW16 crashed into a concrete wall. A front wheel was knocked back towards the cockpit and Senna's helmet visor pierced by a suspension arm. If it had missed him, he would have stepped from the wreck unhurt. Ayrton Senna – the genius of McLaren and Formula One – was dead at just 34.

Murray Walker reflected the mood of the day, saying: 'This is the blackest day for grand prix racing that I can remember.' Senna's body was flown home, and 4 days later, an estimated crowd of half a million people watched the coffin pass by in a state funeral in São Paolo.

It was the end of a dream, and McLaren would also be plunged into mourning. It would be four years before the team finally emerged from the darkness of the Brazilian's death, when Mika Hakkinen brought them back to the top with his world title win. The legendary team that Bruce McLaren had formed and died for had suffered its share of anguish as well as glory.

Ironically, as Hakkinen raced to that title during 1997–98, Lewis was just beginning his apprenticeship at McLaren. After the unforgettable glitz and tragedy of Bruce McLaren, James Hunt and Ayrton Senna, a new era was unfolding, the era of the boy who was born to be its new king at the start of Formula One in the twenty-first century. But Lewis would be the first to admit that none of this would have been possible without the help of his father Anthony and the man whom many called his surrogate father, Ron Dennis. For this was the man who brought Lewis into Formula One and upon whom we shall now turn the spotlight, examining his role in the development of the wonderboy...

CHAPTER 6

BIG RON MANAGER

He may not be the most popular guy in the pit lane, but Ron Dennis, 'Big Ron', as he is known universally on the circuit, couldn't give a proverbial monkeys – brash, confident, looking a bit like the man who owns the joint. Of course, he doesn't: that sobriquet would have to go to Formula One ringmaster Bernie Ecclestone. Yet, as head of one of the era's two most powerful racing team (along with Ferrari), the Big Man carries a definite clout – and, for our purposes, he is the man responsible for the irresistible rise and rise of Lewis Hamilton.

Lewis is the first to admit the debt he owes to Dennis. He said: 'Ron and my father have been the biggest influences on my career. Without them I wouldn't be where I am today. I owe them both a deep gratitude for their faith in me. Ron gave me my big break and I will always be grateful to him for that. He is also my friend, someone I can talk to about anything, someone who always has time for me. He is a great man.'

More of Dennis as surrogate father and mentor – he is directing Lewis' progress in much the same way as football manager Sir Alex Ferguson looked out for his Manchester United stalwart Ryan Giggs in his younger days – later in this chapter. First, let's look at Dennis the man, his background and how he resurrected McLaren after they were struggling to stay on top in the eighties.

Former McLaren No. 1 Kimi Raikkonen echoed the feelings of many in the paddock when he derided his former boss Dennis as a 'control freak' early in 2007. But Dennis, typically managed to turn the tables by declaring that, well, yes, Kimi was absolutely correct: 'I smiled when I heard he said I was a control freak because I am – I don't mind fine attention to detail.'

He is certainly known for that perfectionist streak and for not wanting to have a laugh around the pits. Some think him humourless, but that is only a face value assessment. Get him on his own and he has a dry wit and can laugh at himself. Why, he even admitted that, like Britain's new Prime Minister Gordon Brown in 2007, he had worked a little on becoming more approachable in public. That he did not dislike people; that it was only his commitment to the job that made him appear a dour introvert.

Look at the changes within the McLaren team since the 2006 season if you want the proof of Dennis' attempt to 'spin' himself and his team in a more favourable light. He got rid of the brilliant, but fairly dull Raikkonen and brought in the fierce young reigning double World Champion Alonso as his replacement and then pulled another rabbit out of the hat by giving a relatively unknown rookie – Lewis Hamilton – his head in Formula One. Upon leaving McLaren, Raikkonen, known as 'The Iceman', illustrated that dourness with these few flat words: 'I have been five years with McLaren, but I wanted something else.' He didn't help his own cause while at McLaren by the simple fact that during his final campaign, McLaren failed to win a race for the first time in 10 years. That stark fact made Dennis all the more determined he would get his team back on top of the file – and bring back their first title since Mika Hakkinen last lifted it in 1999.

As the winds of change blew through the team, Dennis also decided that McLaren would begin the 2007 campaign with new title sponsors – only their third in the last 30 years – in communications giant Vodafone. And to cap it all, he laid on a PR extravaganza when he launched his new car, the MP4-22, in Spain. Alonso and Hamilton took to the streets of Valencia on a special circuit in front of 100,000 fans for a few parade laps in a launch estimated to have cost upwards of £4 million. Dennis wanted to show he could put on a launch with style and it went some way towards convincing a sceptical media that maybe he was mellowing a little. The blasts he would give them later in the season for their 'intrusions' into Hamilton's life would make them think twice, but there was little doubt that at the start of the campaign Ron Dennis was working hard to shake off his 'dull, boring, robot' tag. He admitted as much during the Valencia show, saying: 'Before we signed Vodafone over a year ago we had time to conduct an analysis of how people perceive the team. There were positives: integrity, honesty, sporting, cutting-edge, modern… But then came the negatives: cold, not particularly user-friendly, slightly aloof… We were surprised at that because at the circuit we do "meet the team" and we try to be co-operative with the media.

'But however the media might perceive us, we weren't perceived that way by the public, so we said "Let's do something about it". We wanted to make ourselves more human.'

He also spoke of his commitment to revitalise Formula One, which had fallen out of favour with many aficionados during the years of Schumacher dominance: 'Today is really about not just showing the car and the drivers, but more about our effort to practically demonstrate the commitment to Formula One. Don't see it as just a glitzy way to reveal a car. People wanted a dynamic Formula One that reached out – this is our effort to satisfy that need.'

Yet, at the same time in Valencia, he could not hide the more pragmatic side of his nature. Certainly, it had not deserted him when he spoke about his hopes for the new season, although he would enthuse about Lewis Hamilton, the boy he had been nurturing for nine years: 'It's important not to be optimistic or pessimistic, but realistic. So far, everything has led me to believe we are going to have a better car this year, although only time will tell if we're going to be competitive.

'Many people have said Lewis should be in a less competitive team in order that not so much is expected of him, but he's handling it. We've put a lot of work in over the last five months to bring him up to speed, to try to make him the fittest driver, the most knowledgeable driver about the rules. He understands things about the racing car that very few drivers have ever taken the effort to learn.

'He might not be the most experienced driver when he starts the season, but he will be a lot more knowledgeable than most of them about many, many subjects, and superfit as well.' With those words Ron Dennis proved why we Brits are glad to have him on our side in the Formula One battle. Depending on your stance, dull or not, he knows what he is talking about and his decision to blood Lewis Hamilton in F1, when probably no one else would have done so at the time, speaks volumes.

Ron Dennis was born on 1 June 1947 in Woking, the Surrey town in which he also grew up and would one day work as boss of McLaren. At 16 he left school and became an apprentice mechanic for the Thomson & Taylor garage at Weybridge (near the disused Brooklands circuit). He did a part-time Vehicle Technology course at Guildford Technical College. When Thomson & Taylor was taken over by the Chipstead Motor Group, Dennis transferred to another arm of the business: the Cooper Car Company. It was his first big break for they manufactured racing cars. In 1966, aged 19, he became a mechanic for the Cooper Formula One team, whose lead driver was Jochen Rindt. By 1968 Rindt had decided to move to Brabham. It was testament to the skills of Dennis that the ace German driver insisted he move with him. A year later, Rindt was on the move again, this time to Lotus. But now Dennis decided his loyalty was with Brabham and he became his chief mechanic. Tragically, a year later in 1970, Rindt – with whom he maintained a close friendship – would be killed in practice at the Italian Grand Prix in Monza.

The news left him devastated and he was hit by another blow in 1971 when Jack Brabham decided that he would call it a day. At the age of 44, the legendary Aussie had tied with Jackie Stewart for fifth in the points standings in the season. Upon retiring, he explained that he was making a complete break from racing, selling his interest in the team to Ron Tauranac and returning to Australia.

As one door closed another opened for Ron Dennis. Aged 25, he founded his own team in the same year with fellow mechanic Neil Trundle. Called Rondel, it would be based in Ron's stamping ground of Woking. They found sponsors in French oil company Motul and acquired two Brabham BT38s chassis from Tauranac. The team made its first appearance at Hockenheim with drivers Graham Hill and Tim Schenken. Hill won one of the two heats but was beaten to overall victory by François Cevert in his Tecno. A week later, on Easter Monday, Hill gave the team its first outright victory at Thruxton. Later that year the team expanded to a third car with Bob Wollek driving. That winter the same trio went to South America, where Schenken scored the team's second victory at Cordoba.

But trouble loomed. Ron was working all hours and, one

night, driving home late he was involved in a serious road accident. It forced him into a rethink: he decided he would no longer test the cars, turning his skills instead to managing the firm and planning his own cars. This was to be his destiny and soon he would develop his own chassis. A year later he commissioned Ray Jessop to design a F2 car for the 1973 season, to be called a Motul after the team's principal sponsor. The Motul chassis appeared at the start of the year. Henri Pescarolo won the second F2 race of the season and Tim Schenken added a second victory in the autumn. By then Dennis was planning for a Rondel Formula One programme, but his first attempt at the big time was to be spiked by outside sources.

In October 1973 the OPEC (Organisation of the Petroleum Exporting Countries) oil producers created an oil crisis and that winter Motul's sponsorship dried up. Dennis and Trundle had to abandon their dream. The project was sold to businessmen Tony Vlassopoulo and Ken Grob, who established the Token Formula One team. For the rest of that decade Ron Dennis concentrated on F2, quickly setting out the stall of discipline to his staff he demands even today. He explained that he expected cleanliness and orderliness in the traditionally messy garage and paddock, and total devotion and dedication to the job of ensuring the cars were in tip-top condition.

In 1975 he founded the Project Three team and soon he was churning out race winners as he became involved in running the BMW Junior Team F2 cars. By the end of the decade he had set up another new outfit, called Project Four.

The team chalked up success in Formula 2 and Formula 3, taking the British title in 1979 and 1980 with the backing of Philip Morris (Marlboro). They also took the 1980 Procar title with Niki Lauda on board.

Later that year, Dennis stepped up to the role for which he had surely been destined: boss of McLaren. The team's sponsors, who also backed his Project Four via Philip Morris, engineered a merger between the two and the new team was to be called McLaren International.

One of his first key decisions to turn round the flagging McLaren empire was to bring in designer John Barnard, who began work on the team's revolutionary new car, the MP4/1. It was used during the 1981, 1982 and 1983 seasons, and was the first Formula One car to use a carbon fibre composite shell. In 1982 he pulled off another masterstroke as he brought in massive finance by convincing Williams' backer Mansour Ojjeh to support his new set-up with hard cash. Ojjeh, a Syrian-born Saudi Arabian entrepreneur, had a passion for motor racing and did not need much persuading. For Dennis, the beauty of his arrival was that he could now use the $5 million Ojjeh was injecting into the firm for engine development. The new great era of McLaren was imminent as he ploughed cash into a Porsche-built turbo engine. Ojjeh and Dennis established TAG Turbo Engines and in September 1982 announced their first one. It was unveiled at the Geneva Motor Show in early 1983 and raced for the first time at the Dutch Grand Prix in August of that year.

The following year McLaren-TAG drivers Niki Lauda

and Alain Prost dominated the World Championship, scoring 12 wins in 16 races. Dennis was rewarded for all his efforts to turn the firm around as Lauda took the title by a half point from Prost, with both drivers scoring more than double the tally of third placed Elio de Angelis. However, the next year the tables were turned and Prost beat Lauda to the Driver's title with McLaren finishing eight points clear of second-placed Ferrari.

In five years Dennis had turned McLaren from an also-ran into the new kings, a remarkable achievement. At the end of 1984 Ojjeh became the majority shareholder in McLaren, although the deal was not made public until March 1985. It was a fair reward for his investment that had revitalised a company struggling to maintain its seat at the top of the racing world.

The TAG/McLaren empire continued to grow steadily in the late 1980s as more successes followed with Honda engines and they diversified into TAG Electronics and TAG/McLaren Marketing and McLaren Cars. Dennis, who had started out his career as a humble apprentice mechanic in Woking, was literally on top of the world. In 1988 his McLaren team took 15 of the 16 races and both titles, but he had a problem behind the scenes – keeping Prost and Senna from throttling each other. He did a good job, somehow massaging each of their massive egos, but by mid-1989 even he could not keep them at bay. After a controversial collision at the Japanese Grand Prix, which handed the title over to Prost, the Frenchman left the team for Ferrari and was replaced by Gerhard Berger the following season.

Senna continued the victory parade alone and went on to win the title in 1990 and 1991, to add to the one he won for the team in 1988. But by 1993 he too was gone and it would be five years before Mika Hakkinen and David Coulthard took them back to the very top of the sport, with the Finn taking the title.

As he had done so since taking command in 1980, Dennis looked carefully at his team's situation in that mid-90s barren period. He decided what was needed was an injection of new blood and he knew just the man to provide it. In 1996 he approached Williams' brilliant designer Adrian Newey to become technical director of McLaren. Newey agreed and by 1998 McLaren was once more in possession of the Drivers' and Constructors' titles. A second Drivers' title followed in 1999.

Dennis, who lives in Surrey with his wife and three children, was also honoured in his private life when he was awarded an Hon DTech from De Montford University in 1996 and an Hon DSc from City University, London, in 1997. Then, the man who put McLaren back on its feet once more would begin the new millennium in grand style as he received the CBE in 2000. Since taking over the team in 1980, he had guided it to 11 drivers' and eight Constructors' Championships. He had also led McLaren to victory at the first attempt in the Le Mans 24-hour race. At the end of 2000 he earned another notable award when he was presented with the honorary degree of Doctor of the University of Surrey. His citation read: 'Ron Dennis is being honoured for his significant contribution to the automotive engineering industry and for being a supreme ambassador for the UK and Surrey. Through the performance of the McLaren Formula One team, which has been under his direction since the 1980s, he has established a world-class company that continues to push forward the frontiers of technical design and application in many fields.'

Asked how he felt about the award, Dennis said: 'Extremely privileged and fortunate, which I'm sure are feelings everybody who receives a degree can relate to because degrees are a valued acknowledgement of the achievements a person has made.

'The TAG McLaren Group is attached to Surrey in general and Woking in particular. Many of our employees, including myself, are from the local area and have strong ties here. In addition, I am a believer that the working environment is crucial if you are to get the optimum performance from your employees, and the TAG McLaren employees work well in Surrey.'

He also expanded on his core belief that passion is the key to success from the top of the trade down: 'Being a success in industry is to truly care about what you are doing, to be passionate about it. This attitude then filters down through the company as a whole, and ensures that everybody does their utmost to ensure the company succeeds.' In 2001 he was also presented with a BRDC (British Racing Drivers' Club) Gold Medal in recognition for his contribution to motorsport.

As an aside: in June 2007, after the remarkable debut wins by Lewis Hamilton, some members of the public were asking why Dennis had not yet been knighted, that he deserved that recognition after unearthing such a gem. Motoring pundit Steve Robson put it this way: 'I'm pretty sure that the Queen's Birthday Honours are due to be announced sometime in the next week. With everything that he has achieved, isn't it about time Ron Dennis (CBE) was knighted? Frank Williams seems to have been Sir Frank for ages.'

Yet the years from 2000 to 2006 had not been as kind on the track. At least Dennis had the satisfaction of seeing his protégé develop and prosper during that barren spell. His relationship with Lewis Hamilton has always been close since they first met when Lewis was 13, but it has developed over the years into something special. Many trackside pundits refer to him being Hamilton's surrogate father, and it is easy to see why. I know for a fact that he sees Lewis as the greatest find and achievement of his career; there is a special bond between them that will surely never be broken. Ron has said 'You wait all your life for a lad like Lewis to come along. I feel lucky and honoured that I was the one to be with him in his career during his formative years.'

He has certainly become his professional mentor –once even describing Lewis as his '*My Fair Lady* experiment', a comment that may at first seem offhand and patronising. Anyone familiar with the film, though, will know that the protégé outstrips all expectations and the relationship eventually moves on to one of equality rather than mentor and student. That, I am told by a friend of Ron, is what he actually meant by the off-the-cuff remark. In turn, Lewis makes no bones about the fact that his wonderful story may not have happened without his mentor's faith in him: 'I first met Ron when I was 10 years old at an Autosport Awards ceremony. Listening to how he remembers the first time we met is special, and the faith, confidence and loyalty he's had in me over the years since has been key. I think it's a nice story – or the end of one story and the beginning of a new chapter.'

In almost a decade Dennis spent hour after hour with Lewis – teaching him, cajoling him and finally letting him lose on the Formula One track when the majority questioned that decision. Some felt he should have turned to the more experienced Gary Paffett or Pedro de la Rosa. But Dennis would have none of it, saying: 'Since 1998 Lewis has formed an important part of our long-term strategy and we are pleased that we are able to help him take another step and achieve his dream of becoming a Formula One racing driver. Pedro has done an outstanding job for us this season but we felt it was the right time to provide Lewis with this opportunity. It's obviously going to be the biggest challenge of Lewis' career so far but it's one that we are sure he will be able to meet. He is coming into the paddock for the first time as a Formula One racing driver and will have to familiarise himself with the pressures of a grand prix weekend. However, the confidence we have in Lewis' abilities and talent is clear from our decision to give him the chance.'

He also went on to say, with tongue firmly in cheek: 'I'm distinctly unimpressed by the majority of drivers in Formula One. Lewis is well equipped to deal with the drivers who fall into that category. Of course we have reservations – Lewis is an unproven product. But having the World Champion in one of our cars means that we can be less conservative and take the opportunity to give Lewis his chance.'

It was akin to a young lad of 17 being thrown into a Premiership football match for a daunting debut, as was the case with Ryan Giggs when he came on as a substitute for Manchester United against Everton at Old Trafford on 2 March 1991. I was at the match and still remember the gangly lad who was so thin and fragile he looked as if he would collapse if tackled. Until, that was, he danced merrily around the visitors' left-back...

As mentioned, there are strong similarities between the way Giggs' boss Sir Alex Ferguson looked after him and how Dennis has taken care of Hamilton. Both boys were prodigies, potential geniuses, and both had that cool head and fierce determination to make it. That in itself has made it easier for their managers. Both men are level-headed and modest, that is an important part of their appeal, particularly Lewis' as he comes from a sport that is infamous for its pit side arrogance, riches and lack of any humility whatsoever. As pointed out earlier, Lewis is similar in his coolness to his idol Michael Schumacher, but thankfully he does not have the iceman's legendary arrogance and aloofness.

Lewis has, of course, been brought up within the confines of the McLaren training academy for almost a decade. Ron Dennis would point that out to those who implied he had found the boy in the street and thrown him into a racing car. He would also stress, rather modestly, that he had worked with Lewis' father Anthony to keep him on track: 'Lewis gets his basic character from his family values, and we have just supplemented them. He is a well-rounded individual who appreciates not just what McLaren-Mercedes have done for him, but also what his family have done for him.'

British racing legend Nigel Mansell said he was convinced Lewis would not have made such an immediate impact were it not for the cosseting of Dennis and the resources he laid open to his protégé at McLaren: 'McLaren have been way overdue for success. Timing is everything. When a driver can arrive with a team and an engine coming right, it makes a difference. No disrespect to him – I think it was ordained. My story was a lot harder.'

Damon Hill is now convinced, after his initial worries that he would not last the season, that this boy has the lot – and that it is down to Lewis as much as Dennis. Lewis had the receptive abilities to take in what he was being told; he had the sense to listen and learn. Britain's last World Champion back in 1996, said that it was clear that he had also been helped by an excellent McLaren car. Not only this, but he has also consistently shown a maturity beyond his years to keep his cool in the toughest environment in motorsport: 'People should not underestimate what he has achieved in an incredibly short space of time,' said Hill after Lewis' Canadian victory. 'Yes, he's with a good team, and yes, he's got a good car, but to be winning grands prix, and be putting in performances like that, race after race, takes something special. He may be young and in his first season, but this guy is the real deal. If you're good enough in this sport, you're old enough – and, boy, is Lewis good enough!'

Martin Whitmarsh, McLaren's chief executive, gives an insider's view, agreeing that Lewis deserves credit for listening to Dennis. He confirmed that he has the talent and determination that separates him from the average circuit driver: 'Since I joined McLaren in 1989 I've worked with a lot of great drivers, including Alain Prost, Ayrton Senna, Mika Hakkinen and now Fernando Alonso with Lewis. I think it's pretty clear Lewis ticks all the necessary boxes. We set out to ensure that he arrived at Formula One, not only in a competitive organisation, but also as prepared as possible. Lewis has made a great start to his career: it is our continued job to help him cope with the enormous attention in the British media.

'We are sure that it won't negatively impact on Lewis, but we are keen to make sure that in the early stages of his career nothing occurs that detracts him from his focus of getting the job done.'

However, former grand prix driver Martin Brundle believes there is no chance of him struggling under the weight of explanation: 'No doubt, it's going to be a long haul for Lewis and there are a number of things he has to face – his first big shunt, for instance, and all the travel, which can be pretty wearying. But all the ingredients are there. He excites me. Will he be up there one day with the likes of Prost, Senna and Schumacher? He's got a chance, definitely.'

Ron Dennis' decision to hold his boy back from the hordes of press, as Sir Alex Ferguson did with Ryan Giggs, was also a measured move. It meant he did not have extra pressures to cope with; he could continue his burgeoning career and concentrate on improving his driving skills and awareness. Only when he started his grand prix career – and by then he was 22 – did Dennis give him the green light for interviews. By then he had spent those nine years in the McLaren version of the *Big Brother* house and was well aware of what to expect and how to handle himself. He knew how to avoid leading questions and to keep to the script, a tactic that won the admiration of bloggers: Motoring journalist Adam Spurr summed up the success of keeping the youngster back until he was definitely ready for the inevitable blanket exposure in this perceptive way: 'Formula One's newest star is being kept at arm's length from the media and PR agencies. This will hopefully enable the 22-year-old to concentrate on winning races... Time and time again, British sport has appeared to have found a figurehead. Tim Henman (mummy's little soldier), Greg Rusedski (that well-known Canadian – I mean British – superstar) and Jenson Button (rather left out in the cold now) have all failed to impress the most British of solo sports. Hamilton, however, was quietly ushered in to McLaren, and ridiculed the highest hopes and dreams of those of us who watched him enter Bernie Ecclestone's circuit.

'I think that this is a very important part of his success. He has been kept under the wing of Ron Dennis and guarded from the media hype that now surrounds him, so that he can concentrate on his driving. Even ITV F1, that bastion of drivers' interviews, have respected the request from Mr Dennis to respect his privacy. Everybody at ITV F1 seems to be willing Lewis to win, and doing everything in their power not to cause the slightest bit of disruption.'

Let's leave the final word in this chapter to Ron Dennis, the man who built up the McLaren legend into the glory story that young Lewis Hamilton desperately wanted to be a part of, the man who had enough faith in Lewis to push him to the threshold of greatness. Dennis said: 'He now has enough brownie points that he can lose some without getting severe criticism. Confidence is often coupled with arrogance, but there isn't an ounce of arrogance in Lewis. He listened, which frequently young people don't, and progressively built his career...'

CHAPTER 7

WIZARD IN OZ

After all the hype and anticipation finally the time had come for the talk to stop and for Lewis to walk the walk. Or, more precisely, drive the drive. Almost 10 years under the auspices of Ron Dennis and McLaren in Woking had passed and now the world would see whether Lewis could really cut it, or whether he was merely the planet's first 'engineered' Formula One driver, who failed because he was simply a prototype without soul.

Of course, those who had been following his development with interest and hope over that learning decade knew beforehand that he had all the right attributes in abundance. And after 18 March 2007, the secret would be shared by the whole world. Lewis Hamilton arrived at Melbourne on the Thursday before the race and the McLaren team noticed how cool and calm he was. One mechanic remarked: 'We knew he was a lad with composure and self-confidence, but we had not seen anything like the level of his calmness before. He seemed to have no nerves; he was certainly a lot different than Fernando Alonso, who was fidgety and kept asking us if everything was all right, if the car was really ready to go. Lewis acted as if he was out on a Sunday race around a go-kart track – you would never have guessed it was his debut in Formula One.'

The track, at Albert Park in the city of Melbourne, is hardly one of the most exciting on the circuit. If anything, it invites a fairly dull day's racing. There are few opportunities to overtake and David Coulthard once admitted it was far from being the most challenging of circuits. The track, which has been part of the Formula One circuit since 1996, lies within the city's park and its layout is smooth and flowing, with no 90-degree street corners to break the speed. It runs clockwise around a lake, and the scenery and atmosphere is relaxed and peaceful – one of the reasons why it is well liked by the drivers. For Lewis Hamilton, there could hardly have been a better setting for his opening.

One of the other features of Albert Park on a Formula One weekend is its intimacy; drivers tend to sit out and chat with each other behind the garages. Maybe because it's the traditional curtain-raiser, there is a friendliness and empathy between the teams that certainly evaporates by the time the Formula One circus hits Europe three months later, when rivalries have been established and the whole business is much more cutthroat.

At the opener, it's not the end of the world if you don't

win – there are another 16 races on which to stake your claim for glory. Sure, it's a chance to set down a marker, but it's only the aperitif to the main course. For the boy from Britain this was another plus factor: already he could relax without the pressure of being expected to win, being a rookie. But he could also unwind with his father Anthony, having a chat and a glass of soda in a deckchair in between practice and qualifying.

That suited Lewis perfectly. All the limelight, all the attention, was on his co-driver Alonso, the double World Champion, who was soaking up all the interest before his debut for his new team. This was the man who had won at Melbourne the previous season and who was expected to win again, this time for a new team at the start of the 2007 campaign.

It was certainly an unusual scenario: two men making their debut in the same team. Usually, one would be a seasoned pro who had worked for the team for a few seasons. Who knew the team inside out and knew the mechanics and the tech man, and how they worked; was aware of their idiosyncrasies and demands. Ron Dennis was not renowned for being a gambler – he would later contend there was no gamble. That he knew full well what Lewis was capable of, and that Alonso was, after all, a World Champion, who should hardly have needed nursing into a new team.

Typically, he was right on both points although Alonso's questions did surprise the team. He was to settle down after a couple of practice sessions when the car handled well and he knew everything would be OK. Dennis later admitted the Spaniard's previous nerves and doubts were a good sign. Alonso was also a perfectionist, and there was nothing wrong with that – on the contrary it showed the professionalism of the man he was willing to pay £10 million a year to be his No. 1 driver.

In the build-up to the race, Big Ron allowed Lewis to speak a little to the press, to open up a bit and show who he was. Here are some of the more interesting points from a question and answer section.

Asked what drove him on, Lewis replied: 'I am motivated by a desire to be the best at whatever I decide to put my mind to. Once I have decided to take up a challenge, my inner self will not let me give up unless I have achieved my goal. I love motor racing and I have done so since I first watched it on TV when I was about 5. The key element in all of this is that I am not here to take part, I am here to win, and I will do whatever mentally and physically it takes to achieve that in due course. I do not plan to waste this opportunity.'

When asked about Alonso he was Mr Tactful: 'It is truly an honour for me to be given this opportunity to work alongside Fernando in my first year as a Formula One driver. I have a tremendous amount of respect for what he has achieved. The sheer size of the challenge of working with him and competing against him is what is most exciting. All of my former team-mates have been hugely competitive and the challenge and excitement comes from having to find the answers to the most important question, "Just how far do I need to push myself to beat that person and just how far can I go?" With Fernando being a two-times World Champion, I know I have to dig deeper than ever before which is what I love about being a racing driver.'

He admitted it was his dream come true to make his debut for McLaren: 'The feeling is indescribable. Growing up I always dreamed of racing for McLaren and now I am. The thought of racing and working with my team-mates is a great feeling, to be driving a Vodafone McLaren Mercedes is literally surreal.' Ever thankful to his immediate family, whose support he readily acknowledges as playing a key role in his success, Lewis also praised his professional family – specifically Ron Dennis, Martin Whitmarsh and Norbert Haug – for the long-term support and guidance, and of course for the initial opportunity to succeed in a field he loves more than any other.

He also recalled how the history of McLaren was a big attraction: 'Like most kids, I am sure I dreamt of one day racing with Ayrton Senna and Alain Prost. Now my dream has literally turned into a reality and I am driving not only in Formula One but also for the same team as Ayrton and Alain did. I worked hard to make it to Formula One but never imagined it would actually be with a team such as McLaren and in my first year!

Asked if he could possibly emulate his success in GP2 2006 in 2007 in Formula One, his response was typically modest: '2006 was a fantastic year, a year in which everything I had learned through karting, Formula Renault and Formula 3 all came together in GP2. I learned a great deal in GP2 and thank Frederic Vasseur and everyone at

ART for their support. At the end of each year, I sit down with my manager and we review and evaluate the year and come up with a plan for the following year. 2007 will be no different to any other year. Once I have a plan, I always follow it to the end. I know I have to work harder to be stronger, mentally and physically, and to prepare myself for whatever may come my way in Formula One, but I am ready and relishing the challenge.'

And what made him tick – what was his ambition now that he had finally made it into Formula One? He replied: 'If you want to be the best at whatever career you choose in life, then you have to compete at the very top. Formula One is the pinnacle of motorsport. From the time I started my racing career in Cadet Karts in 1994, right the way through to Formula Renault, Formula 3 and GP2, I have dedicated my life to achieving my goal of becoming a Formula One World Champion. I am now another huge step closer to reaching my ultimate dream.'

Unashamedly, Lewis stated that his aim is always to win but, aware that it was still his debut season, he recognized there was work to do to learn as much as possible from Alonso and the whole team: 'I aim to do a steady job for the team and help them progress towards both Constructor's and Driver's Championships.'

He then revealed a little more about his personal life, his ambitions, loves and hopes in a Q-and-A session with the Formula One Complete website team. Asked what he would wish for if he were granted three wishes, Lewis replied that the first one would be for more, and then for the health and security of his family. 'Finally, I would wish that I could do something positive for others less fortunate. I am not sure what or how just yet, but I'm sure the answer will come to me in time.'

The journalist enquired what items he couldn't live without if stranded on a remote island; the reply being music ('My MP3 player as I couldn't cope without having any music'), his girlfriend, and unsurprisingly, a super-fast form of transport: 'A speedboat with a full tank of fuel would be useful.'

If he weren't a racing driver, Lewis identified music as the field he's be most interested in working in. He plays the guitar and when he was younger he tried to set up his own band. A lot of his friends are involved in music so it is a big part of his life. Failing that, he would have probably pursued another sport.

The questioning quickly returned to Formula One, and gave Lewis the opportunity to talk about what he liked about his job: 'The feeling you get when you are really driving on the edge and pushing beyond the limit. The rush you get, the feeling of speed, the force that your body is under, all of that coming together gives the biggest adrenaline buzz and it's something that you can't experience anywhere else.'

At the time of the interview he was driving a Smart Forfour Brabus, which he described as great fun to drive. But he was keen to extend his collection and getting a Mercedes-Benz was a high priority. His ultimate dream car would be the orange McLaren Formula One LM housed at the McLaren Technology Centre.

Lewis' dream holiday destination would undoubtedly be somewhere in the Caribbean. With family in Grenada he had the developed a love for visiting the island. 'Maybe someday I'll visit some of the other beautiful islands of the Caribbean, but for now Grenada is the place.

'I have a fairly extensive training programme that takes up a lot of my time away from the track. When I do have some downtime,' continued Lewis, 'I like to spend it relaxing with my family and friends, in particular catching up with my younger brother Nicolas.' Away from work, Lewis named golf and basketball as two sports he liked to play to keep in shape.

The website team ended by asking Lewis about his favourite track (Monaco) and whether he had a hero: 'I would say that I haven't really had a hero since I was very young as a hero is someone that seems invincible. There are people that I greatly admire, though. In Formula One Ayrton Senna was really inspirational to me and I didn't think Michael Schumacher would ever be counted as a hero, but I really do look up to him for what he has achieved and what he has done for the sport.' Outside of racing, he named his Dad foremost, then hip hop star P. Diddy, whom Lewis cites as a motivational role model for he way in which he has built up his empire. 'Finally, Martin Luther King who was just a great person and continues to inspire many people, including me.'

Then, this unassuming, eminently likeable boy went out for practice in his first grand prix weekend. During the first and second sessions both he and Alonso turned in fine performances, proving McLaren were in fine fettle and that the team was well on the pace. After practice, Lewis was buzzing with adrenaline, his first taste of Formula One action had left him wanting more. He said: 'I was so excited when I drove out of the garage for the first time this morning; it was an incredible feeling as I have wanted to be a Formula One driver since I started karting, and now I am and enjoying every single moment. The track is good, particularly as I love street circuits and the whole atmosphere is amazing. Back at the McLaren Technology Centre we have done a lot of simulation work to prepare me for this weekend but it was good to actually drive it for real. The car feels good and the two sessions today were really useful.'

He would also do well in his first ever grand prix qualifying sessions, ending up fourth on the grid. Eventual race winner Kimi Raikkonen, in the Ferrari, took pole position in a time of 1:26.072, Alonso came second in 1:26.493 and BMW's Nick Heidfeld third in 1:26.556. Lewis clocked 1:26.755.

After qualifying he said: 'I'm overwhelmed to be on the second row for my first grand prix – a huge thank you to the team who have worked so hard, both here at the track and back at base. This weekend is what I have been preparing myself for during the past 13 years and I'm enjoying every moment. I think we are in with a good chance in the race. Basically I want to get a good start and then work hard to score as many points for the team and myself. I'm not going to make any predictions because anything can happen, but so far, so good.'

The race itself would see the same four who finished top in qualifying finish in the top four, but with Lewis and Heidfeld changing places. A crowd of 105,000 people flocked to Albert Park for the season's opener – and the first race of the 'post-Schumacher' era; the German's final race being the Brazilian Grand Prix on 22 October 2006.

Beforehand, a nervy Ron Dennis had asked that TV companies refrain from conducting pre-race interviews with his boy. Instead, the TV scenes during those vital last few minutes before the start would show Lewis and Ron, student and mentor for the previous decade, together in the pits. Lewis is all ears as the Big Man gives him some last words, some final encouragement as the moment for which they had been building so long edges ever closer.

This was a poignant moment. It could also, conceivably, have been the moment when Fernando Alonso first questioned whether he had made the right decision in joining McLaren. The Spanish boy who loved, nay demanded, the limelight and all the fuss and minute attention of his team saw his boss spending those last key seconds before what was, after all, his big debut too, with a rookie. The rookie he had imagined would be his easy No. 2 on the way to an easy third world crown.

Afterwards Big Ron revealed he had been using those last few minutes to advise his protégé that the start was the key to the race and success: 'I told him to hold his position at the start and not do anything stupid.' Lewis certainly took in the advice, indeed, he even improved on it, taking a calculated gamble to head past Alonso into third place in the early seconds. The *Guardian*'s Paul Kelso explained it in this way: 'What Hamilton did announced the nature of his prodigious gift. As a declaration of intent and talent it has rarely been matched.'

Throughout the race, the youngster never looked out of his depth. Ice-cool, decisive and brilliant, he even matched the fierce pace of Raikkonen's Ferrari, while driving with a fine judgment and maturity to keep Alonso at bay for the best part of the 58-lap race. He would only drop to third when Alonso pulled off a short second pit stop to come out in front after Lewis had been previously been held up on his own in-lap.

For Raikkonen, this was the perfect start in his role as Michael Schumacher's replacement. The Finnish driver led from start to finish and lived up to his pre-season label as title favourite. Kimi said: 'We didn't need to really push as hard as we could have. My biggest problem was the radio – it stopped working just before the start. It is special moment with a new team, everything is new, to win in the first race. I am really happy with the team and the way things are going. It couldn't be any better than it is now.'

But his glory was short-lived for his win was overshadowed by Lewis Hamilton's display as the world's press quickly woke up to the fact that Formula One finally had a new hero, a new phenomenon after the era of Schumacher. Quite simply, it had been an incredible result by Lewis to finish on the podium in his debut race. It also continued the sequence of glory for British drivers at the circuit since its opening in 1996. Damon Hill won the inaugural event that year in the Williams and the following year Britain struck gold again – this time David Coulthard triumphed for McLaren, their first, incidentally, with a Mercedes' engine.

Colourful Eddie Irvine was to win in 1999 – his first Formula One win for Ferrari – and four years later Coulthard notched up his second victory at Melbourne in the McLaren. As this book went to press, that remained David's last Formula One win, and will probably turn out to be his final one.

Damon Hill summed it up: 'Lewis qualified well, and he raced brilliantly. He was at the sharp end in his first grand prix and was competitive with his team-mate – really, really good.' Hill was, of course, Britain's last Formula One World Champion, and he admitted he had seen some fine driving by Lewis; enough to convince even him that the boy had what it took to follow him. He was particularly impressed by his brilliant start: 'The weight of expectation was massive on Lewis and it seemed to me he didn't really show any sign of weakness at all. He was on it right from the word go. His start was just a classic, fantastic, pulling that move on the first corner. It was a brave, but committed overtaking manoeuvre.

'It's very, very easy for someone in their first grand prix to make a hash of that, but he never looked like he was fazed by what he was doing – he just did it and it came off. And when he was in front of Fernando [Alonso], you could see he was really using the entire road. He was right up against the wall going into the switchback at the back of Melbourne and he was using all the road on the exit.

'He was pushing, he was confident, and he never looked ragged. It was good. He looked very happy on the podium. I think he knew he'd done a bloody good job. He was in the race at the sharp end in his first ever grand prix and competitive with his team-mate. Tremendous – really, really good!'

Former Great Britain hope Jenson Button suffered a frustrating weekend in his Honda, finishing 15th in Melbourne. At least he had the good grace to congratulate the man who had taken his place as the nation's new Formula One idol: 'He did a fantastic job. Lewis had a great first race and was lucky enough to be in a good car, but there is no getting away from the fact that he did a great job.'

Lewis was pleased with his weekend's work in Australia and the result enthused him with new confidence – he now felt able to predict that he would one day become Formula One Champion, although modesty forbade him from saying it would be in his first season. He admitted he had enjoyed every moment of the big debut: 'Formula One is the highest challenge I've ever had. I am very competitive and winning is what I want to do. My dream is to win and become a World Champion. Three years is a good time to put on my goal to win a world title.'

His third-place finish proved to be the best debut performance by a British racer in 41 years since Mike Parkes took second place in the French Grand Prix. Lewis finished 11.3 seconds behind Alonso who, in turn, was 7.2 seconds behind the flying Finn. His result meant that he had also become the first Formula One rookie to claim a podium finish since Jacques Villeneuve in 1996, but don't forget that the Canadian already had previous motor racing pedigree in America's Indy Car series. To be fair, Raikkonen also claimed a record: becoming the first driver to win in their first race for Ferrari since Nigel Mansell in 1989. It was also the first race in World Championship history (obviously apart from the all-time opener in 1950) when all three podium finishers were making their debut for their team.

The Finn took the maximum 10 points to lead the Driver's title with Alonso close behind on eight. Lewis had picked up his first grand prix points in his first race, yet very few would have backed him to be third in the race for the Championship with those six points.

Mark Sharman, head of ITV Sport, was understandably also delighted with Hamilton's performance in Melbourne. He knew this would mean increased viewing figures during the season if Lewis could maintain his excellent start and said it had convinced him that the 22-year-old was surely destined to become the next British sporting icon: 'If Lewis begins to win races he will become the biggest sports star in Britain in no time. He's one of a new breed of young sportsmen like Theo Walcott and Amir Khan, who are a breath of fresh air, and he's hugely exciting.'

Former Formula One driver Mark Blundell, now working as ITV's main analyst, agreed and also voiced the opinion that Lewis was on the way to becoming a superstar with McLaren: 'This is a multi-million pound outfit... All their work and all the expectations of the sponsors rest on Lewis' shoulders. He's the first black driver, he came with a lot of expectation, having won the support series GP2 last year, but all we're talking about is a great new driver. This is a sport that lost a superstar in Michael Schumacher last year, and people are wondering if we might have found the replacement.'

Lewis said how much he had enjoyed the race and paid tribute to the effort of his mechanics and technical support: 'I'm absolutely ecstatic – today's result is more than I ever dreamed of achieving on my grand prix debut. A big thank you to the team who have worked so hard during the winter to make sure I was as prepared as I could possibly be. I made a good start, but the BMWs were quick off the line and Kubica managed to get past. There was no room on the inside so I got on the left and managed to outbrake both Kubica and Fernando coming into the first corner to take third. The race was intense, and I was working very hard. I made a few mistakes, but nothing major and really enjoyed myself. It was great to lead the race for a few laps, but I knew it was only a temporary thing. Fernando got past me at the second pit stop as he was able to stay out a bit longer and I lost some time behind backmarkers. We now have a lot of work ahead of us with the Malaysia test and the rest of the season, but there is no doubt that we can build from what has been achieved today.'

Fernando Alonso claimed to be delighted with his McLaren debut, saying it had set down a marker: 'What a great way to start the season and my career as a McLaren Mercedes driver! Of course it's always better to win, but

Kimi Raikkonen was a little bit quicker than us today. However, I'm really pleased. My start was a bit strange, with both BMWs being very quick off the line and I was so busy defending my line from Heidfeld on the outside that it was not possible for me to stay ahead of him. I was then behind Lewis for a while and was just focusing on keeping up with him and sometimes dropping back to allow the car to cool down. I took second after the second pit stop as I was able to stay out for an additional two laps.

'Originally it was meant to be one lap, but because I was behind Lewis I managed to save enough fuel for 1 more lap. We will now continue to work hard to give us the best opportunity to beat Ferrari at the Malaysian Grand Prix.'

Ron Dennis admitted he was pleased with the showing of his two drivers, but typically of his perfectionist zeal, was disappointed not to have won: 'Of course as always we came to Australia to win, but a somewhat unexpected strategy adopted by BMW was very disruptive to our race. Following Heidfeld's first pit stop the gap was just too big to realistically close it and the additional range from our strategy was subsequently wasted.

'Both drivers did an excellent job giving us a narrow lead in the Constructors' Championship. A special thank you to the test team and the workforce back at the McLaren Technology Centre, who have worked so hard during the winter and contributed so much to the faultless reliability that we have enjoyed throughout the weekend. The coming Malaysian test should give us every opportunity to further improve the competitiveness of our cars.'

Norbert Haug, competition chief for McLaren's engine partner Mercedes-Benz, took time out to give both Alonso and Lewis a vote of confidence, saying: 'The season started well with Fernando and Lewis scoring 14 points on their debut race. Fernando showed with his performance exactly why he is the double World Champion whilst Lewis made a perfect start to his grand prix career and proved absolutely worthy of the confidence we have had in him for the past 10 years.'

An interesting sidebar to the Australian Grand Prix of 2007 is that two other drivers were making their Formula One debuts – Heikki Kovalainen and Adrian Sutil. Sutil is considered one of the drivers who could push Lewis in years to come if he gets the right car – he was to finish 17th in Melbourne. But Kovalainen's experiences there sum up just how brilliantly Lewis did to finish third, and just how competitive and unforgiving relative failure is received within Formula One.

The 25-year-old Finn had been promoted from test driver to replace Fernando Alonso at Renault after the Spaniard's move to McLaren. But he spun at the Jones Chicane on his 40th lap, which led to him losing a place to Felipe Massa. He then ran wide on several occasions during the early part of the race, finishing tenth, and received a public wind-up from Renault team chief Flavio Briatore, with the unforgiving Italian describing his debut as 'rubbish'.

Meanwhile, phone-ins and website forums in the UK were buzzing after Lewis' dazzling debut. The BBC prompted a flurry of responses on the 606 site after proclaiming: 'Given that the McLaren was comfortably the second quickest car in Melbourne – and only one of the faster Ferraris was in with a shout at the front following Felipe Massa's problems in qualifying – third is about where Hamilton should have finished. Far, far more remarkable was his performance in comparison with team-mate Fernando Alonso.

'This is the finest all-round driver in the world, a double World Champion. Someone who last year took on and beat in a straight fight Michael Schumacher – who some consider to be the greatest ever and who was certainly the greatest of his generation.

'And yet Hamilton had the temerity to pass the illustrious Spaniard around the outside at the start, and make him work hard for the rest of the race. You could count on one hand the number of drivers who could do that to Alonso in the same car, let alone on their grand prix debut. He made his mark in quite emphatic style and there is no doubt that Alonso, and the rest of the Formula One field, will have taken notice.'

The remarks prompted Formula One fan Graham Parkin to say: 'I was fortunate enough to be able to watch Lewis in GP2 at Silverstone last year and remember a manoeuvre that was surprisingly reminiscent of the one he did at the start in Melbourne as he went past Alonso. The only difference at Silverstone was that he managed to pass *three* cars on a corner you supposedly cannot overtake on. For the rest of the race, he then received a standing ovation for every single lap he completed.

'I don't think I have ever seen a situation where there has been more interest in the "warm-up" race than the actual main event, the Formula One. Everyone was talking about Hamilton and how that if he wasn't in a Formula One car within two years, someone was missing out on a great talent. He is the UK's greatest hope of another Championship winner.'

Karting fanatic Alan Dove said it was about time Lewis received his rightful acclaim: 'It is nice to see that finally everyone is witnessing just how good Lewis Hamilton is! The UK karting scene has been singing his praises for over 10 years. I raced the kid when I was 10 and he was an absolute genius. I would go as far as to say he hasn't really improved much since he was 10.... he has *always* been that good!'

The excellent website, grandprix.com, summed up Lewis' display in fine style by comparing it to a Hollywood movie debut: 'Lewis Hamilton's start was straight out of Hollywood. He edged away off the line and was aware that Robert Kubica, a career-long rival of Lewis', who looks like one of those Nordic villains that Bruce Willis would have shot in the 94th minute of the movie, was alongside him. Worse still (cut to slow motion), Kubica was getting ahead and switching across in front of our hero.

'Lewis did what Sylvester Stallone would have done and jinked the wheel to the left and swooped around the outside in an elegant arc, passing not only the evil Polish villain (who actually seems like a very nice chap) but also the double World Champion Fernando Alonso to grab third place. (Cue stirring music).

'We were watching the birth of a new star as Lewis Hamilton kept Fernando Alonso at bay in the finest traditions of comic books heroes of yesteryear. The double World Champion was being held back by the plucky young chap on his grand prix debut. People in newspaper offices across the world with no interest in Formula One were perking up. This was a news story. Lewis was on his way to the front cover of *Sports Illustrated*, following the path cut recently through the media jungle by Danica Patrick.

'It was the most impressive debut in Formula One for more than 10 years. Hell, that's rubbish! This was much more impressive than what Jacques Villeneuve did back in 1996 because he had much more experience with big powerful cars when he took the Williams to second place in Melbourne.'

Great stuff... Now all Lewis had to do was continue to prove he was worthy of the growing adulation and hype, that his third place finish in Melbourne was no fluke – he was the real thing. Here was the new cool-headed Schumacher mixed with a liberal sprinkling of the adventure of that legendary daredevil Senna. He now had three weeks to contemplate his initial success and rev himself up for another test on the other side of the world. Sepang, in Malaysia, eagerly awaited the young star, but would he survive unscathed and retain his cool in the heat and humidity of a circuit built on land that was formerly a jungle?

CHAPTER 8

THE RUMBLE IN THE JUNGLE

As he approached the second Formula One grand prix of his life at Sepang on 8 April 2007, the heat was on for Lewis Hamilton. If Melbourne had been a relatively easy-going introduction to the high-stress of top-level motor racing, and given that little was expected of him in his debut race, it was now a different story altogether in the humidity of Malaysia. Now the whole wide world knew Ron Dennis and McLaren had been hiding away and cultivating a phenomenon, and that Lewis Hamilton was no traditional young man thrown into the Formula One inferno. No, here was someone who was the virtual finished article before he had even properly started. A one-off who could not only live up to the hype, but exceed it.

Sepang was a prime example of how Formula One ring-master Bernie Ecclestone envisaged the sport developing.

The track had been specially built in 1999 on land that had been jungle. It was a shimmering, shining circuit – the first of Formula One's new generation of ultra-modern, high-tech circuits. It was also part of the Malaysian government's attempt to bring riches to the country: in the mid-1990s the Prime Minister, Dr Mahathir Mohamad, determined that by 2020 Malaysia would be a fully industrialised nation. He decided that the best way to achieve this would be through the auto trade.

The nation's biggest oil company, Petronas, began investing heavily in Formula One when Sauber and Malaysia's national car company, Proton, bought Lotus Engineering. Dr Mohamad ordered a grand prix track to be constructed as part of the vision and not just any track either. In conjunction with Bernie Ecclestone, he wanted to create a new-style circuit that would be the envy of the world in terms of facilities and technology. Just 2 miles from Kuala Lumpur, the circuit did not disappoint – its combination of long, high-speed straights and tight, twisting corners made it a challenge for drivers. Overtaking was possible but you had to be top-notch to master the circuit.

That humid Sunday the circuit of the future would welcome the driver of the future. Lewis Hamilton arrived in sweltering heat on the Thursday before the race and was taken aback by the level of interest in him. His incognito lifestyle was now a thing of the past; everyone in Sepang was asking about him. Interest was not just from the UK – the Americans and the Germans were also keen to learn all they could, as were his Far Eastern hosts. He was in big demand. His third place finish in Melbourne ensured this would be the case, but his personality and easy-going charm was also a massive lure for a press and Formula One following that had found itself distanced from the drivers during the heyday of Schumacher.

The young black British wunderkind provided a welcome antithesis to the ice-cool arrogance, some might say lack of soul, of the German. In contrast, Lewis was very approachable and full of smiles; he was welcoming and, most of all, down-to-earth. It was a remarkable landshift in the world of Formula One and it was clear as early as the second grand prix of the season.

Lewis was asked how he felt on his arrival: could he emulate his success in Melbourne, or did he concede that it had maybe been a mere fluke? His reply was telling: he said that he was not in Sepang to make up the numbers, no, he was here to win: 'There's no rush as there are 16 races left. But I'm here to win and whether it's the first weekend or the last, as long as I get one in, then I'll be happy. From what I had seen of the track before arriving for the test I thought it looked like a great circuit and I was not disappointed. Its layout means you can build up a great rhythm, with all the corners running into each other. It is also really wide, which I imagine will lead to exciting racing.'

And how was he coping with his new fame? He admitted: 'I'm still relaxed about it all but it is a bit like an out-of-body experience. It's like I'm sitting out there watching myself. Just yesterday in town, I saw a big poster of myself. It is a bit strange with all the attention.'

Of course, he was at a natural disadvantage to Alonso and most of the other drivers at Sepang: apart from testing the previous week, he had never driven around the track. It would be the same story when they finally arrived in America. Sure, he had an idea what it would be like from his time in the McLaren simulator at Woking, but his only first-hand experience had been during testing, whereas Alonso, for example, had won in Malaysia in 2005 and was second behind Giancarlo Fisichella in 2006. Yes, he was at a distinct disadvantage but was he concerned? By Sunday night he finished runner-up to his team-mate, with another 8 points in the bag in the title race. As Murray Walker might say... remarkable.

Lewis was pleased with the way things went during practice and felt he had acclimatised well: 'This is my first Malaysian Grand Prix, but I got to know the circuit well during last week's test. The heat and humidity are as I expected and have trained for. The practice today was pretty straightforward and we made further steps. The circuit conditions are constantly changing, which makes it challenging to find the right balance. I'm looking forward to qualifying tomorrow.'

In qualifying, Ferrari's Felipe Massa had taken pole after a brilliant final lap. The Brazilian made amends for his qualifying failure in Melbourne by clocking 1:35.043, 0.267 secs ahead of Alonso. Raikkonen was third in 1:35.479 and Hamilton fourth in 1:36.045. As an illustration of just how superbly Lewis was driving, his vastly more experienced fellow Brits David Coulthard and

Jenson Button were thirteenth and fifteenth respectively on the grid, come Sunday.

After qualifying he admitted he had eased off a little as the rain had started to fall; that he could possibly have done even better, but did not want to gamble on a wet circuit. He said: 'It went pretty smoothly. I think the car performed well and we look forward to the race. I'm optimistic about the race and I'm on the clean side of the track. The car is working well and I think we could have had two cars on the front row. However, when I came to Turn 7 it had started spitting with rain a little bit. I had experienced this at the test last week and knew it could be slippery, so I eased off a small amount.'

In the race he delivered another fine display of measured, mature driving, finishing in 17.5 seconds and runner-up to Alonso. This was the Spanish ace's first victory for McLaren and elevated him above Kimi Raikkonen in the title race; it was also the team's first win since Japan in 2005. Hamilton held off a late challenge from Raikkonen to confirm his second successive podium appearance. After going from fourth to second on the first lap, Lewis also saw off a determined Felipe Masa. The Brazilian had tried to charge past Lewis on lap six but overshot the corner, slid off the track and finished in fifth position.

The McLaren 1–2 finish was an emphatic declaration of intent to Ferrari after their triumph in Melbourne. Ferrari themselves conceded they had a faster car, but their drivers had not matched Alonso and Lewis. Afterwards, perhaps predictably, given the heat and humidity, Lewis was drained but still coherent and making a lot of sense in what he said. It had been, he admitted, easily the toughest race and challenge he had ever faced: 'I was defending my position for a lot of the time and I'm so pleased that I managed to keep both Felipe and Kimi behind me. However, it was hard work and it was just so hot inside the cockpit. I made a good start and was able to get past Felipe and Kimi to take second. At one point Felipe was attacking and ended up going slightly off the track, and I was able to keep second. Kimi was catching towards the end as I was struggling with the balance a bit, but what a race! I now have experience of racing in these conditions and will be even better prepared next year.

'To see two Ferraris behind you, two red blobs in the mirror, knowing that they had started lighter than you and were quicker than you... I had to keep pushing all the way to the last lap and not make any mistakes. I had to bite my tongue and dig as deep as I could, and yet preserve the energy I had and pull the car to the end. Defending is 10 times harder than trying to overtake someone when you have two guys lighter on fuel and perhaps slightly faster. I'm now looking forward to Bahrain. Congratulations to Fernando, very well done.'

Even before the cars had been packed away in the trucks, Ron Dennis was also planning ahead for Bahrain. He took time out to say a few words about Hamilton's second place finish: 'Lewis continues to demonstrate why he has warranted the enthusiasm of all of us who have worked with him over the years.'

Bahrain was just a week after Sepang, giving Lewis little time to recover from the ordeal of Malaysia. Another new, hi-tech circuit, the Manama – located in desert land in Sakhir – was designed by Formula One's in-house architect with the aim of opening up the sport to the Middle East. In 2004 Bahrain became the first country in the region to host a Formula One grand prix and it did not take Lewis long to acclimatise. Then again, he was no stranger to it: indeed, this had been the circuit where he had achieved one of his best ever results prior to joining Formula One. In December 2004 he won the first ever Bahrain F3 Superprix after starting eleventh on the grid. In a superb drive, he moved up to fourth by the end of the opening lap, and on the final lap sped past his two main rivals, Nico Rosberg and Jamie Green, to take victory.

The memory of that race gave him hope that he could repeat his glory run. As in Malaysia, he showed an incredible coolness in searing heat. Those months of fitness training back in Woking had clearly paid off – his body had shown a remarkable recovery rate from a week previous when he had clearly been exhausted after finishing his work in Sepang.

As they got down to business back in Bahrain, his father Anthony expressed his own excitement and apprehension over Lewis' start to his grand prix career. That second place in Malaysia had also made him the first man to finish in the top three in his first two races since another Brit, Peter Arundell, did so in 1964. And that prompted Anthony to say: 'I'm frightened what's going to happen next. It's crazy.'

Once again, Lewis was the focus of attention for the world's media who had gathered in the desert. And he did not let them down – giving a confident soundbite when asked what they could expect of him: he was out to make history by becoming the first man ever to record three straight podium finishes in Formula One. And, no, he wasn't ruling out the possibility of winning his third race. Jenson Button, the previous blue-eyed British boy, had needed 113 starts to earn his first win, but Lewis was quietly confident: 'I'm pushing and working as hard as I can. It may be this weekend, it may be the last race of the year; it may be next year.

'So far I haven't made a mistake. But we all make mistakes trying to put the car through everything and trying to better ourselves. It is inevitable when you are pushing the car to the limit that you are going to make mistakes and it will happen at some point.'

Practice went well as Lewis' uncanny knack of adapting swiftly to any circuit continued apace. After a steady few laps getting to grips with the Sakhir circuit, he said: 'It has been a positive session today. In the first practice the track was very dirty and slippery so there was no point spending too much time looking at the set-up. In the second session we began our fine tuning and completed a couple of long runs. I think I was quicker and more consistent than previously in the long runs, which is positive and there is definitely more to come. We now have quite a bit of data to look at, but so far, so good.'

So far, so good indeed! Lewis was third in the drivers' standings, four points behind Alonso and Raikkonen, and

McLaren headed the team standings with 32 points, nine ahead of Ferrari. Could he maintain his dynamic start? Qualifying suggested yes, he could. Massa would once again take pole, but Lewis also qualified on the front row of the grid for the first time in his career. Significantly, there were also heavy brows and mutterings from Alonso – the rookie had outpaced the double World Champion, his senior co-driver, for the first time, and he had done so in the same car. This was a watershed in his relationship with Alonso. While the Spaniard had been happy to go along with his less experienced team-mate, now, for the first time, he looked at him through different eyes – of grudging respect and, possibly, fear.

After qualifying, Lewis was, inevitably, on a high: 'To go into my third race in Formula One and get a front row is amazing. But the lap was not that great. Earlier in the session I had better laps. Qualifying is tough, really intense, and you need to pull out absolutely everything in that final flying lap. The wind is always changing – sometimes there is a tailwind, sometimes a crosswind. I feel pretty relaxed about what has happened so far. It feels natural. I am happy to be where I am. But the race is going to be tough. The first corner here is always tricky; it is such a tight corner.

'But I have been here before and feel a bit more comfortable with the circuit. I am sure we'll have a strong race tomorrow.'

But he did better than that. By the end of Sunday's race, he was joint leader in the battle for the Driver's title. Massa took first place from pole in his Ferrari for the third win of his career, but Lewis was runner-up, just 2.3 seconds behind the Brazilian, with Raikkonen third, 8.5 seconds behind Lewis. A distraught Alonso finished fifth. The result meant that he, Raikkonen and Lewis were all now on 22 points, locked together at the head of the Championship.

Lewis acknowledged his place in the record books: 'I'm very pleased with today's result. To have finished on the podium three times out of three is fantastic. We have definitely closed the gap to Ferrari and I know everybody will continue to push hard to improve even more in time for the Spanish Grand Prix.

'I was able to keep up with Felipe in the first stint but I really struggled with the balance of the car in the second. I had a lot of under steer and wasn't able to brake as late as I would have liked. However, after the second pit stop – when I changed to hard tyres – I was able to push again. I really enjoyed the race today and with a few more laps I might have been able to challenge Felipe for the lead.'

Alonso tried to put a brave face on what had been a poor result for him, blaming the car and saying he would make things right when they reached the next stop on the tour: Barcelona in his Spanish homeland: 'In a way I feel happy as I came away with four points and I am still leading the Championship, which is what is important. This was not a great race for me but these things happen. I was struggling for pace and overall grip, which means that you can't drive the car as well as you would like. You always start the race believing you can win, but after six or seven laps I knew that it would be tough. I couldn't keep up with the Ferraris and Lewis, and in the end had to settle for fifth.

'I now look forward to the next couple of weeks where we will all work hard to further improve the car in time for my home grand prix in Barcelona.'

Ron Dennis tried to take the heat off by not making too much of Lewis' brilliant achievement: 'Even though it was not a perfect day, we can leave Bahrain leading both Championships, which is a great achievement for the team. Fernando struggled a bit with the balance of his car and we never really managed to perfect his set-up. Lewis was more comfortable with his car and had a great race.'

It was time for a break in the hectic schedule. Lewis and the McLaren team flew out of Bahrain soon after the race on 15 April and headed back to England. He now had almost a month away from the circuit until the Barcelona race on 13 May. But this was not a month off by any stretch of the imagination. It was time to go home and unwind for a couple of days, and then go back to Woking for more training and testing on the car.

Alonso was also busy – recovering from the shock of being beaten by his No. 2. He returned to Spain to lick his wounds and determined that he would once again be top dog when battle resumed at the Circuit de Catalunya.

Half an hour north of the city of Barcelona, the track had opened in 1991 and already held a fond place in Alonso's heart. It was there, in 2006 that he had won the race in his Renault and he approached the 2007 event with much confidence. He also applauded changes made to the circuit for 2007: a tight chicane had been added to help overtaking by slowing cars through the last corner: 'I will miss the final two corners, because as a driver I prefer the high-speed turns, which are more fun to drive. However, it should enable us to get a good slipstream onto the main straight and have a go at overtaking on to Turn One, which is always a good thing.

'One of the downsides of Barcelona is that overtaking has always been very difficult as the two corners that led onto the main straight were always very high speed, and it was difficult to get a tow and get close to the guy in front. This will now change.'

He also made it clear that he did not expect Lewis Hamilton to get one over on him on his home territory, claiming the near month away had helped him get over the disappointment of Sakhir. He said: 'The race in Bahrain was not great for me but we had a strong test at this track earlier this week, and we got to understand how the car performs at the Circuit de Catalunya and the changes to the layout.'

When Lewis arrived for work in Barcelona, it seemed he could not have cared less what Alonso was thinking or saying in public. The years of training under the McLaren regime had taught him that the only focus that mattered was on oneself. As practice began he was his usual approachable self, although he admitted the fame game had surprised him. The change in his own fortunes had become clear when he spent some time during the break between Bahrain and Barcelona at his family home in Tewin, Hertfordshire. He admitted: 'It was strange going back as what people describe as a "celebrity". When I got home there were photographers outside my house. They are there from eight in the morning until six at night, just sitting in their cars. It's really weird but there's not much you can do about it.

'Fortunately for me I've not just shot to the top, and I've not got hundreds of people coming up to me every day. It's bit by bit that people are noticing me in the streets.'

Here was a young man you could take to your heart. There was none of the usual moaning about the drawbacks of being a star, simply a comfortable acceptance that if you are in the public eye in a big way, it is acceptable. It was an example some 'stars' would certainly do well to follow: Piers Morgan once told me that the thing he most detested about celebrities was when they whined on about being photographed and questioned about their lives. It was all part and parcel of the celebrity package. If they couldn't stand the heat, they should get out of the kitchen – and sharp. And it's a view I endorse totally.

Talking of stars, the Formula One mega names of the past were queuing up to salute the youngster as practice loomed in Barcelona. Motor racing legend Sir Jackie Stewart led the way: 'He is, of course, driving for one of the best teams in the world at the present time, with a competitive car, but nevertheless he's been able to accomplish more in a shorter time than any driver I've ever seen enter Formula One.

'It's no easy matter, getting into Formula One and attacking the great talents that are out there. For a new driver to do that with such consistency and not to be making the kind of mistakes that new drivers usually make is in itself a remarkable achievement.

'It's not unusual for a driver to do very well in his first year and have a bit of a dip in the second year – that's par for the course. But I think within the next three years, Lewis Hamilton will certainly be in contention and could easily win the World Championship.'

And Michael Schumacher – in Spain to watch his first Formula One grand prix since his retirement – joined in the chorus of approval. He admitted he had been keeping an eye on Lewis even when he was racing and winning in GP2: 'He's doing a very good job – he's well prepared and he's quick. It's not a surprise to me after seeing his races last year. Maybe it's a surprise that he's so consistent, but there you go.'

Schumacher certainly was correct in that last statement: in the first practice session Lewis was the star man, recording a lap four-tenths of a second faster than Alonso. Yet another sign of the times came when you saw Jenson Button celebrating after he had posted his best showing for a while – with the tenth best time.

Lewis knew he had thrown down a gauntlet to the Spaniard and said, with a big smile on his face: 'We completed our pre-planned programme focusing on tyres and set-up work. Everything went well. I set my fastest time early in the session and was able to be consistent throughout, so I'm fairly confident for the rest of the weekend.'

By the end of the qualifying session the next day he was brought down to earth a little. Massa gained yet another pole by finishing in 1:21.421, while Alono secured second position on the grid with a time of 1:21.451. Raikkonen was third in 1:21.723 and Lewis finished fourth in 1:21.785.

The Spanish crowd seemed disappointed Alonso had not taken pole but he himself was surprisingly upbeat. Had that anything to do with the fact that he had reclaimed the limelight from his No. 2, whom he was increasingly seeing as a potential rival rather than the lapdog he had expected? Alonso said: 'It is a good weekend for us so far. The car is performing really well and the first row is confirmation of the competitive pace we have had all weekend. Hopefully we can see a very good race. It was a really close fight and that is confirmation of how tight things are. There was nothing more I could get from the car. Both my qualifying laps were pretty good so we will see tomorrow.'

Once again, he appeared to be blaming the car, not himself for going faster or doing better. There were no comments from Lewis; he just went back to his motorhome and planned how he would improve the next day. From him there were no words of remorse or blame, just a gritty determination to show his worth when it really mattered. And didn't he do just that on the Sunday? Belying his fourth spot in qualifying, he beat Alonso on his home turf, another brilliant landmark. Massa clocked up another win, roaring home in 1hr 31m 36.230s. Lewis was runner-up, 6.79 seconds behind the Brazilian, and Alonso came third, trailing Lewis by almost 11 seconds.

This was hardly the victorious homecoming Alonso had envisaged. Worse still, was the fact that Lewis' fourth consecutive podium finish – and his third second place in succession – meant that he was not only the clear Championship leader but also the youngest ever. More bad news followed at the McLaren inquest as they confirmed that the Spaniard had only himself to blame for losing out to Lewis: his brush with Massa at the first corner on the first lap had caused him to run wide on to the gravel. The mistake pushed him down to fourth and left one of the aerodynamic deflectors on the right-hand side of his chassis damaged.

Lewis' elevation to clear title leader was a moving moment for all at McLaren. He was, of course, taking a record formerly held by the team's founder, Bruce McLaren. Lewis was just one month and two days younger than the New Zealander had been when he won his legendary grand prix in Argentina back in 1960. Though it was hard to play down the sense of euphoria he felt at the situation, Lewis did his best to try to pour some calm on to what had by now became a frenzied widespread belief that he would be World Champion in his first season. He said: 'I wouldn't really say it fuels my belief that I can win the World Championship in my first year but it is a positive development. This is only my first season and there will obviously be some ups and downs. If we can keep scoring podium finishes, we can do well.'

He had made a fine start, swiftly banishing the blues from his qualifying result and roaring past Raikkonen on the way to the first corner to move into second place as Alonso and Massa blundered together. Lewis admitted getting off to a flyer had been instrumental in his plans to finish higher than his qualifying fourth: 'The key was to get the best position at the first corner. It was very close when he [Alonso] came back on the track but we got through it. In the early stages I was struggling to get heat into the tyres and had a bit of oversteer, but things improved considerably a few laps into the race – however, the gap to Felipe was already too big.

'In the second stint I was a bit unlucky with the traffic but that happens sometimes. We certainly had the pace in the closing stages. Things just keep getting better and I continue living my dream. To come into my fourth grand prix and come out leading the World Championship against all these great drivers is unbelievable. The team has worked really hard since Bahrain and while we didn't win, I still think we can take some satisfaction as we are leading both Championships.'

Alonso found something else to blame for his defeat: the tyres. Although he did accept that he made a mistake on the first corner, he had no words of encouragement or praise for his young team-mate: 'My chance for victory disappeared after the incident at the first corner. I got off the line OK at the start, and was able to get a tow from Felipe and challenge into the first corner, as I was already half a car length in front. But we touched, and I had to go on the gravel to avoid an accident. We were both lucky to finish the race. As a result by the second corner I was fourth. I also sustained a bit of damage to my car, which upset the balance for the rest of the race. I lost additional time in the second stint as the tyres were not working as well.'

Once again Ron Dennis was in a situation he could have hardly envisaged, with his young 'upstart' once more beating the man he had brought into the team at a cost of millions. Again, he showed his tactical skills by refusing to blame Alonso for that first lap mistake. He kept the praise of Lewis to a measured: 'Coming into the Monaco Grand Prix being first and second in the Drivers' Championship and leading the Constructors' battle is a good achievement for the entire team. Our pace was a little weak in the middle sector. Fernando's race was hampered by having damaged his deflector during his efforts to get past Massa in the first corner.

'Another solid performance from Lewis. As you would expect, we will continue to push hard in our development programme to put the team in the best possible position to win as many of the remaining races as possible.'

'Another solid performance from Lewis'... If you hadn't known the result, you might have thought he had finished something like fifteenth! Norbert Haug, Mercedes Motorsport boss, was a little more liberal in his praise: 'It's great that Lewis and Fernando are at the top of the list in the Drivers' Championship after the fourth race here in Barcelona. Well done and thank you to all the team members for leading the Constructors' rankings too. Lewis again did a great job – we will keep pushing and will increase our performance further. We are now looking forward to the next race in Monaco in two weeks' time.'

An editorial on the F1 Pit Box pointed out that Hamilton could now win the title in the opposite way to Alonso in

2005: 'Lewis Hamilton leads the Championship. His astounding rookie year continues with another fabulous race; even when his tyre choice looked to be hurting him in the final leg he refused to let up, keeping Alonso way behind, regardless of his increased pace on harder tyres. I seem to remember Alonso cementing his first Championship win with a string of second places after punching in a few wins – I see no reason why Hamilton couldn't do it the other way around.'

An interesting point: yes, Lewis Hamilton was already looking forward to Monaco. He was leading the Drivers' title race with 30 points, ahead of Alonso on 28, Massa on 27 and Raikkonen – who had retired on the tenth lap with a mechanical problem – on 22. Not only this but in the past Monte Carlo had always turned up trumps for him: the previous year he had won in Monaco in the GP2 race and triumphed in the Monaco Formula Three Grand Prix in 2005. Now he was aiming for the hat trick. Yet what started out as a dream was to turn into something much more disturbing; something neither he, Alonso nor Ron Dennis could have anticipated in his first season by the end of a contravesial race in the gamblers' paradise. As Monaco loomed, there was another, more positive element to Lewis' first season, however. It was becoming clear he had changed the landscape of Formula One for the better. In fact, some even claimed he had *saved* it...

CHAPTER 9

THE BOY WHO SAVED FORMULA ONE

As the season progressed, it became clear that Lewis Hamilton had done much more than make an enormous personal impact on the sport: his exploits also transformed the fortunes of motor racing. From a sport that had been struggling, it suddenly became trendy. For the first time in many years it was once more compelling viewing and Lewis' daring brought in new fans that would hardly have been dreamed of in the predictable days of Michael Schumacher. I myself experienced the jaw-dropping impact Lewis had made when my mother phoned me out of the blue to ask me how he was doing during the Italian Grand Prix in Monza in September! Even my young sons Frankie, 9, and Jude, 7, had been captured by the magnetic charm of Britain's latest hero, tuning in to ITV1 on Sundays to see what was unfolding during the second stage of the season.

Lewis Hamilton had magically turned motor racing from a peripheral viewing sport for the few into a must-see for the masses. And some people, motor experts among them, would even argue that the Stevenage Rocket had emerged as an unlikely saviour for Formula One and the British leg of the season at Silverstone, which had been under threat for a couple of seasons. Put simply, Lewis has sparked a level of interest in Formula One unseen in the UK since the mid-1990s when Damon Hill won Britain's last World Championship. Even at grassroots events the Lewis ripple had its effect: karting tracks, for instance, reported a surge in the number of kids turning up.

A spokesman for ITV, which has the contract for Formula One racing, summed up the Lewis effect in this way: 'Lewis Hamilton appeals not just to the core petrolheads, but to the average Joe Bloggs on the street. He has attracted a new demographic to the audience because he is young and black.' As the season progressed, ITV grand prix viewing figures almost doubled and Autosport magazine reported its best sales for many years... admitting this was also down to Lewis Hamilton.

With all that in mind, I asked Chris Hockley, an F1 expert and journalist at the *Sun* newspaper, to investigate how Lewis had changed the landscape of Formula One and opened it up to a much wider audience. He came up with some interesting explanations and revelations: 'It's no coincidence that in the stressed-out, information-overloaded twenty-first century, fairytales have once again become big box-office. And as Harry Potter and the Hobbits' mythical quest have captured our imagination at the cinema, so young adventurer Lewis Carl Hamilton, named after one of the great Olympic heroes, has us glued to the small screen to watch the latest episode of his incredible journey.

'Not only has Lewis single-handedly restored Formula One to the pinnacle of world sport, he has set it on fire… and thrown petrol on the flames for good measure. With the heat has come cool, Hamilton style. He's calm, conscientious and collected, despite the pressure cooker lifestyle he has been hurled into. After taking the Formula One grid by storm in the space of a few weeks, he has gone showbiz by appearing on the star-spangled pages of newspapers. When the *Sun*'s pace-making *Bizarre* column pictured him out on the town with rappers P. Diddy and Pharrell Williams, Lewis knew he had arrived not just as a racing driver but as a celeb-britt-tee.

'Now girls want to kiss him, mums want to cuddle him, dads admire him and boys want to be him. His rocket-ship rise to fame has bumped up British TV audiences for grands prix by a whopping 50 per cent. And enthusiasm for Formula One is soaring across the world – even in the stock-car domain of America, they were forced to sit up and take notice when this upstart rookie kid beat off the reigning World Champ to win the US Grand Prix.

'It's a fairytale, you see, enacted across the globe.

'And all of a sudden everyone, from barmaids to vicars, from paperboys to company directors has an opinion on Lewis, and asks after his progress. No more is Formula One the preserve of anoraks, petrolheads and techno-junkies who salivate at the prospect of a 0.63 per cent increase in front aerofoil downforce eked out by Ferrari's engineers.

'Now, wives who decades ago gave up trying to understand their husbands' weird obsession with "watching cars go round in circles" are dallying at the telly and asking: "How's Lewis doing?" Surely it won't be long before traffic cops tell speeding motorists: "Who do you think you are? Lewis Hamilton?"

'In a nutshell, Lewis has returned motorsport to the masses. But it's not as if he has changed its physical make-up, or intrinsic excitement value. Formula One racing, for years mired in aerodynamic über-technology that makes overtaking all but impossible, is still largely comprised of a dash to the first corner followed by a high-speed procession and the odd change of order through pit stops. Superhero or not, Lewis can't change much about that.

'So what is it about him that is pulling in the crowds – and saving the skins of TV commentators who were beginning to splutter on empty as another drone-a-thon unfolded before them?

'The answers, of course, are many and varied – each contributing to what Formula One folk like to call "the package". Like a state-of-the-art grand prix car, it's possible to break it down to its components. But be warned, the list is growing longer by the day...

'*The Charm.* Fast becoming legendary as looker Lewis fields yet another barrage of questions with a polite, easy-going manner way beyond his 22 years. "How do you explain your brilliance?" he is asked. "I'm just doing the best that I can," comes the reply. Guaranteed to make him a favourite of mums and grandmas. What a nice young man!

'The Modesty. The shy smile as he is interviewed in the run-up to the British Grand Prix by a hard-nosed TV news anchorman, more used to dealing with terrorist atrocities, who describes him as a "global phenomenon" and compares him to the superlative Tiger Woods.

'The Belief. An unshakeable and fearless conviction in his own ability to drive cars as fast as they can be driven, and to dive through gaps that lesser mortals would not dare. It would be a cliché to say this belief is "hidden" behind his self-effacing attitude. It would also be untrue. For all his humility, Lewis constantly emanates an aura akin to what toothpaste ad makers would call "the glow of confidence".

'I remember meeting him at last year's *Autosport* Awards show, the Oscars of motor racing, at which Lewis, recently announced as a 2007 McLaren Mercedes Formula One driver, picked up yet another gong. McLaren chief Ron Dennis made a bizarre speech in which he warned Lewis that the British media would likely build him up with the sinister long-term aim of knocking him down again. As a tabloid hack myself, I felt duty-bound to tell Lewis this was paranoid rubbish, and that he would have our 110 per cent support.

'I waited while Dennis introduced Lewis to the evening's guest of honour, former Ferrari Formula One star Carlos Reutemann, now a leading politician in his native Argentina, then stepped in to voice my reassurance in the manner of kind uncle to naïve nephew. Lewis listened patiently and thanked me with an understanding nod. Yet, although he didn't say it, the calm look in his eyes left me in no doubt that having the support of the media was all very well and good, but he didn't really need it to achieve what he wanted to achieve. That would be done on the track, thank you very much. He was far too polite to accuse me of being patronising but that's how I felt, guiltily, as I left his side.

'*The Family*. The support Lewis has received from his family has been well chronicled – and his dad Anthony is as familiar a sight at the circuits as his son. Lewis' long-time mentor Ron Dennis is widely regarded as a second father figure, though it did not stop paddock gossip suggesting the determined Hamiltons would walk to another team, had Dennis not put Lewis in a McLaren for 2007. The devotion from family and team seems to have given Lewis a sense of obligation admired by millions of parents more accustomed to ungrateful children who habitually throw their toys out of the pram.

'Lewis' upbringing and nurturing has also resulted in a refreshing lack of ego and disarming honesty. Asked how he keeps his snowballing fame in perspective, he replied: "You've just got to be yourself. That's the best advice I could give anyone. It doesn't matter who you meet – the Queen, anybody."

'*The Attitude*. It has come to be a dirty word used to describe sneering youth. But it doesn't have to be so. Lewis has attitude – but in a positive way. He discovered his remarkable talent soon after his father bought him a go-kart when he was 6. But though he raced hard, he continued to study hard at school, too. He was 12 when Dennis signed him up to McLaren's young driver programme. And ever since, you get the feeling he has been dedicated to achieving success because so many people were supporting him, and he felt duty-bound to try his hardest to pay them back.

'*The Rookie.* Part of Lewis' attraction emanates from him "coming from nowhere" to take on the giants of grand prix. It's not really the case. Despite his youth, Lewis has had a long and illustrious career in the lower reaches of motor racing, and his speed and daring have come as no surprise to keen followers of the sport. Yet although motor racing is a massive global industry with countless categories, it's also true that the vast majority of the population know nothing of it apart from Formula One. And therefore they were barely aware of Lewis' existence until his startling grand prix debut in Australia. So, even though under the patronage of McLaren he is the best-prepared rookie in Formula One's history, he is still perceived as a newcomer – an incredibly exciting one at that. And what timing! He is following in the tyre smoke of one Michael Schumacher, a peerless driver who was never able to capture the public imagination like a Senna, a Mansell – or a Hamilton. Formula One fans wish – oh, how they wish – that Schuey had delayed his retirement by a year so Lewis could go up against him; I reckon the pair of them feel the same. And who knows, Schumacher may yet take it on. Wouldn't put it past him.

'Look, also, at the contrast between Lewis and his team-mate Fernando Alonso – a fantastic racer, a double World Champion, universally admired by Formula aficionados, yet unable to command a wider audience beyond his native Spain.

'*The Normality*. Matt Bishop, editor-in-chief of the respected *F1 Racing* magazine, reckons the hoo-ha about Lewis is down to him being "so damn normal". An unprivileged lad from the Home Counties with "an engaging humility as unforced as his astonishingly natural driving style" – I'd go along with that ... with one rider, which is that Lewis has the true superstar quality of making the abnormal seem normal.

'I take you back to the comparison with Tiger Woods. Wins golf tourneys effortlessly, doesn't he? He doesn't, of course. There are hundreds of brilliant golfers out there on the fairways ready to put one over on him – and he has to try like hell to overcome them. He just makes it look like the work of a moment, then shrugs his shoulders afterwards. Recognise the trait?

'*The Tributes*. It's not just Ordinary Joes who have been gobsmacked by Lewis' astonishing arrival in Formula One. Past greats of the sport have been even more impressed. And they have said so, too, which in turn feeds back into the public consciousness. Take, for example, the astonishing assessment by Stirling Moss, who said: "I'm flattered people are comparing me with Lewis."

'Nigel Mansell calls Lewis "the Chosen One". Damon Hill says: "I've never seen a rookie as good as he is." And

Niki Lauda reckons he is "the best guy around with even more potential than the British media expect." And that's saying something!

'Fortunately, through pure ability, Lewis was quickly able to shake off the monicker as "the first black grand prix driver". But former team boss Eddie Jordan put it succinctly when he said of him: "All the indications border on the sensational. He's black, he's attractive, he's rock'n'roll."

'Which, in a roundabout way after all the analysis, brings us back to Lewis as Mr Cool. He even uses the word a lot, which makes him, well, cool! For instance, talking about his party night with P. Diddy & Co, he said: "The weird thing was, there were all these celebrities there – and yet I seemed to be the main attraction. I expected to be the big nobody, the guy they didn't know all that much about.

'But people were coming up and asking me for my number – and asking if I wanted theirs. How cool was that?'

'Very cool, Lewis, is the answer. Cool enough for David and Victoria Beckham to wish you well on the British Grand Prix starting grid. It seems as if the man himself cannot quite believe what's happening to him. And he admits as much in all his post-race interviews and TV appearances.

"I'm living my dream," he repeats, again and again.

'It's a theme vigorously exploited by McLaren's main sponsor Vodafone, whose TV adverts show a young Lewis piloting a spaceship as he chases his wildest wish. And as other kids crash out, one by one, Lewis remains stoically at the helm of the craft as it morphs into a McLaren Formula One car.

'But, heck, we lesser beings know we can't all make it. We know our limitations – we're just glad *someone* can do it. To prove that, yes, by crikey, it *can* be done! And by someone so "damn normal" and pleasant... So we join Lewis in the fairytale and it goes on for us all. We're living the dream, too. And it feels good.'

Indeed it does, Chris... indeed it does. As I have followed Lewis' fortunes in Formula One over the last year, I have also noticed how he has caught the imagination of many youngsters. In June 2007, for instance, pupils at a Norfolk school enjoyed a motorsport day as a direct result of the influence Lewis was having in Formula One. They had seen him roar to the top of the Driver's title on TV and the school's headmaster had been only too happy to invite along a local motor racing company to show them a real racing car.

Pupils at Spooner Row Primary were spellbound at the sight of Comtec Racing's 175mph World Series single-seat car. Based near Attleborough, Comtec won the Drivers' Championship at their first attempt in the World Series in 2006. Jonathan Lewis, owner of the Norfolk-based team, talked of how motorsport had played a major role in his life – and let them sit in his £250,000 pride and joy. He also spoke of how Lewis Hamilton had fired the imagination of the youngsters – and encouraged their interest in his visit. He said: 'It was surprising how knowledgeable they were about motorsport. All of them knew Lewis Hamilton – he's done great things for the sport. The reception class loved it and were just in awe, but the older ones asked some really difficult questions. They were proper little switched-on individuals. The best question was "Why do you do it?" How do you answer *that?*'

Headteacher Simon Wakeman said: 'The children thought it was fantastic, very exciting, particularly the younger children, who were thrilled to get the opportunity to sit inside the car and pretend they were racing drivers. They all want to be Lewis Hamilton when they grow up!'

Lewis' father Anthony is also delighted at how youngsters are jumping on his son's bandwagon – and how he is opening up the sport to a new generation. He says this particular spin-off of his son's success is making both him and Lewis 'very happy indeed': 'I remember when I was a kid I didn't have anything. When Lewis was a boy we still had nothing. We got this opportunity to do something and now we're here. Every day is a dream and is something to enjoy and cherish.

'I want Lewis' story to be an inspiration to other kids that if you do have a dream, and you work hard at it, then you could make it happen. He made a lot of sacrifices as a kid to follow his dream. But his success hasn't changed him – he's the same guy now he's on top of the world and he will stay like that forever.

'It is important that he keeps focused and keeps winning for the good of the other young guys and girls who have nothing and want to achieve something. I want them to look at Lewis and see that if you work hard, you make sacrifices, your dreams could come true.

'Lewis says he doesn't feel like a superstar. At the end of

the day he's just Lewis and it's important for him to stay like that. He still lives with the family. There's no yachts or wild parties – it's all about hard work and his dream to win the Drivers' World Championship.

'He is a fully committed Formula One racing driver, not a half-hearted "I'm there now – I am going to live the lifestyle and be a playboy racing driver". His view is "I'm here to race and that's all I want to do". He has said it himself, "I'm not here to come second." If he was here to do that then he could live the lifestyle, afford to go partying, enjoy the sun, then think, oh I'm racing this weekend, am I? I will be there in five minutes'. No way!

'It was his dream to get to Formula One and the next dream was to win. The ultimate dream is to win the World Championship. We have been blessed. We have been given some great opportunities and Lewis is making the best possible use of them.

'It's not like winning the Lottery, buying the ticket and hoping your numbers come up – it's about having the dream and staying the course. We are really lucky to be here: we're not going to be arrogant and waste the opportunity. That is why I want kids with hopes and aspirations to look at Lewis and see him as an inspiration.'

Just a couple of weeks into the season, before Lewis' impact had been truly realised and had taken hold of the sport, Renault boss Flavio Briatore voiced the feeling even from within the sport that it had become a dull spectacle. He said: 'Normally it's boring.' It was certainly a demoralising view.

A couple of months later, the Italian would have reason to feel grateful to Lewis Hamilton, but at the start of the campaign Briatore went on: 'A 1-hour 30-minute race is too long because the last 30 minutes – 90 per cent of the time – is really boring. Every time there's excitement it's because something's happened outside or because it's heavy rain, or there's some accident or stuff like that. I still don't understand why we don't try to make excitement in every race.'

Mark Sharman, head of ITV Sport, naturally disagreed with the idea that motor racing had become boring although he also had reason to be grateful to Lewis Hamilton – particularly for the way he had drummed up an avalanche of new interest and, consequently, increased viewing figures for the independent network. By the time of the British Grand Prix, ITV's viewing figures were significantly up on the previous year, with 7.7 million watching the United States Grand Prix compared to 5.4 million in 2006. And figures for Silverstone proved just how much of an effect Lewis was having: the ITV1 audience peaked at 5.1 million for the British Grand Prix, while over on BBC1 the men's singles final at Wimbledon drew in just 2.2 million when the two events clashed.

Former Formula One driver Mark Blundell, now working as ITV's main analyst, agreed that Lewis was the superstar the sport urgently needed to take it forward. He said: 'He's the first black driver, he came with a lot of expectation, having won the support series GP2 last year, but all we're talking about is a great new driver.' The *Independent*'s TV columnist Chris Maume summed up Lewis' impact after the

US Grand Prix: 'As the camera panned across the serried ranks of petrolheads at Indianapolis in the minutes before the US Grand Prix, Mark Blundell remarked to Steve Ryder that Lewis Hamilton has brought a whole new audience to Formula One. Quite right: in 10 years of this column I don't recall writing a single sentence about it (unless that sentence was "Christ, I'm bored!"). And until the Saturday before last I'm sure I'd never watched a second of qualifying. Which, for a male of the species born five days after Fangio's last grand prix, is just weird. So the Hamilton kid has got me hooked...'

Damon Hill was in no doubt that Lewis Hamilton would play a major part in guaranteeing the future of the British Grand Prix at Silverstone for years to come. The Lewis effect led to a record 42,000 fans attending on the Friday, followed by a Saturday best of 80,000, with race day an 85,000 sell-out. Ticket prices that day ranged from £99 to £260. It was also reported that online retailers had been inundated with customers buying £19.95 Lewis baseball caps and replica T-shirts at £27.95. Hill said the ticket sales – a direct consequence of Lewis' impact in the run-up to the 2007 race at the Northamptonshire site – proved just how vital and relevant the British leg remained.

Damon said: 'I am as excited as everyone by his proven potential and promise, and for the first time since I did it in 1996, a British driver will arrive at Silverstone leading the World Championship... Sorry if I'm banging on about Lewis too much, but as president of the British Racing Driver's Club (BRDC), it's my job to bang on a bit...

'The extension of the grand prix contract beyond 2009 will require a development programme of the facilities to keep pace with the kind of venue sports fans are getting used to expecting around the world. This is a crucial time for the British Grand Prix. Failure to achieve our goals and to reach a viable, sustainable agreement with Formula One's management could mean the event will be lost. I am not in any doubt that Formula One will move on without us, just as a driver would lose the pack and never look back – but we also have a duty to protect our venue for all motorsport. It's a tough call.

'Little wonder then that I am excited by the arrival of Lewis Hamilton. I would be lying if I did not regard his appearance as somewhat timely. But he just goes to prove the power of an individual in the world of organisations.'

BRDC chairman Robert Brooks echoed those views: 'Members like Lewis are helping us. The Hamilton factor is very positive and helpful in keeping the British Grand Prix.'

Business analyst Alan Switzer backed both men in their belief that Hamilton's success could propel Silverstone to new heights of popularity. Switzer, a director of the Sports Business Group at Deloitte, said: 'Local heroes can have a huge impact on the financial health of a sport. Lewis Hamilton's success has helped lift the British Grand Prix to become the third highest attended event in the UK's sporting calendar after Wimbledon and Royal Ascot.

'Should Lewis consolidate his success, motor racing can expect a significant revenue boost, particularly once existing broadcasting and sponsorship contracts expire. Broadcasters and corporates will compete to be associated with such a potentially attractive global sporting icon.

'ITV's current Formula One television rights contract is reportedly worth around £25 million a year. But the success of Lewis means that could increase substantially when it expires at the end of the 2010 season.'

He also believes Silverstone will benefit as circuit owners, the BRDC, look to secure a new contract once the present deal expires in 2009: 'At a more local level, the increased ticketing revenue and secondary spend will form an important part of the funding mix for the redevelopment of Silverstone. This is almost certainly necessary for Silverstone to retain its grand prix in 2010 and beyond. Indeed, if extra capacity could be added to Silverstone, Lewis' success suggests it would be matched by demand.

'Fernando Alonso's success has been the main factor for the Spanish Grand Prix now attracting more than 340,000 spectators over the extended weekend, the highest of the Formula One races.'

The Hamilton effect was also apparent in a sustained betting spree in the run-up to Silverstone. Bookies reported that in the same race the year previously there was not half so much interest because of the lack of a genuine British title challenger and competitive action in races. According to Ladbrokes' spokesman, David Williams: 'Even before Hamilton's first race there was little to suggest a betting boom but his first podium finish saw a huge upsurge. Betting on race two increased by 75 per cent across all channels and this year has broken all previous records on turnover. Already on the British Grand Prix we have seen more money bet on Hamilton than on all the other drivers combined.'

There were a series of other bets you could have made on the brilliant young Briton before Silverstone. Again, this all showed the enormously positive influence he was having on the sport in so many different ways. The odds on him winning the Drivers' title were now 8–13 as against a pre-season 25–1, for example. You could also find odds of 9–2 that he would finish on the podium in every grand prix. Also, 11–10 that he would win more races than any British driver (Nigel Mansell held the record with 31) and 10–1 that he would go on to break Michael Schumacher's record 91 grand prix wins. Everywhere you looked was Lewis Hamilton. He was the main man and the man to whom a whole host of workers within the Formula One 'industry' owed a mighty debt.

It was boom time again for Formula One – and the public was not slow in admitting their interest was all down to one man. Already a Formula One fan, Neil Adamson of London admitted Lewis had taken things to a new level: 'None of my friends like Formula One so I got into it by accident. I started watching it on TV and I got a passion for it. I've tried getting friends to watch it with me, but they say they haven't got time for it. Maybe it's a different buzz for them. I watch it all the time on TV, even if it's on at 2am. My daughter is into it too. I wish I could go to all the meets, but I have a family and a shop to run, so I don't have the time. I went to Silverstone years ago in Nigel Mansell's time. It was absolutely marvellous – not even the race, just the spectacle. I was walking around, admiring the people and the vibes.'

Julian Phillips, of Bury, near Manchester, said: 'Whether you like the sport or not, you have to admit it is incredible what Lewis has done. The sport itself is boring, but you cannot take anything away from him. Would you say that Tiger Woods has done "OK", only because you don't like the sport? Nobody – however good they are – comes in, wins and finishes on the podium so many times. It takes someone special to break the win barrier that soon.

'Jenson Button is not as good as Lewis – because he does not have his mental strength. Hamilton just wants to win. And don't tell me it's just down to him being in a McLaren. Even in a Honda he would do better than *their* current drivers! He is, without doubt, set to become the greatest sportsmen *ever*. He will have more of an impact than Tiger Woods, and I'm saying that as a golf fan.'

Finally, Louis Graham, of St Ives, Cornwall, summed up the remarkable effect Lewis has had on motor racing: 'Lewis Hamilton is great news for British motorsport – in fact, he is the saviour of it. He has raised the profile of a sport that lags massively behind in the viewing ratings when compared with the likes of football, bringing in thousands of new converts, and making it fresh and new.

'And he is a nice guy too, which is unusual among today's usual prima donnas. Lewis Hamilton is the living proof that good guys do sometimes win. We are proud of you, Lewis, and will follow you for years to come – now go and win more titles than Schumacher!'

Sentiments certainly echoed, Lewis...

CHAPTER 10

MONTE CARLO – AND BUST

'Mugged in the streets of Monte Carlo' – that's one way to describe what happened to Lewis Hamilton in Monaco on the weekend of 27 May 2007.

Yet it had all started so differently when they arrived at the so-called playboy paradise the previous Wednesday. As already noted, Lewis loved it there: indeed, later in the season he admitted that he could easily live in the principality. The sun was shining, the atmosphere relaxed and the race around the streets is one that every Formula One driver I have ever spoken to admits to enjoying. They thrive on the challenge of the tight and twisty streets and the specific demands of road racing. Lewis had his own views on the circuit: 'Well, there is no room for error and it's all about knowing your braking zones, knowing where the bumps are...'

And how was he getting along with Alonso? Had he noticed any change in their relationship as they got down to business again? 'I don't think it's changed. I think with the team, the relationship grows constantly. I've been at McLaren for a long, long time and it just gets better and better – we're very much working extremely hard together to succeed and it's going extremely well. As you can see, it's getting better and better. I think with me and Fernando the relationship is growing. We're sort of starting to understand each other. Obviously we've got a huge amount of respect for each other as we always have. But it's doing fine.'

But was Alonso still top dog; was he the pupil to Alonso's master? 'I never actually thought it was a master-pupil thing, to be honest. I think that as in every team, there's a little bit of rivalry there but that's only on the track. We're professionals. Off the track we're friends – we can talk, we're relaxed, there's no tension there.' And how was he adjusting to his newfound fame? 'Well, it has been a roller coaster, the whole journey. One, getting to Formula One, and then having four podiums in my first four races – it is unknown, but it is difficult. You know, I don't think it has kicked in really. You look at the races and you think wow, I finished second to Felipe Massa! It is just that these last few years, I have been watching these guys racing and I was admiring them. And now I am amongst them. It is really difficult to come to terms with...

'I don't read much about what is going on back in the UK in terms of what is being written about me. I think it is the way I deal with it. I don't feel I particularly need to read it.

The hype is growing, but that is the way I control it. It is nice to see your face in a magazine or a newspaper. It is good to see that you have the support, but I hear they are very good stories so that keeps me happy.'

'Good stories' they certainly were. The boy was a clean-shaven hero of our times and what would surely become known as The Hamilton Brand – in the same way as the Beckham Brand – was already taking shape. He was different; a nice, normal, steady sort of guy in a sport more used to excess and hedonism. To his credit, he also laughed off the suggestion made a few days earlier by Eddie Jordan that he perhaps did not have the necessary aggressive side of a World Champion to his character. Jordan said 'Lewis is fortunate to have a well-grounded team with a structure he probably wouldn't have got anywhere else. But if he needed to do what Schumacher did to Villeneuve or Hill, would he do that? You need to do that to win. Winning is in the mind, and you have to do it at all costs.

'Anyone who tells you different is either lying, or hasn't achieved what they're capable of. There has to be a steely aspect that we haven't seen, otherwise Hamilton will be swamped. He needs to have that arrogance otherwise he will not succeed. Does Alex Ferguson have it? Yes. Does José Mourinho? Yes.

'Winners generally are not nice people. They try to be, but they are immensely selfish, immensely arrogant and have a total belief in their own ability. Nothing else matters to them when they are at work.'

Lewis just shrugged his shoulders when told of Jordan's

words: 'I don't know if I particularly believe that "win at all costs" is the way forward. Yes, we are here to win, so you prepare yourself and you work as hard as you can, but I don't particularly agree with win at all costs. Sure, every driver has a different way to look at it.' It was a brilliant putdown of the Irishman whom over the years had sometimes seemed to believe his own publicity that he was the oracle and saviour of Formula One.

Ron Dennis also waded into the row, saying 'There are drivers who are prepared to do anything to win. They've been in Formula One and left, but Lewis isn't one of them. People relate to the fact that good guys can win. For us, he is not just a great racing driver snapping at the heels of a double World Champion, but he is also, along with Fernando Alonso, a great human being. These guys are fun to have in the team, with the popularity of Lewis very much about living the dream.'

Confident and assured, Lewis then joined his father for a light supper and a little rest before the business of practice. In the first session he was second to Alonso – the Spaniard setting the fastest time with a lap of 1:16.973. Earlier in the day, Lewis had actually been ahead but a problem with the starter motor meant he could only complete 14 out of 32 laps. The gap between the two men was six-tenths of a second.

In the second session the McLaren team were thrown into a panic when Lewis, trying desperately to overhaul Alonso's time, crashed. Almost an hour on, he ran into trouble as he raced too close to the barriers, losing control as he braked on the approach to the first corner – the Sainte Devote right-hander – and crashed into the tyre barrier. Clearly concerned, Ron Dennis was observed looking grimly at the scene and his relief was tangible as his boy jumped out of his car and signalled he was not hurt.

Lewis, shaken by the incident, said 'Today was the first time I have ever driven a Formula One car around Monaco and it was awesome. I have obviously had experience of the circuit from Formula Three and grand prix two, but in a Formula One car it's very different.

'Everyone makes mistakes, and I'm only human – these small things happen. I was pushing and right on the limit, which is something you always have to do at Monaco. I then found the limit – at the mid-point of the second session – and found out how unforgiving this track can be. I just locked the rear wheels, and as it came before the apex, I lost the back end, tried to brake too quick and went off into the wall. There is just no room for error in Monaco. To be honest, it was a light impact, even if it looked quite quick. I'm obviously sorry as there will be a bit of work for the guys.'

The colour had also returned to Ron Dennis' face after practice was complete – with Lewis third behind Alonso and Raikkonen. Big Ron said 'This is a mistake all drivers make of all standards. It's not something I will level any criticism at. I'd obviously rather not have a bent racing car but, under the circumstances, we're pretty comfortable with his contribution to this season.' And with tongue in cheek, a big smile on his face and a wink, the paternal McLaren boss added in a conspiratorial whisper: 'He still has a few Brownie points in hand!'

By the end of qualifying, Lewis had proved just how mentally tough he was. The crash had no impact on his performance as he finished second only to Alonso in determining his place on the grid for the race itself. For the first time in the season Alonso took pole after rocketing to a time of 1:15.726. Lewis was second in 1:15.905, but had been ahead of his team-mate with just 4 minutes left on the clock. Alonso pipped him at the last after being delayed in traffic by Mark Webber. Massa was third.

It was the first time McLaren had claimed a clean sweep of the front row in the season and Alonso's first pole since the China Grand Prix the previous October. Lewis was glad to have made that front row but conceded he could even have snatched pole: 'To start my first Formula One race in Monaco from the front row is amazing and for the team to have a 1–2 is just fantastic. I have really enjoyed my weekend and qualifying was no exception. It's hard to explain, but around this circuit you are just constantly on the limit. My last flying lap was affected by traffic and I lost a lot of time but that is just the challenge of this place.

'I was three-tenths up on my previous best but I was held up by Webber. I don't know if he saw me. I lost half a second behind him but I managed to pull it back to within a tenth, but after that the tyres were gone. The car felt great. It was exactly the same time I did on heavy fuel. So we did a good job and I am happy with that. It will be interesting to see what happens tomorrow. We want to finish the race in the points and continue as we have been going this season.

'The car has been super all the way through, and I believe we have a strong strategy. I think it will be a great race, and hopefully Fernando and I can provide the team with a 1–2 finish.'

Alonso was more delighted than usual with his pole position – he was now in the unlikely position of having to chase for the title with Lewis out in front in the standings, and he was determined to hunt down and conquer his young rival. He admitted 'This is a very important pole position. There was a little bit of everything going on. We were expecting rain at the start but that only affected 1 lap and then we were at normal speeds as usual. Monaco is very stressful for everyone.

'All weekend has been good for us and the car seems very competitive, but you know Monaco is a very special race. It could be very difficult. Starting from pole is good, but it is a very long race. And the weather is changing so much. Obviously pole position gives you the best possible start to the race but there are 78 laps, and as it's Monaco anything can happen.' Clearly the master was feeling the pressure. He needed a win if he was to reel in Hamilton; even the weather was starting to worry him.

By the end of Sunday night, the Spanish driver was feeling more at ease with himself as he once again led the drivers' standings. Both he and Lewis were now on 38 points after Alonso won his second successive Monaco Grand Prix, at the same time notching up McLaren's 150th success. He took the lead in the standings courtesy of his two wins in the season so far, as opposed to none by Lewis.

It was also the fourteenth time that the team had won in Monte Carlo and McLaren's first 1–2 finish at the race since 1989, the heyday of Ayrton Senna, who won in that year, and Alain Prost, who was second. The stark facts of May 2007 show Alonso beat Lewis into second place. For Lewis, consolation was found in his fourth successive second place in his maiden season, and in that he beat Massa into third. But the youngster was clearly upset that McLaren's unusual strategic requirements – requesting their drivers maintain their positions so as not put each other at risk on the notoriously demanding and dangerous track – had meant Alonso took first place.

For Alonso, it was a seventeenth career win as he came home in a time of 1 hr 40m 29.329s, 4 seconds in front of Lewis. The lead had yo-yoed between the two McLaren men in a thrilling contest in front of a crowd estimated at more than 120,000. Among them were Hollywood actors Jude Law and Jonny Lee Miller, Juventus and Czech Republic soccer star Pavel Nedved and the German tennis legend, and now sports commentator, Boris Becker. But on Lap 58, with 20 to go, the two men were told to conserve their equipment and settle for McLaren's second 1–2 finish of the season.

Alonso also set the fastest lap on Lap 44 in 1:15.284 and at the end of the race he was beaming. Top cat once again: 'It has been a fantastic weekend, no doubt, and to score this hat-trick of pole, fastest lap and win is something very special and even more here in Monaco.

'I enjoyed very much today's race, with a perfect car all through the race. It was so good to drive such a nice car for 78 laps and win at the end. This win means a lot to me – I have never had the experience of being more than 1 minute ahead of the competition, which probably makes this one of my best victories.

'I didn't get off the line brilliantly from pole position, but as there is such a short run to the first corner I was pretty sure that I would be able to keep the lead. However, as I was able to save fuel in my first stint I was able to stay out for two more laps than originally planned. After that the race was pretty quiet with only the backmarkers causing a few problems, especially shortly before my second pit stop when I lost a lot of time. I will enjoy this victory and look forward to the races in north America.'

In public at least, Lewis put a brave face on it, saying: 'I knew we were both extremely quick, so I could only apply pressure, but he's a two-time World Champion and he doesn't really make mistakes.

'I tried to attack him and wanted to win if I could, but I have to accept that I am in my rookie season and he has number one on his car and I have number two. I am the second driver and so I must accept that and respect that for the team.

'I had good pace at the start, but then I had some graining on my front tyres which didn't help. It was an exciting race which also saw me tapping the guardrails a couple of times, fortunately without influencing the handling of the car.'

These were stoical, resigned words that hid an inner hurt.

The decision by McLaren to rein him in would cause a public storm. Alonso benefited on this occasion but it would have the effect of denying him the same opportunity again. Public disquiet told McLaren they had dropped a clanger and it was a mistake they were keen not to repeat. Ever the diplomat, Ron Dennis tried to play down the possibility of any resentment: 'Both Fernando and Lewis drove so well and responded excellently to the team's wishes of bringing both cars home safely in what was a memorable 1–2 result and our fourteenth victory in the principality. However, there is some disappointment because of the different strategies we needed to follow to cope with a potential deployment of the safety car – which has happened four times in the last five years. Consequently you virtually have to decide in advance which one of the team's two drivers will claim the victory.' Team orders that interfere with a race result were outlawed in October 2002. Dennis cited safety issues as the reason for keeping Lewis behind Fernando. 'Once the first round of pit stops had taken place we reverted Lewis from a one-stop strategy to the faster two-stop strategy and at the same time slowed both cars down to conserve the brakes. As a team we would like to race but this circuit requires a disciplined approach and as a result we can leave Monte Carlo with the maximum amount of points.'

Massa paid tribute to the blistering pace of Alonso and Hamilton: 'McLaren showed really an incredible pace – even if I'd pushed like 150 per cent on the limit it would have stayed the same. There was nothing to do. I was just thinking about finishing third and scoring points. Five points [deficit] is nothing in the Championship, so let's work hard for the next race and try to be in front there.'

A plethora of fine words and plaudits but the fact remained that Lewis was disappointed at having to play second fiddle to Alonso. At the end of the race he even handed his trophy to his brother, Nicolas. Asked whether there was any significance in that – did it perhaps mean he thought it was small reward in light of what could have been? – Lewis again stonewalled the suggestion that he felt hard done by 'My brother supports me in every race and it is good to have him there and he loves to be a part of it. I am proud to have him with me and it is great when he comes up and I can give him the trophy to make him feel important – and just show him that he is.'

The British public remained unconvinced. They felt that from now on Lewis and Alonso should be given equal billing and equal opportunities. We had been told they both had the same car so let the fastest man, and the better driver win. Then there could be no questions of favouring one against the other, could there?

Radio 5 Live presenter David Croft started a fevered debate on the rights and wrongs of Ron's tinkering, saying: 'Now I know how much regard and respect Ron Dennis has for Fernando Alonso, and I know how hard he's trying to make the double World Champion welcome at his team.' But Croft believed that this tactic, 'Demoralises Hamilton for one thing, and secondly sets a precedent that Alonso may expect to be repeated in the future... Hamilton wasn't happy after the race and I didn't expect him to be. His flying start in the sport has increased his and the media's expectations. He wanted to win, to make his mark and become the first rookie to do so in Monte Carlo.'

Racing fan Paul Hurley, of Burton in Staffordshire, responded by saying Dennis was well out of order: 'It just wasn't a fair thing to do. We all know he has got to protect his investment, but surely he can see that Lewis deserves to be set free? He's lucky that Lewis didn't give him a right earful, prodigy for 10 years or not!'

And Karen Pugh of Birmingham was similarly scathing 'He spends all those years bringing him through. He should have allowed them both the same rights. Why does Alonso need nursing if he is so good? I thought he was the man who said he wasn't scared of anything, or anyone? Well, little ol' Lewis seems to be scaring the living daylights out of him!'

Dave Butler of Romford spoke for those who believed Big Ron had made the right decision in putting the team first: 'Sure, Lewis had a chance of winning this weekend, and he's proved he is just as quick as Alonso, but to have allowed them to race to the end and push each other to the limit would have been suicide for a team. They would have been getting hammered in the press if they had allowed that and the drivers had taken each other off of the circuit. Monaco is not an easy place to pass, so if Lewis had caught Alonso it would have taken a brave move to stick your car where it was at risk of being chopped.

'Well done RD and everyone at McLaren.... A silver car looks better than a red one at the front.'

Rony, a Brazilian Formula One fan, claimed the furore showed Lewis was getting too big for his boots: 'Your daring Hamilton has started to show some new colours, hasn't he? He not only wanted to go for the win, he also felt he was entitled to rant over the radio when his team told him to stop being foolish. Furthermore, his attitude and noise brought about the Fédération Internationale de l'Automobile (FIA) investigation that could have cost his team dear. And then, when asked if he was surprised with Ferrari's lack of performance, he sported a smile and said "Not really, no." One could not but feel a hint of arrogance in his answer. He is starting to believe in his own myth – the first step towards a fall.'

The debate raged on and Formula One bosses entered the fray. They were also unhappy with McLaren's strategic decision to hold back Hamilton and launched an investigation into a possible breach of their rules after learning that Ron Dennis had admitted he prevented Lewis from challenging Alonso after their first pit stops. But Dennis then denied favouring Alonso, and the FIA subsequently vindicated the team, stating that: 'McLaren were able to pursue an optimum team strategy because they had a substantial advantage over all other cars. They did nothing which could be described as interfering with the race result.' The FIA had examined radio communications between McLaren and their drivers, data from the team and a report from the official observer.

Big Ron breathed a sigh of relief at the verdict and declared it to be the end of the matter as far as he was concerned. He said: 'The entire team was understandably disappointed that outstanding drives from both Fernando and Lewis, resulting in a great 1–2 victory and McLaren's 150th win, was temporarily tarnished.

'The efficient intervention and subsequent inquiry of the FIA into the allegations of the last three days has removed any doubt about the manner in which the team ran its cars during the 2007 Monaco Grand Prix.'

He was glad to be able to turn his back on what had been an unpleasant interlude but the one major plus to come from it was that hopefully Lewis Hamilton would never again be ordered to play second fiddle to Fernando Alonso. From now on the double World Champion would have to beat his arch-rival in a really convincing way, starting at the next race on the calendar... in Montreal on 10 June 2007.

CHAPTER 11

CANADA HIGH

It was make or break as Lewis Hamilton arrived in Canada for the sixth grand prix of what was becoming a thrilling Formula One season. A fortnight on from Monte Carlo and his dismay at being brought to heel by McLaren as he contemplated taking on Alonso, the boy dubbed 'the Stevenage Rocket' in the pit lane now had to put up or shut up.

Although his clear annoyance at being made to play second fiddle to the Spaniard resulted in a FIA inquiry into Ron Dennis' tactics as previously noted, it also created a situation where he would now no longer be expected to handle the car for McLaren's tactical advantage. That was the unexpected bonus of Monaco, but in another sense it put him in an unenviable position. Now, there could be no excuses if Alonso beat him; they were both in the same car and so it would be down to driver quality. Also, there were mutterings from the Alonso camp that maybe he was getting too big for his boots – what had he actually done to warrant equal billing? How many races had he won?

In some quarters, he was labelled with another nickname: the bridesmaid. Second best, never the No. 1. By 10 June in Montreal and for the first time in his short F1 career, the pressure was truly on for him. But his magnificent, and now typical, response was to turn up on the Thursday to 'bed himself in'. There, he met and greeted both press and fans as though he was about to take a gentle stroll in the park rather than hurtle round a circuit at death-defying speeds of up to 203mph in front of a crowd pushing 105,000 on 70 punishing laps. And, at the end of it all on the Sunday afternoon, he was to stand on the podium once again; for the sixth consecutive time, but this time would be the first as the winner. The 'bridesmaid' had eventually reached the altar. For Lewis Hamilton, genius rookie driver, it was the end of a long hard road: he was the No. 1 driver in the world that day, no question about it.

The Circuit Gilles Villeneuve, named after the late, great Ferrari star, is one most of the Formula One drivers can take or leave. No great test, it is, however, a favourite with the fans – its combination of straights and slow corners making for fast, furious, action-packed racing.

Lewis also arrived in Montreal with yet more criticism of his style ringing in his ears. But whereas prior to Monaco Eddie Jordan had knocked him for not being sufficiently aggressive, another 'name' from the past – former World

Champion Jacques Villeneuve – now accused him of being... not aggressive enough! It just went to show how unreliable some of the pundits were.

For Lewis Hamilton was becoming big business. Merely being associated with his name could bring benefits aplenty. Jordan talked about Lewis at the launch of his autobiography, which helped to gain vital column inches of publicity in the following days' newspapers. The onset of his native Canadian Grand Prix saw Villeneuve appear in a rare public outing since his retirement fromFormula One at the end of the 2006 season.

Villeneuve accused Lewis of being too aggressive in his driving at the start of races, saying it was reminiscent of Michael Schumacher, who was attacked for 'dirty driving'. 'When will these chopping moves stop?' he asked. 'Lewis is not getting penalised and his behaviour off the start has started to look the way Michael used to.' The Canadian said he was surprised officials had not waved a black flag at Lewis, calling him into the pits for potential disqualification for dangerous driving. 'So far, he has been lucky, so we'll see if it carries on,' said Villeneuve – who won the title for Williams-Renault in 1997. 'He makes progressive moves that would have got some of the other drivers black-flagged.'

He also questioned whether Lewis was in the same league as Alonso, who had won in Montreal the previous year, and whether he would crack under pressure: 'Lewis is very fast, but he still has to step up to the plate and beat Alonso. And we still haven't seen how he reacts under pressure – that will be interesting to watch.'

Of course, Lewis would answer the barbs in the best style possible: by blasting Alonso out of the water come the race that Sunday, at the same time proving indisputably that he could handle the heaviest of pressure.

In the first practice session on the Friday he was two-tenths of a second slower than Alonso, but let's put that into perspective: this was the first time he had ever seen the Montreal track, let alone raced around it in a Formula One car. By the end of the second session in the afternoon some were questioning whether he was struggling in the heat and with the pressure growing on him by the day. He finished third behind Alonso and Massi, and made a few minor errors of judgment as he roared around the track.

So was he about to crack? No way! He seemed cool and collected as he talked about the day's work, explaining it had been as much about properly familiarising himself with the track as setting new records: 'Today was the first time I had the opportunity to drive here and I really enjoyed myself. We had done a lot of work back in the UK with our simulation programme and also I have watched a few of the past races here but you can't beat the real thing.

'We worked on set-up, tyre evaluation and also looking at the brakes as this circuit is notoriously hard on the brakes. There were no problems and it looks like we are in good shape.'

Indeed he was... By the end of Saturday's first qualifying session, Lewis was the fastest and that propelled him into the second session with a breezy confidence. In the morning, he finished four-tenths of a second ahead of Kimi

Raikkonen's Ferrari with Alonso third and Massa fourth. This set him up nicely for the final scramble for pole position in the afternoon's qualifying sessions and he did not disappoint, claiming the first pole of his F1 career with a fine display of driving. He set the fastest time of 1:15.707 and McLaren team-mate Alonso was unable to beat it with his final lap, finishing on 1:16.163, with Nick Heidfeld third in the BMW on 1:16.266. The Spaniard led earlier but lost six-tenths of a second in the final section.

Afterwards Lewis said: 'I feel fantastic; I have never felt so good. I had to wait for a few anxious seconds before discovering that Alonso had not beaten his time. It has been a fantastic day; it is already a fantastic weekend. It is not easy when you have a two-time World Champion hunting you down.

'I stayed strong and I did it. I owe it all to the team – we worked very hard to get it right. You come to that last corner at 200mph and on the final lap I went quicker than I have ever been; I almost touched the wall. For the final lap the car was sweet. I did not make a mistake and I got the time – I am thrilled.'

The result gave him the hope and confidence to believe he could now translate his brilliant form into a first grand prix victory the following day. 'It is going to be tough,' he said. 'I have not yet started from pole so that is another new experience for me. We have the car and strategy, and I just need to get a good start, get to that first corner first and stay consistent.'

Alonso, who started the race second on the grid, would

pay dearly for the mistake in final qualifying at the L'Epingle hairpin that cost him pole. He said: 'I was really going for it and was fastest for the first two sectors but went off the line and touched the gravel.' To give him his due, he did have some gracious words for his co-driver: 'I'm happy to be on the front row for tomorrow's race and for Lewis to be on pole next to me. The first row will be enough for today and tomorrow I will have another chance to try and win the race. I obviously want to win, but also I'm not going to win the Championship this weekend, so I will be sensible.'

Ron Dennis could not contain his excitement at Lewis' first pole: 'A fantastic qualifying result for the team for the second time in a row and for Lewis to achieve his first ever Formula One pole position. Fernando was unlucky on his second qualifying lap not to have improved following two great first sectors. We are confident that we will have a strong showing in tomorrow's race but certainly will not be complacent.'

And Mercedes boss Norbert Haug was equally effusive, saying: 'Lewis will start from his first Formula One pole position in only his sixth grand prix. Fernando was fastest in both the first and second sectors and until the final sector it looked like he would make it. Lewis and Fernando achieved the best possible qualifying result for the team for the second time within a fortnight.'

Not surprisingly, Ferrari team boss Jean Todt was in the doldrums, saying it had been the 'poorest [qualifying] of the season so far' and that he feared the worst in the race itself. Todt had always been a perceptive realist. He said: 'We were no match for our main rivals. Of course, the points only get given out in the race but the overall picture after today is not a favourable one and I hope that changes for the race.'

It wouldn't. Lewis gave a faultless show to take his first Formula One victory in only the sixth race of his career in a time of 1hr 44m 11.292s. He led throughout, maintaining his focus and concentration as the other big guns of McLaren and Ferrari seemed to lose theirs. He also survived four interventions by the safety car to earn an eight-point lead in the Championship over Alonso, who could only finish seventh. BMW's Heidfeld finished second, 4.343 seconds behind Lewis, with Alexander Wurz third in the Williams, their success finally breaking the McLaren-Ferrari stranglehold on the podium. Wurz's podium was Williams' first since Heidfeld finished second in a Williams-BMW at the Nürburgring in 2005.

Alonso set out like a man possessed, but overextended himself as if he were trying too hard, running wide at the first corner, and slipping down to third place behind Heidfeld. During a nervy ride, he overshot that corner another three times. The Spaniard also suffered when Adrian Sutil's Spyker was involved in a crash. Alonso was low on fuel and forced to make his first pit stop at the same time. Unfortunately for him that broke Formula One rules stating drivers cannot pit until the field has formed up behind the safety car – bringing him a 10-second stop-go penalty, and dropping him to thirteenth.

Fair credit to Fernando, he now set the fastest laps in his attempt to catch up, including the fastest of the day at 1m 16.367s on Lap 46, but he had too much ground to make up, despite the three further appearances by the safety car. The very fact that he finished meant McLaren maintained their record of completing every racing lap in 2007, with 768 so far.

There were other facts worth noting down in Montreal: Lewis became one of only nine drivers to win in his first year of competition. The others were Juan Pablo Montoya (2001), Jacques Villeneuve (1996), Clay Regazzoni and Emerson Fittipaldi (1970), Jackie Stewart (1965), Giancarlo Baghetti (1961) and Giuseppi Farina and Juan Manuel Fangio (1950). The win meant he had 11 races remaining to beat the record for the most grand prix victories in a debut season – the total of 4 set by Jacques Villeneuve in 1996. The Canadian Grand Prix was also the eighteenth occasion when a race featured a first-time winner and pole sitter, the last being Turkey in 2006 when Felipe Massa won from pole.

Lewis arrived back in the pits, fist aloft after his glory lap. Making his way up to the podium he came across the men at McLaren who had guided his career over the decade to this, the highest point: Ron Dennis, Martin Whitmarsh, and Norbert Haug. He headed straight for Big Ron and gave him a bear hug, before running up the steps and out on to the podium to celebrate his win. He said he was 'over the moon' as he savoured the sweet taste of victory: 'I've been ready for the win for quite some time. It was just a matter of when and where. I have to dedicate this win to my Dad because without him this would not have been possible.'

He then explained that holding off Alonso on that first corner had been key to his moment of glory. 'I didn't make a great getaway,' he admitted. 'Fernando got a better start and I had to make sure I didn't leave a gap for Nick behind me. Then I saw Fernando come flying down the outside and thought, oh no, I'm going to lose the lead, but he just went straight on at the corner. I continued on my line and got a fantastic exit, and then Fernando came cutting across in front of me. It was pretty exciting!'

He was talking ten to the dozen, like an excited schoolboy, and who could blame him? Now he had achieved the dream he had worked towards since he was first caught by the racing bug as a young boy of 6. All those years of hard work had paid off. He continued, 'I'm on another planet after this – I simply can't find the words to describe what it feels like to win my first Formula One race. The team has done a fantastic job and I'm so happy to be part of the Vodafone-McLaren Mercedes family. It seemed like every time I opened up a bit of a gap the safety car came out and I had to start all over again. It was only a few laps from the end [that] I realised that victory was within my grasp and I started noticing things like the fans cheering, and when I crossed the finishing line it was amazing. I now have to stay focused and keep up the good work.

'It's been an incredible start to my Formula One career so far, but I know there is a tough season ahead of us. Finally, thanks to the entire team at McLaren and Mercedes-Benz for all the hard work they have put into the car – it's an absolute pleasure to drive and be part of such a winning combination.'

Alonso's offered his congratulations, saying: 'I think this was a strange race with the safety car being deployed so many times, which worked to Lewis' advantage today – and my disadvantage. I came into the pits for the first time on Lap 24 as I had no more fuel so basically there was nothing I could do.

'It was a shame as this resulted in a 10-second penalty but I guess that unfortunately those are the rules but there was no alternative other than to stop on track with no fuel. After that I had to push as hard as possible because I was stuck in the middle of the field, and when you push to the maximum you sometimes go off track but at that stage there was nothing to lose. Whilst it was a difficult race for me, I'm pleased for the team and Lewis that we were able to secure some important points and Lewis winning his first race. I hope for a bit more luck for the US Grand Prix next week and at least I can leave Montreal with two points more than Massa.' And they say you have to be selfish if you want to be a champion...

Although Ron Dennis was beaming at the realisation that his boy had finally done it, once again, he was initially concentrating on the Spaniard's 10-second penalty and claiming he had been hard done by. He said, 'The whole team worked so hard to achieve the optimum result today. The frustration and disappointment of receiving a stop-and-go penalty, having been forced to stop in the pit lane when the pit lane was closed in the first safety car period, was obviously immense.

'However this in no way should detract from a mature and disciplined drive by Lewis to claim his first grand prix win. It's a very long time since the British national anthem was played for a race winner. His family should be justifiably proud of his achievement and whatever McLaren and Mercedes-Benz have contributed only compliments his talent and commitment. Lewis has done a great job, he deserved it and I am happy for him. Fernando was truly unlucky today but there is still a long way to go in the World Championship and we appear to be extremely competitive.'

Lewis was asked what could better this – was there an even more impossible dream to come true? He said: 'The next dream is obviously to win a Formula One World Championship but at the moment we have to be realistic again. It's always good to bear in mind that I'm still a rookie and this is my first season. There are going to be some hard times. I hope that there aren't, but it's just bound to happen – it's just the way it goes in this business and there'll be good days and bad days. But at the moment it's been consistent and that's down to the team and all the people around me. I've got a very well-grounded family and I think it works perfect.'

A lively question-and-answer session followed at the traditional post-grand prix press conference. One section of amusing answers from the Stevenage Rocket, involving also Heidfeld and Wurz, is worth recording here. It highlighted how the boy was developing, becoming much more assured, independently confident and able to handle being in the public arena.

Q: I read this week that you said pole position was better than sex, where do you rank this? (Laughter among the Press corps)

A: Heidfeld: He's too young still.

A: Hamilton: Yesterday it was a joke, it's a completely different feeling but... (More laughter)

A: Wurz: Did something change since yesterday? (More laughter)

A: Hamilton: It's definitely another level of feeling from yesterday, that's for definite.

Lewis was also asked what his father had said to him immediately after the race. His reply and gratitude to the man who had sacrificed almost everything to see him on that pedestal was certainly touching. 'I haven't seen him but obviously I could see him in the crowd while I was on the podium and it looked like he had a tear in his eye. So it's obvious that he was extremely proud and you wouldn't believe the amount of work he's put into my career. He had nothing when he was younger – just to see his family be successful is a real pleasure to him.'

Anthony was too choked with emotion to speak after Lewis' win, but a few minutes later he sufficiently composed himself and was told his son had dedicated the win to him. 'I hadn't heard that,' he said. 'But I'm glad I didn't hear it because who knows what would have happened? I was trying to hold it back as it was. This was the ordinary guy makes good. It's a special day for us but also for lots of other people, Formula One people and not Formula One people.'

He admitted the strain of the race had left him drained. 'Today has been hard work,' he said. 'I had to go through winning that race four times today. I did four grands prix today. Forget Lewis! He has just been laughing in his helmet and enjoying the race. That is what he does – nothing scares him.'

Would he and Lewis now be sitting down to make plans for a real assault on the world title crown? He smiled and shook his head: 'We never made plans to get to where we are; we just made plans to always do the best at what we were doing at that time. Getting to Formula One was just the next step that came along. We never, ever look ahead and say, "Right, we are going to do this, this, this and this".

'Wouldn't it be really painful if you start setting your heart on winning the Championship and it doesn't happen? We have plenty of time to win that championship, and if it happens this year, then that is a bonus.'

He conceded Lewis himself might be thinking about winning the crown now, but said he would be doing his utmost to keep him on the straight and narrow: 'What Lewis is going to think about is bringing the car home. Keep your mind straight, keep your feet on the ground and just bring the car home every time you take it out. And if we get a win along the line, that is brilliant, and if we win the Championship, that would be great.'

After his press conference, Lewis showed another side to his character by insisting he went to greet the fans from the UK, and indeed the rest of the world, who had waited patiently for him to emerge. They had cheered him to victory and now they wanted to congratulate them. He, in turn, wanted to meet them, thank them and celebrate a little with them even though, as the McLaren team was already reminding him, the next grand prix, in America, was only a week away.

Lewis insisted 'There's plenty of time to enjoy this win before going to Indy, and we'll obviously go there with great confidence. I've no doubt we can do well there as well. I just want to also thank the crowd; they were fantastic today.'

It was yet another illustration of how he differed from the stereotyped Formula One driver. He would never have dreamt of rushing off and locking himself away in his motorhome. Instead, he wanted to thank the people who paid his wages and whom, in the majority of cases, watched the races in what are often, let's be honest, uncomfortable surroundings – often fields with meagre facilities and zero comfort. Monza especially springs to mind...

By nightfall after his first Formula One Grand Prix win Lewis Hamilton was rapidly acquiring a new title: the People's Champion... It was party time for him in Montreal and the tributes and accolades poured in as the night progressed. Sir Stirling Moss led the way, saying of the young man who had become the 19th British driver to win a grand prix: 'He is a very impressive young man, the most impressive young driver I've seen in a long while. He has the car control and he has the calmness when he is driving, but he is also a fighter and has a great manner about him. He'll go a long way. I was impressed with him at the beginning of the season, but even more so now. It was obvious how good he was, but I never thought – and I don't think anybody thought – he would be leading the World Championship.

'For a guy who has just come into the sport, that is unbelievable, so I am terribly impressed and what has impressed me more than anything is that he is a racer.'

Another of racing's knights in shining armour, Sir Jackie Stewart, went even further, saying: 'He is probably the brightest star that has entered Formula One – ever!'

Damon Hill paid tribute to the way Lewis managed to maintain his cool in the heat of the battle: 'People should not underestimate what he has achieved in an incredibly short space of time. Yes, he's with a good team, and yes, he's got a good car, but to be winning grands prix, and be putting in performances like that race after race, takes something special. He may be young and in his first season, but this guy is the real deal. If you're good enough in this sport, you're old enough – and, boy, is Lewis good enough!

'He's leading the World Championship and winning races, so his confidence will be sky-high. And he's shown he can handle the pressure. We shouldn't get too carried away, but we could be looking at the next British World Champion.'

Another former World Champion, Niki Lauda, admitted he had the feeling that he was witnessing a new epoch in motor racing, thanks to Lewis' win – one that could take the sport to a new exciting level. He said, 'This was the best result ever, for him and for Formula One. I've never seen a guy driving such a perfect way. If he continues like this, he will be Champion. We all expected him, with no experience, to make mistakes under pressure, but he doesn't do any mistakes.'

Sir Frank Williams – who saw his own driver, Alex Wurz,

finish a distant third – said, 'He is absolutely a brilliant driver. You could almost describe him as a phenomenon, given that he is achieving so much with no Formula One experience. He is very, very remarkable.'

Simon Barnes, chief sportswriter of *The Times*, summed up best what the press back in the UK were thinking; his prose typically brilliantly flowing and rich: 'There was a sense of inevitability about it, almost a sense of serenity. Lewis Hamilton won his first grand prix in his sixth race and the dominating emotion was well, of course he bloody well did! What do you expect? The only mystery was why it took him so long– because Hamilton does not seem to be anything to do with precocious talent. By an extraordinary illusion, he looks exactly like the mature article, like the complete athlete: calm in himself, happy in his skin, as certain of his abilities as if they had been tried and tested a hundred times.

'No wonder his team-mate at McLaren, Fernando Alonso, has got the jumps. Being a World Champion is no defence against Hamilton's slightly spooky sense of self-certainty... Hamilton just drove. He drove with that sense of affinity for his conveyance that you occasionally see in very, very good horsemen – an almost passive sense of competitiveness, as if the driver or rider were merely a kind of vector for victory.'

Writing in *F1 Racing* magazine, Peter Windsor was also full of wonder at how easy Lewis had made such a difficult accomplishment appear: 'Lewis won this race because he won the pole; and then, from a slowish start, won it at the first corner – when Fernando blew it. He won it, in short, with a display of perfect braking, feel and balance on a torrid day. He won it with consistent precision at the big braking areas – at the hairpin and into Turn 1. He won it with a confidence level about which most drivers can only dream – with a quick trip to the circus on Saturday evening, followed by an early night, then a satisfying day at the races. It was simple. He made it look ridiculously simple. Such is his stature.'

The public was also eager to add their salute to the wonderboy, at the same time stressing how he had resurrected a sport many had turned their backs on. David, of London, said 'This guy Lewis Hamilton is really something else. His sudden appearance and success on the Formula One scene is reminiscent of Tiger Woods in golf. Both are mature, highly talented, no-nonsense professionals who have taken their respective sports by storm and just do the business. Formula One is worth watching again.'

And Derek, of Horsham, commented: 'Hamilton is showing great stability and consistency in every race. Alonso didn't become World Champion twice by being rubbish and this all makes for a very, very exciting season. Thank God the two are in the same car! No one can say that the other won because the car they were in was better... although Alonso is already trying to make his excuses.'

Catherine, from Powys, said, 'Lewis seems dedicated and modest. From the interviews I've seen with his father, he comes from a well-grounded background. I'm a 33-year-old woman and thanks to Lewis Hamilton, I've become interested in Formula One.'

There was even a surge of interest and admiration from overseas fans of Formula One. Pancho Villa jnr, from Mexico City, joked: 'Hopefully you Brits can be champions at one thing, since you all have not won a football championship since 1966 and we all know that it was rigged...LOL!' And Freddi, of São Paulo, conceded: 'Although I'm a Brazilian and a big fan of Massa's driving style, seeing Hamilton win yesterday was very nice and it perhaps gives us an idea of how the next few years of Formula One will be. I believe it will be exciting – with a nice competition among the new talents such as Massa, Hamilton, Kimi, Alonso and others. That's good news.'

It sure was. And while Lewis Hamilton was making fans as far away as South America, the good times were really about to roll in north America. Cue Indianapolis, one week on...

Above left: The McLaren Formula One team was formed in 1963 by New Zealander Bruce McLaren. Here he is pictured in his debut year, 1966.　　　© *PA Photos*

Above right: Lewis with team principle and mentor Ron Dennis.　　　© *Getty Images*

Below: In Australia ahead of the opening race of the 2007 Formula One season with McLaren team-mate Fernando Alonso.　　　© *Reuters/Mark Horsburgh*

Two men Lewis thanks for their long-term support, (*above left*) Martin Whitmarsh, Chief Operating Officer at McLaren and (*above right*) Norbert Haug, Vice-president of Mercedes-Benz Motorsport.
© PA Photos /© Rex Features

Below left: Lewis poses for pictures with fans in the paddock prior to the Spanish Grand Prix at Circuit de Catalunya track in Spain, May 2007.
© PA Photos

Above right: Nick holding Lewis' second-place trophy from the Monaco Grand Prix, May 2007.
© Getty Images

Above: Victory at last! Celebrating his first win with his team in Canada, 10 June 2007.

© *PA Photos*

Below: British fans showing their support at the US Grand Prix where he gained his second win, June 2007.

© *PA Photos*

Above: Enjoying a night out with Natasha Bedingfield and Pharrell Williams.

© *PA Photos*

Below left: Attending P.Diddy's launch dinner for the Sean John fragrance 'Unforgivable' at trendy bar Fifty with his father, July 2007.

© *Rex Features*

Below right: With Hollywood actress Thandie Newton and his brother Nicolas at the F1 party on behalf of Great Ormond St Hospital, London, in July 2007.

© *Getty Images*

With the prospect of a British driver winning his home grand prix, record crowds flocked to Silverstone to show their support for Lewis on home turf.

Above left: Focusing for the race.   © *Rex Features*

Above right: British fans have waited years for a figure like Lewis to bring new life to the sport.   © *Rex Features*

Below: Anthony on the track with Kimberley Walsh, Nicola Roberts and Sarah Harding from girl band Girls Aloud.   © *Rex Features*

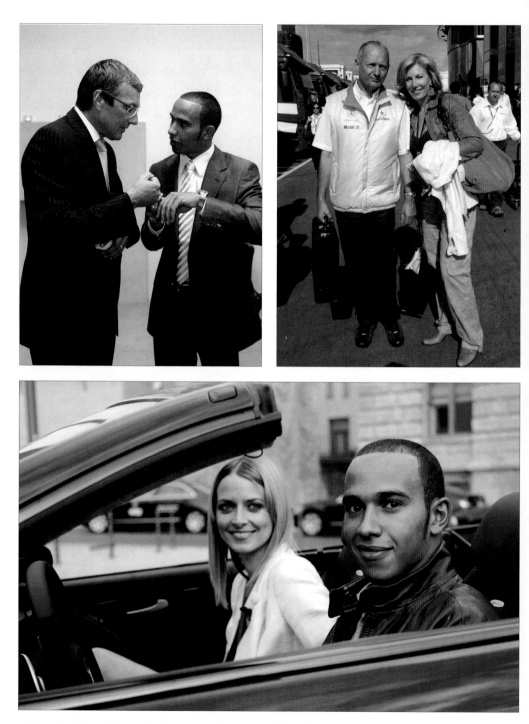

Above left: Tag Heuer Ambassador Lewis and President Jean Christophe Babin compare their watches, photographed at a party hosted by the exclusive manufacturer in London, July 2007. Lewis is rapidly becoming a brand name to rival the likes of David Beckham.

© *Rex Features*

Above right: Ron Dennis with his wife Lisa.

© *Rex Features*

Below: With Eva Padberg at the 'Power Meets Fashion' event on the opening day of Mercedes Benz Fashion Week 2008 in Berlin, July 2007.

© *Rex Features*

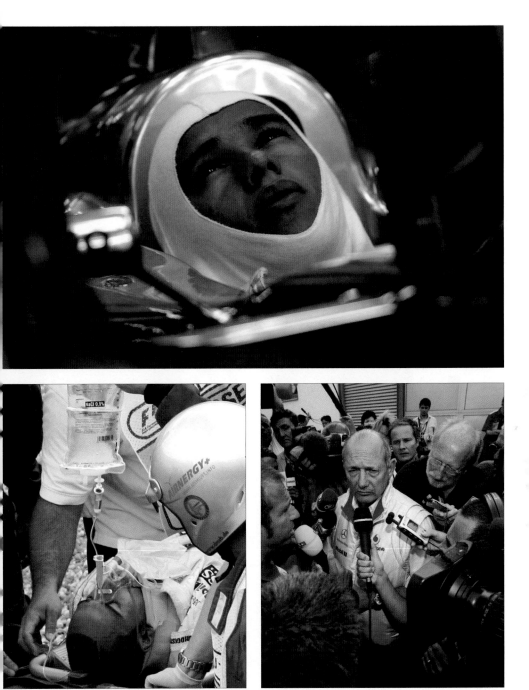

The European Grand Prix at the Nürburgring in July 2007 saw Lewis crash into the tyre barriers during Saturday's qualifying session.

Above: In his car for the Friday practice session. © *PA Photos*

Below left: Lewis is transported on a stretcher after the crash. He gave a wave and a thumbs-up sign as he was taken into the ambulance. Remarkably, he sustained no injuries and was able to race the following day. © *PA Photos*

Below right: An emotional Ron addressing the media after the crash, July 2007.

© *PA Photos*

Adding another trophy to his collection. Lewis Hamilton at *GQ* magazine's Men of the Year Awards in September 2007, where he received the Sportsman of the Year gong.

CHAPTER 12

AMERICAN IDOL

So, was it a one-off, or would Lewis Hamilton now take advantage of what had been a growing momentum? That was the question being floated wide and far as he arrived at the Brickyard for his Formula One US debut in the middle of June 2007. Obviously, the win in Montreal had filled him with confidence, but now he was in among the big boys. There could be no more hiding behind the 'rookie' tag; that was clearly a misnomer. No, as he revved up for the seventh Formula One race of his fledgling career, he had now become one of its hottest properties. The secret was out; the secret anyone connected with his career for the previous 10 years could well have guessed, that anyone who had watched his all-conquering season in GP2 the previous year would have acknowledged: Lewis was a natural and would take Formula One by storm.

He arrived in the States on the Thursday before the race to acclimatise himself after his Canadian triumph. In truth, this did not give him as much time as he would have liked, especially with this being another circuit he had never visited, let alone raced around. But needs must. After his win in Montreal he found himself much in demand. He explained his late arrival in this way: 'I was in New York for a couple of days – I had an appearance for Mercedes-Benz. Then I went to Washington yesterday for another appearance for Exxon-Mobil and getting back the flight was delayed from 4 o'clock to 8 o'clock, then eventually it was cancelled at 9. So we ended up staying in a hotel and luckily we flew out this morning.'

Not ideal for a man who, as already noted, is big on detail and likes to prepare himself fully, both mentally and physically at his own pace before a race. But he was also mature enough to accept that life would never be the same again after that thrilling triumph in Canada: 'I know that I had the front pages back in the UK after the race, which is awesome. I have had something like 200 text messages from friends and it's almost impossible to reply to them all, but I'm trying.

'It's a big stepping stone in my career and in my life. It was a great feeling to get the first win and definitely not expected going into my sixth grand prix, especially at Canada, which wasn't one of my strongest circuits. I think Fernando [Alonso] was probably quicker than me there but I did a solid job. It's obviously very positive for the team – we've extended our lead in the Constructors'

Championship... Great points for me... and coming here we've got to continue with that performance.'

His first impression of the Indianapolis Motor Speedway, also known as the Brickyard, was a good one. He admitted he felt a thrill of expectation shiver down his spine as he surveyed the track: a high-speed oval with tight twists and turns and a long straight made for putting your foot down. The home of American motor speedway and the world-famous Indy 500 shimmered in the sun as he put on his helmet for practice on the Friday prior to the big race. Even back then he admitted to a gut feeling: this was a race he could win; he could be the new King of America once the 73 laps had been completed on the Sunday, no doubt about it.

He also knew victory would put him in the history books, along with Graham Hill and Dan Wheldon, as British winners at the track. Hill, a legendary Formula One driver, had won the Indy 500 as a rookie in 1966 and Wheldon emulated his glory race in 2005; the first Brit to win at the Brickyard during those 39 years since Hill's romp. Lewis said, 'I am very excited about the race. It's an amazing opportunity for any driver to come here and compete. Watching the Indy 500 over the years, it's an awesome race and I've always wanted to go and watch and be a spectator. But to be here, racing on the circuit, is pretty cool. Just flying over, I could see what the track was like. It's quite a nice complex.'

But would the new level of expectation weigh heavily on him? Might it adversely affect his performance at the Brickyard? 'To be honest, I try not to focus on that,' he said, scratching his head. 'I came into the season with a very open mind and being realistic of the fact that I am a rookie and I've got a lot to learn, it is still a very steep learning curve. And yes, I have a great opportunity as I'm in the best team and have one of the best drivers to compare myself to.

'But I still feel there's going to be times during the season when there will be some lows, as well as the highs, and I think it's way too early to talk about the Championship. There are 11 races to go and I just have to approach every race exactly the same as I always have and try and do a solid job.

'Each time I go out in the car, I learn something new. I'm becoming more and more comfortable in the car, with the team, with the controls, and with the rules and the regulations and just the whole racing. I'm always learning bit by bit and I will continue throughout the season.'

It was that level-headedness that convinced many that he could push Alonso and Raikkonen down to the wire in the battle for the Driver's title. A cliché maybe, but for one so young, he had a wise old head.

The first day of practice at Indianapolis was spent studying the track, learning its bumps and curves; how to avoid its pitfalls. Fernando Alonso set the fastest lap in the first session with Lewis seven-tenths of a second behind him. The Spaniard was also top dog on the afternoon session, with a best lap of 1m 12.156s. But there were now ominous signs from Hamilton: as he got to grips with the circuit he was closing in on his team-mate. By the end of that day the gap was a little more than one-tenth of a second.

He knew he was once again on the brink of something big: 'As this was the first time I have ever driven here I spent some time just getting to know the circuit. The really tricky bit is the mid-section as it's very tight and twisty. We spent our time fine-tuning the set-up and evaluating the two different tyre options provided by Bridgestone this weekend.

'In the first part of the second session I ran a little wide and did some minor damage to the aerodynamic fences, which took a little time for the guys to repair. We have a pretty good idea of where we are going, and it looks like we should be competitive, but as always, Friday is only the start of the weekend – there is a long way to go.'

Alonso was fastest again on Saturday morning, with Lewis third, but by the end of the day the tables had turned dramatically. It was Lewis who grabbed his second consecutive pole after turning in a time of 1m 12.331s, 0.169 seconds ahead of Alonso. The Ferraris of Felipe Massa and Kimi Raikkonen would make up the second row. It was a terrific result for Lewis, who admitted he had not slept well the night before. Some pundits believed this could be down to hay fever, but he admitted: 'No, I wouldn't say I've got hay fever. I haven't been getting much sleep lately, probably just enjoying it too much! But yes, I didn't feel great.' Maybe not, but he couldn't conceal his delight at the outcome of qualifying: 'I'm quite surprised, to be honest. Going into qualifying we hadn't found the optimum set-up and I knew Fernando was quick here.

'To be on pole once again within a week is fantastic – I like north America! The fans here have been so enthusiastic and supportive for the team, and I hope they enjoyed today. I screamed into my helmet when I got the confirmation from the team of the pole position. It's a challenge to come to a track for the first time, and I have learnt new things every single corner and every single lap. I knew I had to push very hard in my second run in the final qualifying session. The car is working well, and the team has done a great job.'

Things got even better on race day as Lewis roared home first in 1hr 31m 09.965s to take his second victory in a row and forge 10 points clear of Alonso. It was also his seventh appearance on the podium in his seventh Formula One race. And he did it in style, completing a grid-to-flag victory and coolly dealing with Alonso's two attempts to pass him. Alonso, who would finish second, tried to get past Lewis as they pulled away from the grid, but it was the boy from Stevenage who won the tussle.

They clashed again after making their first pit stops 1 lap apart. The two cars went down the main straight side by side but again it was Lewis who emerged in front as they hit Turn One. After that, it was race off as he kept his position as leader until the chequered flag. The victory also meant Lewis entered the record books as only the fourth rookie, along with Jacques Villeneuve, Nino Farina and Juan Manuel Fangio, to win at least two races in their debut season.

Afterwards he was glad to be out of the searing heat of the day. He admitted he had been boosted by local fans backing him with noisy klaxons and the presence in his pit lane of American rapper Pharrell Williams as his VIP guest. Looking slightly dazed, Lewis admitted: 'It just keeps getting better and better – what an amazing week this has been! I can't believe that I have won. To come to two circuits [Montreal and Indianapolis] that I didn't know and to really come out with such pace and to see the team moving forward is great.

'The last 15 laps seemed a lifetime, but I was in the lead – I was able to do it and I'm very emotional now. Everything went right: start, pit stops, strategy… and I'm really happy. I was under pressure all the way from Fernando and we were both pushing as hard as possible. I made a good start to maintain the advantage but Fernando was right there. In the second stint Fernando managed to get really close when my tyres were graining, and he had a go at the end of the straight, but I was able to keep him behind. It's been a long and hot day, but I have really enjoyed myself and the support from the fans.'

Ron Dennis was at his most diplomatic, congratulating both drivers on their 1–2, but also pointing out that this time he had told them both to cut down their revs. Big Ron said, 'During the middle stint Fernando pushed hard and caught Lewis, and this created some positive but tense moments on the pitwall. We were obviously happy to let them race but had to be mindful of the fact that our competition was not threatening our 1–2 finish. Fifteen laps from the end both drivers reduced their revs to save the engines for the French Grand Prix but still continued to race. Their sporting behaviour, both on the track and especially during the podium celebrations, made the team proud to have two such great drivers.'

Lewis was told it was Father's Day and asked did he have a special message for Anthony? He said, 'I didn't even know it was Father's Day – I've just been so focused. I remember someone told me but I didn't know if it was Father's Day over here, or Father's Day back home. I'm never aware of those dates, but now it's even better.

'I dedicated the last win to him, but I don't really know what to do with this one. I think there's going to be – I hope – many, many more to come. I can't just keep on dedicating to a different... there are so many people in my family! As I said, I'm grateful to all of them. I hope he's happy, and I will say Happy Father's Day at the end.'

But he did not realise how big a star he had become until he arrived back in the UK. Now he was the talking point around the pubs and workplaces – he had become a national celebrity and a national treasure. The fans were desperate to send him their congratulations. Joe Neill of London said: 'Firstly well done Lewis! Your two wins in Canada and America are fantastic for Formula One. Also, full credit to McLaren for giving a British driver a chance – and for giving Alonso a run for his money! To me it looks like he is more than equal! It's great to see raw talent get a chance – let's hope he keeps it on the road all year – and that he goes on to win the title.'

Another racing enthusiast, Tim Leach of Burnley said it was time for Alonso to give a bit of credit where it was due: 'I have the greatest respect for anyone who drives a Formula One car, but after seven races Hamilton is 10 points ahead of Alonso. They are equal partners with the same backup and resources, which means that driving skills are the main criteria that separate the two team-mates.

'Alonso has to accept the fact that possession is nine-tenths of the law and barring a major disaster, he has his work cut out to catch Hamilton.'

Tom Bray of Dublin paid tribute to Lewis' cool style: 'It is really satisfying to have Lewis win these two north American races. His two wins from pole were solid – extremely high-quality calm execution with chaos often around him. I'm just glad to see that if he indeed does close up the Championship this year, it will include quality wins. I was worried for a while that we may have a non-race winning champion with this point system. But the cream does rise to the top. And has it ever!' Meanwhile Bill Lowe, of Banbury, was similarly effusive of Hamilton's driving skills: 'How much of the emerging gap between McLaren and Ferrari is based on Hamilton's skill as a driver? The Indy race, which I saw in person, was a masterful exhibition of driving ability.'

And tributes were also paid to Ron Dennis and McLaren for their gamble in bringing the youngster to world fame in such a short time. Alan Davies of Chester said: 'Win pole, protect your line, put your foot down, don't make any mistakes, bring it home! Five essential ingredients that make superb racing driver – yesterday at the Brickyard, Lewis was superb.

'Fernando will need to re-adjust his strategy and driving style in order to get back into the running. It's good to see that he opted to play it safe and bring home maximum points. However the star of this race is not just Lewis: it is also McLaren. The team has gone from being side-of-the-track scenery in the last few years to a dominant Ferrari-eating outfit. Five wins in seven races, three 1–2 finishes, and a bag full of podiums.

'They are clearly running away with the Constructor's title, leaving Jean Todt scratching his head and wishing for a Schumi resurrection. As far as the Driver's title is concerned, in 2008 McLaren might have *two World Champions* under one roof! What a combo that will be.'

And Jody Smith of Ipswich said that after his 2 wins in north America Lewis would surely now go on to pinch the title from Alonso: 'He has been consistent, got podiums, pole positions and two victories. Hamilton has shown his armchair critics that he is for real and is the new dominant force in Formula One today.

'Long-shot overtaking manoeuvers at the start of grand prix races are costing him dearly – Alonso had better learn to live with Hamilton's speed and consistency, and up his game, or the double World Champion will be left in his wake.

'Personally, I don't think Alonso can catch him now – Lewis is too consistent and will surely go on to capture the world title.'

Jonathan McEvoy of the *Daily Mail* also paid tribute to Lewis' showing in America – like others particularly admiring the way in which he dealt with all that came his way in such a mature, composed manner: 'Nothing seems to faze the new star. He arrived at a track he had never seen, following a nightmare journey... He charmed the crowd by waving, signing autographs and saying all the right things whenever a microphone was pushed under his nose. He is a natural.

'He was equally sure-footed in the cockpit. Yes, Alonso had the edge in practice and the first two sessions of qualifying, but when it counted in the shoot-out for pole, Hamilton banged in the fastest time on Saturday afternoon – all that in high temperatures and with hay fever. It was a masterclass in managing the weekend.'

Finally, the *Daily Telegraph* printed a note of congratulations that must have just about iced the cake for Lewis after his US win – it was from his cousin Michelle and read: 'Hi Lewis! This is your cousin, Michelle Hamilton, daughter of Randolph Hamilton, who is the son of your grandfather's (Uncle Davidson) brother (you know him as Uncle Fleet). Congratulations on your big win! We watched you all the way from the United States and we're so proud of you. Aunty Irva is here with us for the summer and she cheered you on the whole way.

'I hope the newspaper will forward this message to you. If not, we'll get in touch with your Aunt Vanessa. Again, congratulations and enjoy your big win!'

The ripple of applause continued all week, with tributes and accolades pouring in en masse. But Lewis knew he had to put it all to the back of his mind; it was not his scene to play the big 'I am'. No, he had another important date looming in his bid for world domination: it was less than two weeks until a 1 July showdown with Alonso & Co. in France.

The heat had been on in the US and now it was off as they

travelled back to a rain-swept Europe, but it would reach boiling point as the Formula One circus finally touched down at Magny-Cours for the eighth leg of an unrelenting pressure-cooker campaign. Alonso was agitated and fired up after losing out to his 'rookie' team-mate in north America and he was determined to avenge those defeats in Europe. Lewis knew he would have to pull out all the stops once again to keep at bay the man who was, after all, a double World Champion.

As events unfolded at Magny-Cours it became clear that Lewis now had to face up to a new problem as well as Alonso, and, like his team-mate, this one would not go away. It was the re-emergence of the prancing horse... as Ferrari finally put their early season problems behind them and put on a weekend's showcase of dazzling racing to take the limelight off Lewis and Fernando.

British fans hoping for a Lewis Hamilton hat trick of wins were disappointed when he struggled to live with the rejuvenated Ferraris. Kimi Raikkonen arrived at the French circuit clearly meaning business: he was fastest in the first practice session on the Friday and his dominance would continue right up to the end of the race on the Sunday afternoon. Even as he arrived in France, Lewis seemed a bit disorientated, claiming to 'quite like the track' and saying 'I've had some very interesting experiences here' before adding, 'I have always liked racing here, when you hear people talk about circuits that are technical, Magny-Cours is definitely one of them.

'It is important to have good speed in the slow corners, as

they tend to lead on to long straights. You have to have good mechanical set-up for the corners and the same with traction for the exits. My favourite sections of the track are the two high-speed chicanes at the back of the circuit. We go through them at speeds of up to 200kph, which is very fast for a chicane; very special to drive through and unique in Formula One.'

The bit about liking the track puzzled me, especially in light of his visits in Formula Three and GP2. Maybe it was just part of the ever-maturing Lewis Hamilton, putting on a diplomatic show for his French hosts? Certainly, his record at the circuit did not inspire his fans: he crashed there in F3 and had a similarly tough learning lesson there as he cruised to the GP2 title in the 2006–7 season.

He conceded: 'The French round of the GP2 Championship last season was not my best weekend as I had a coming together in the first race that led to me starting race two from nineteenth. I did make my way up through the field to fifth to score some points, so it is possible to overtake here. Although you always want to be on pole, you can pass at Magny-Cours, while there is a short pit lane that means there are more strategy options.'

The jinx seemed to have struck again on the first practice session – he was sixth fastest. Yet by Saturday night his fortunes appeared to have turned: he had done well enough to start from second on the grid. Lewis set a time of 1m 15.104s and missed his third pole position in a row by only seven-hundredths of a second, and he would have sneaked it, had he had not made a braking mistake in the final section of qualifying. He admitted: 'You can't be perfect all the time. On my final lap I braked a bit late into Turn 15 and ran wide. Without this mistake the pole position would have been possible for me today – I had it there.'

Was the pressure of leading the World Championship by 10 points and being hunted by Alonso, getting to him, maybe? Lewis said: 'I don't feel any more pressure, I just feel that I approach every weekend the same. It is great to be in the lead, but obviously there are 10 races left and it is way too early to consider winning the Championship.

'I am still in my first season. A lot of the other drivers obviously understand that I am still a rookie but as you go through the season they see that you are doing a good job or you have a close battle with them, and they can see you are fair or something like that and they build the respect that they have for you; it grows. But I still think they obviously know I am a rookie, they expect me to make a mistake at some point...'

Massa had won pole and Raikkonen would be No. 3 on the grid. Alonso suffered gearbox problems in the final section of qualifying, meaning he would start from a disastrous tenth position. As he wound down after qualifying he was in a grumpy mood, but managed a smile a little later saying he hoped the heavens would open in France overnight! Alonso said, 'I will pray for rain tonight. We know wet conditions are difficult and produce mixed results. But if you are quick in the dry, you can be two or three tenths of a second quicker than the guy in front. If you are quick in the wet, maybe it's two seconds so you can make up places much, much quicker. So I really hope it's wet tomorrow because it might lead to some uncertainties we might be able to benefit from.

'Starting tenth no doubt that makes it difficult for me to close the [points] gap to Lewis. I need points, but I also know that finishing higher than fifth might not be possible, but it is what I will try to do.'

He also smiled grimly when the word Ferrari was mentioned and said he himself had never written them off in the title race: 'After winning three races in Monaco, Canada and Indianapolis, people seemed to forget Ferrari, but not me. I know they are quick, that they can do a very good job and they are always strong. To beat Ferrari is always difficult, and it will be difficult until the last race.'

At least for once this enigmatic, often difficult man was spot-on. Ferrari would transform their season as Kimi Raikkonen and Felipe Massa finished first and second at Magny-Cours to end Lewis' run of victories. But the Stevengage Rocket was still in there battling, taking third place to extend his lead to 14 points at the top of the drivers' standings in what was his eighth consecutive podium finish.

Raikkonen took the lead on Lap 47 on his way to victory in a time of 1hr 30m 54.200s. He had overtaken Lewis by the first corner – the first time the Brit had been overtaken in Formula One – and powered on from there, finishing 2.414m ahead of Massa and another 32 seconds beyond Hamilton. Alonso put in a battling display to finish seventh, but out of the points.

Lewis tried to put a brave face on the weekend in France: 'I am sure we can bounce back at the next race, without a doubt. Going into my first British Grand Prix with the team I've always wanted to drive for, and leading the World Championship is one of the greatest feelings a driver can have.

'So long as we maintain reliability and consistency I don't see why we can't keep going for the win. At the start of the season such a thing was unimaginable, while I have said before that I never expected to finish on the podium in my first race, never mind to do so now for eight races. So I'm very, very happy with the job I've done, and the job the team has done. Even after the fact I was overtaken for the first time in a race, I am not disappointed. I don't like being overtaken, which is the same for everyone, yet it was inevitable it would happen at some point. But the fact is we have finished on the podium again. We are the most consistent team and I do think we are doing the better job. Obviously, you can't win every race, but I've extended my lead in the Championship so I couldn't be happier.'

McLaren team boss Ron Dennis admitted he had switched Lewis to a strategy to guarantee third place, recognising it would be impossible to overtake the Ferraris. He also tried to downplay the impact of the boys in red, saying: 'Obviously we are delighted that Kimi won over Massa (who would have been just 1 point behind Alonso had he won).

'We flattered them this weekend. They did a good job and probably improved the car a little, but we made them look a lot better than they were. Hopefully we will demonstrate that at Silverstone.'

Ah, Silverstone... There was just no let-up in what was becoming a punishing test of stamina. Lewis was certainly looking forward to the next stage of his examination: the journey home but even he was feeling the strain with the knowledge that the Prancing Horse was alive and kicking. Raikkonen and Massa had resolutely proved that to be the case with a dominant weekend for Ferrari in the wastelands of France.

Lewis was about to find out just how big a name worldwide he had become when he arrived back in England – and how he was being talked of as a pioneer for blacks who had never previously considered Formula One as a spectator, or indeed participant sport. Before we land back in England, let's now take a slight detour to examine the effect Lewis Hamilton was having on Formula One as its first black driver.

CHAPTER 13

RACE DRIVER

When Pharrell Williams joined Lewis Hamilton as his VIP guest at the US Grand Prix, the focus inevitably moved to the effect the young racing driver was having on the black community in terms of the sport. It seemed clear that as well as opening up Formula One to a younger, more vibrant audience, Lewis' achievement in becoming the first driver of black heritage to win a grand prix had encouraged other black people to follow the sport and, in some cases, to dream of breaking into it as he had done. As mentioned before, the natural role model comparison in the early days of his arrival on the scene was Tiger Woods. Just as Lewis was to storm to glory quickly, appearing nine consecutive times on the podium, so too had Tiger done in golf. Woods won his fifth Pro tournament and was World No. 1 just 42 weeks after he made his professional debut. It was also anticipated that, just as Tiger had opened up golf via his dominance over the years, so too would Lewis widen out motor racing.

But was that an altogether too simplistic view of affairs? Would the Lewis effect have black hopefuls queuing up to follow in his footsteps through Formula One's previously closed door? Of the Tiger Woods' comparison, Lewis himself would say: 'I'm not Tiger Woods, I'm Lewis Hamilton, but I think he's a sensational athlete. I hope I can do the same in Formula One.'

'The same in Formula One'... Yet even before his extraordinary wins in north America had been fully taken in, some pundits decried Lewis' achievements, arguing that even if he did turn out like Tiger that was nothing to shout about – after all, what had Tiger really done for the ethnic minorities in golf?

Matthew Syed led the doubters in *The Times*, arguing it must be said, with considerable aplomb and armed with convincing statistics to illustrate that Tiger had not changed golf one bit in terms of racial progress: 'The truth is that Woods has not had anything like the influence on global black consciousness that his cheerleaders suggest. Not one black player has joined the PGA tour since Woods turned professional in 1996 and there has not been a black player in the Ladies Professional Golf Association since 2000. There are today no home players from an ethnic-minority background playing on tour and of the 60 teenagers in the English Golf Union's elite programme only two come from minorities.'

Yes, that's quite an argument – well constructed and, on the surface at least, difficult to debate. I asked Ash Hussain for his views on Syed's contentions. Ash, 36, of east London, is an ideal man to talk about breaking down barriers. A national newspaper picture editor of Asian descent, he told me how he himself had to struggle to break through 'traditional barriers within the newspaper industry' to reach the top. He also admits he had to break through barriers within his own community: 'When I started out 15 years ago, the Asian community wanted doctors, engineers and lawyers, not photographers! But since then a few Asian youngsters have seen what I have achieved and have been inspired to pursue a career in media.'

He vehemently disagrees with Syed's view that Tiger has achieved nothing in breaking down those same barriers in golf, arguing that just because no one else has emerged at Tiger's level this does not mean he has failed as a role model for blacks. Ash said: 'I feel it is a bit too harsh because you get a lot of people who watch golf, especially in the ethnic groups, because of Tiger – he has actively encouraged people from ethnic minorities to follow the sport. I know of many who do so who did not previously and I also know many who have taken up golf because of Tiger Woods. OK, they are not champions like him but he opened the door for them; opened the door for a brand new audience and new participants. An audience who previously may have thought of golf as a rich man's domain, but who were enticed in by Tiger's success and personality.

'Tiger was the first black man in golf to win the Masters

at Augusta, the first to wear the green jacket. If that is not inspiring to youngsters, just what is? In the same way, Lewis has opened the floodgates for ethnic minorities in motor racing, which, like golf, was considered by many to be purely a rich man's sport.'

Ash believes the impact of Lewis Hamilton and the dynamic young Asian boxer, Amir Khan, is already opening up sport to minorities who might otherwise not be drawn in. He said, 'I think Amir Khan is another Lewis Hamilton in the sense that he is an absolute inspiration for the ethnic minorities. Amir is a new modern trailblazer for would-be black boxers in this country, having taken over the path already laid by Prince Naseem, and I strongly believe Lewis will similarly inspire kids from ethnic backgrounds into motor racing. In fact, I think what he has already achieved in the last few months has already inspired a whole generation of young ethnic drivers to compete in motor racing.'

In his forcefully-argued piece Syed also contends that Lewis will probably do nothing to help the lot of deprived black children. That he will, inevitably, become a 'yes-man' to the corporate giants who pay his wages rather than using his undoubtedly privileged position to try to improve the lot of ethnic minorities. Syed cites the example of Michael Jordan as a warning as to how Lewis could turn out; he argues the basketball star showed a 'shocking reluctance' to enter political debate in case it upset the sponsors who indirectly beefed up his massive salary. He claims Jordan could have used his position in his home state of North Carolina to unseat the Republican senator Jesse Helms in 1990. This would have been a noble cause as Helms once helped to create a campaign slogan that read: 'White people, wake up before it is too late. Do you want Negroes working beside you, your wife and your daughters in your mills and factories?'

Syed dismissed Jordan as being politically impotent, saying his response to the chance to get rid of Helms was to dismiss it out of hand: 'Republicans buy sneakers, too' – a reference to his shoe-manufacturing paymasters Nike. It leads *The Times'* journalist to conclude: 'Lewis Hamilton will soon become familiar with the rules of this depressing game. Even now the 22-year-old is being schooled in the art of saying nothing. His handlers recognise that by presenting their client as a blank canvas it will be easier to persuade multinationals to emblazon him with their logos. Like Jordan, he will soon become a walking billboard.'

Again, Ash Hussain has no time for those sentiments, arguing Jordan is given a particularly harsh assessment: 'I disagree with the idea that Jordan did no good – he did a lot for deprived ethnic minority children which has not been reported in the press. He also regularly helps out with children's charities and, of course, he did a film called *Space Jam*, which was aimed at the children's market – and many kids found its theme of achieving freedom inspiring. So just how is Jordan not an inspiration for coloured children? Much of what he does in his life is aimed exactly at helping and encouraging children.'

Syed also claims that, like Tiger, Lewis will be forced to pay lip service to his sponsors. He writes: 'It will be astonishing if Hamilton — a kid from Hertfordshire who has already signed lucrative deals with Vodafone and the watchmaker Tag Heuer — does not follow the example of the man destined to become the world's first billion-dollar sportsman. He will soon become accustomed to having a slick agent or two at his side during interviews, ready to deflect any question that might impact upon the sanitised image of his corporate clients.'

Ash Hussain believes Lewis Hamilton is no one's mouthpiece and that he is a young man of principle who will always say what he believes. He argues should he ever step out of line then his father Anthony will be there to help him: 'I think Lewis is a person who can speak for himself and always will – and the only person who will be at his side through thick and thin will be his dad, not some slick agent. His dad will keep him on the straight and narrow. He has steered him in the right direction so far, so why should things change now? He is a loving dad to him, not domineering, just loving and concerned his boy does not make mistakes.'

Amir Khan also believes Lewis is big enough, strong enough and wise enough to look after himself, and that he will not be taken for a ride by any 'slick-talking agents' or manipulative sponsors. The boxer, from Bolton in Lancashire, also believes that he and Lewis *are* opening doors for kids from ethnic minorities, and indeed all creeds. Amir, who has been car mad since he was a kid and even had motorsport ambitions of his own before he plumped for boxing, said: 'I truly believe Lewis and me are the future of

British sport. We are both pushing the boundaries and keeping alive the British sporting tradition.

'I want the pair of us to inspire young British kids to take part in more sport. And I'm not just talking about boxing and racing, because I think kids will look at us and take up all types of sports. We are natural winners and kids will look at us and say, "I can do that. I could be a winner like Amir and Lewis."'

Ash Hussain also had something to say to those who claimed Lewis was getting carried away by stardom and celebrity, that Pharrell Williams' appearance on the scene and the gradual emergence of other stars in Lewis' camp such as P. Diddy and Beyoncé was symptomatic of such a malaise. He said: 'People are questioning why Lewis is hanging around with people like that as if they are bad guys. But P. Diddy has got a school for deprived children in New York that he funds and Pharrell is a real nice guy. They are not as shallow as some would tell you; they have an altruistic side, and I know Lewis likes them for that as well as their company. I just can't be as cynical as some people seem to be towards Lewis and his friends. At the Goodwood Festival of Speed, Lewis came out and signed autographs in driving rain. He could have gone off home but he spent the whole day there. That is the sort of person he is – he is an ambassador for the sport; he's not just in it for the money or the fame – and he is also an ambassador, and an absolutely fantastic one, for the ethnic minorities.'

One celebrity 'knocked out' by the charms of Lewis Hamilton was renowned Buddhist Maxi Jazz, the singer in

Faithless and a motorsport fanatic. He admitted Lewis had become his hero, saying: 'As a 50-year-old man I never thought I'd have a 22-year-old hero. I met him last year and he shook my hand so hard he crushed it. He is manna from heaven. I want our children to be revering someone other than 50 Cent. To hear about Lewis and his dad's struggle to get somewhere, that's positive.

'The Government should be subsidising karting instead of going on about ASBOS. Kids won't have any energy for joyriding after they've been round the track. There are no affordable facilities for kids. Britain is the home of motor racing and yet we're not doing enough for the future of this sport.'

Writing in the *Observer* before the British Grand Prix at Silverstone in July 2007, Anna Kessel voiced the widely held opinion that Lewis' VIP guests and fans were merely a sign of the remarkable landscape change he was bringing about in Formula One. She said: 'Two weeks ago he appeared on cult urban music channel MTV Base and at Indianapolis hip hop mogul Pharrell Williams and singer Beyoncé hung out with Hamilton's family in the pits. In just four months Formula One has gone from hip – a fashionable playground for the super rich – to hip hop, and the predictions are that Hamilton's stock will yet grow.'

Two journalists from rival black-focus newspapers were quick to back up her belief that Lewis was the best thing in years to happen to Formula One. 'Lewis will be more popular than Tiger Woods,' said Michael Eboda, editor of the *NewNation*, a paper that serves the Afro-Caribbean community. 'He's turning the whole community on to the sport. People are glued to their screens when previously they would never have considered watching Formula One. One of my friends can't even drive and he's calling me up to talk about Lewis.' And Rodney Hinds, sports editor of the *Voice*, said: 'I get emails and phone calls after every race. There's a buzz about Lewis; people who don't know a goalpost from a lamppost are talking about him. He's uniting and exciting people. It's the relate-ability factor. I know Richard Williams [father of Venus and Serena] and he'll be over here around the same time as the British Grand Prix. I wouldn't be surprised if someone from their camp went to meet Lewis.'

The journalist revealed that the *Voice* had applied for Formula One media accreditation for the first time in its history following the news that Lewis would be racing. Yet Hinds admitted some of his friends were still wary of going to races live at the circuits: 'I had a phone call this week from two sisters who have followed Formula One for years. They've done the European circuit but they tell me there are no other black people there. We are the people watching sport via the remote control. We need to get a group down there to show solidarity. But there still remains that thought – how comfortable would we feel at these events? I would love to go to Silverstone and see large numbers of my community watching Lewis Hamilton.'

Three former England footballers – John Barnes, Luther Blissett and Les Ferdinand – were so inspired by Lewis that they set up a project to encourage young people from ethnic and disadvantaged backgrounds to get involved in motorsport. Luther told the *Observer*: 'Lewis is someone I can really identify with as a black man. In England we have a multicultural society, but that is lacking in motorsport, which is elitist and limited in its diversity. There is a lack of black faces, from drivers to mechanics. It was the same in football at one point until myself and Cyrille Regis made it common to see black faces.'

And Les Ferdinand said: 'Black kids are always looking for someone to aspire to and beyond football we have struggled to provide them with someone. Now kids will hear Lewis' story of how he got started, parents might start thinking they'll take their kids karting on the weekends.' Meanwhile, Michael Eboda came up with a vision that, if realised large-scale, could be even more far-reaching – and arguably the most remarkable of all the pluses from Lewis Hamilton's rise to the top: 'The most important thing to come out of this is Hamilton's relationship with his dad. Many of our young black kids don't have that and it may just make some fathers think again.'

Others within the black community were quick to praise Lewis and the way in which he had opened previously closed doors. Ron Shillingford of Operation Black Vote (OBV) said, after Lewis' first Formula One race in Australia: 'We hail the magnificent debut of grand prix sensation Lewis Hamilton who raced to glory on Sunday... For a black kid from humble beginnings just getting a coveted Driver's place was an amazing feat. It doesn't surprise me though because I first featured Lewis in the

Voice 14 years ago when he was embarrassing much older kids, thrashing them in karting races... I remember [his father] Anthony telling me when he was 8 that beaten adults were so astonished they thought Lewis was a midget! They just couldn't believe someone so tiny was so brilliant.' And OBV director Simon Woolley added: 'We're usually carrying negative stories about our community so it's refreshing for OBV to applaud in no uncertain terms the achievement of this talented black man. Lewis deserves nothing but praise.'

The *Voice* also lauded his achievements in a special comment before the British Grand Prix in July 2007, saying: 'The *Voice* celebrates 25 years this year and without question no sportsman or woman has so quickly captured the imagination as Lewis Carl Hamilton. Remember the name, as the rookie Formula One driver looks to replicate the achievements of some of the sport's true greats. Yes, his career is still fledgling and he has lots to learn – in and out of the car. But at a time when black youth grab headlines for negative reasons, here is a young man who quite simply is young, gifted and black... Congrats too should go to Lewis' family and father Anthony in particular, who has been the perfect role model for his own son.'

But the last word on the race issue must go to Lewis himself: 'It's going to be a pain, the whole fame thing, but I'm strong enough to handle it. When I'm at a race now I don't think, "Oh man, I'm the only black guy here!" I noticed it more in karting. On the day Senna died there was another black family at the track. But they weren't doing anything big because they didn't have the money. In karting, because some of the kids were immature, the odd racist thing would pop up. But I channelled my aggression; that's one of my great strengths. I was also taught that the best way to beat them is out on the track.'

Truly a great attitude from a great young man – and a real trailblazer and role model for coloured people in general as well, as those now taking an interest in Formula One. For bringing in newcomers from ethnic minorities who would not normally have taken an interest, as well as thousands of others who had deserted the sport because it had become dull and predictable, motor racing will always owe a mighty debt to Lewis Hamilton. Now let's return to his thrilling debut season and first appearance at Silverstone in front of 85,000 of his adoring home fans at the British Grand Prix...

CHAPTER 14

SILVER LINING

Lewis Hamilton would only realise the full impact of his extraordinary success on the world at large during a warm sunny afternoon in the Northamptonshire countryside at the start of July 2007. The heavens had been opening without relief for what had been a rain-soaked summer, but his return to Britain even brought an end to the mini-monsoon, or so it seemed. The sun shone brightly and everywhere you looked around Silverstone there were smiles.

And why not? The conquering hero was returning home after his exploits in north America. He had left as a minor name, but was returning world famous as the latest member of the celebrity club. It was amazing how a few heady weeks in Canada and the States had transformed his status. Lewis knew he had 'made it' when he appeared pitside after the race and was approached by the man whose crown as the world's most famous sportsman he was now confidently tipped to one day take. Even the king of bling, the comeback kid himself, appeared a mite nervous as he smiled and warmly shook Lewis' hand. David Beckham had certainly met and become friends with bigger worldwide names, but he had probably not come across one so ordinary, 'normal' and humble. His wife Victoria also seemed caught up in the magnetism of the day's star attraction, shaking Lewis' hand as if he were a long-lost friend.

After commiserating with him briefly on his third place finish in the race that day, the couple headed away into the late afternoon sun, but only after telling Lewis that he was always welcome to pop in, should he ever be 'passing through' Los Angeles. It did not go unnoticed that they had deliberately sought out the new star of motor racing, especially as they were actually at the circuit as guests of Honda and former British glory boy Jenson Button, not Lewis and McLaren! Still, even the high-flyers at Honda didn't seem to mind too much – it was, after all, Hamilton's big day. For it was Lewis that the record crowds of the weekend had come to see and he was bringing in the readies that ultimately, if indirectly, paid their wages.

David Beckham said that he thought Lewis was 'brilliant, a star and definite champion in the making' and admitted he had enjoyed the day: 'The atmosphere is breathtaking. It's different to a soccer stadium where fans sit in a very compact space.' And Posh gave her congratulations to Lewis on his win in America, saying he had 'helped prepare the ground' for their imminent move to LA, and admitted the whole day had been 'sexy': 'It was music to the ears and the eyes! To be on the grid just minutes before the race starts, to see those polished cars and the guys get ready – and then hear the noise as they start their engines...'

'Commiserations'... the Beckhams offered Lewis their sympathy – that was another puzzling, ethereal aspect to contemplate as the trucks were loaded and the Formula One circus moved out of Silverstone that Sunday afternoon. Just nine races into his top-level career, and nine podium finishes that had left him 12 points ahead of his nearest rival in the Drivers' Championship, a third place in a debut British Grand Prix was being viewed as failure. The BBC's Andrew Benson summed up the sighs of disappointment that could almost be heard throughout Britain after Lewis trailed in behind Raikkonen and Alonso: 'He denied it, but it looks as if the British Grand Prix opened up the first tiny cracks in the phenomenon that is Lewis Hamilton.'

The *Guardian*'s Alan Henry took a sympathetic line as he considered Lewis' admittedly rather lacklustre performance, proclaiming: 'The Silverstone race reminded the Formula One community of how relatively inexperienced Hamilton is. It was only his ninth grand prix and it was understandable if he were to make the wrong choice when it came to detailed car set-up.' *The Times*' Edward Gorman was much more severe: 'At Silverstone, it was more evident than hitherto the penalty that Hamilton can pay for his lack of experience,' and suggesting Lewis was suffering because of his activities away from the track:

'Hamilton has begun to look tired and perhaps McLaren should rethink his off-track schedule to give him every chance of producing the goods on the track.

'Promotional events for sponsors – sponsors whose logos already cover his driving suit and his car – seem hard to justify, given the historic nature of the prize at stake. Hamilton may also need to reconsider whether mingling with pop stars between races is the best way to preserve his energy for the battles ahead.'

The *Sun* also zoomed in on his off-track, albeit in a less censorious way, with a picture of a Page 3 girl to set off its back page story about Lewis and these nudge-nudge, wink-wink words: 'The reason behind Lewis Hamilton's pit-stop boobs at Silverstone may have been exposed last night – Nicole Baker's 32DD bumpers. Lewis, 22, blamed a couple of errors on his disappointing third place finish in the British Grand Prix. But we can reveal that Nicole's bodywork was the last thing the Formula One ace clapped eyes on before the race. The *Sun* Page Three Idol contestant was representing Lewis as his pit girl when she caught his eye.'

The coverage in the press summed up the level of expectation that now travelled with Lewis Hamilton, the superstar. After Silverstone, he explained in a little more detail just how surprised, and caught unawares, he had been with the massive fan base he now had. He was becoming more in-demand off the track, being snapped out and about with singers and models. And on top of this, past and present drivers now queued up to praise him, as well as team bosses, with Sir Frank Williams describing him as 'superhuman'. This all led Lewis to say: 'It is still a very difficult experience to get used to – I don't believe I have got used to it. It's good that it's always fresh, always new and always exciting for me, and I hope that continues but it has been tough. As for the good things I hear from people like Sir Frank Williams, and all the people in the Formula One world, it's overwhelming.

'When I came into the sport, I came here to do a solid job. There's been a lot of pressure on from day one, but there's not been that many negative comments so I have been able to keep all this positive energy. It's definitely comforting to hear such nice things but having my world turned upside down... I'm very lucky I have good balance and a sense of awareness to get on with my life.'

Traditionally, Britain is a nation that loves to build up its heroes... then knock 'em down with equal fervour. Was that to be Lewis' fate? Some pundits now openly claimed this was the end of the road for the wonderboy's season, that it would all be downhill now. It seemed a harsh, destructive thought process, maybe even based on envy and jealousy. Let's rewind a few days and examine more closely how Lewis coped with his first British Grand Prix in Formula One...

In the build-up to the race it became clear that Lewis was carrying the hopes of a nation on his muscular shoulders. Day after day the newspapers were packed with stories about how he could win on his Formula One debut at Silverstone and items about how he was coping with the new pressures of stardom. Twenty-four hours before he was due to set up camp for the race weekend, he admitted his life had changed dramatically with his newfound fame: 'On Sunday night I was invited to the Princess Diana party (after the memorial concert at Wembley in her honour) but I didn't get back in time. Then I could have gone to the after-party but I was too tired, so I had dinner and went off to bed.

'Then on Monday I was playing golf in Woking and on the ninth tee I got a call saying P. Diddy has invited you to a special dinner. There was me, Pharrell [Williams] and Natasha [Bedingfield], we got in Pharrell's car and took that to an after-party thing. Pharrell got out first and I got out second and, just being a gentleman, seriously, I gave Natasha my hand and helped her out. Then somebody says something and next minute it's all over the place, and I don't even know the woman!'

He said he was coping well with the new stresses of fame and that he was relishing the idea of the race: 'Without a doubt, the British Grand Prix will be the biggest race of the year for me, as it's my debut home race. It is going to be another new experience, and I expect the atmosphere will be incredible. I cannot wait to race in front of my home fans.'

He asked his growing army of fans to be patient, but promised he would do his best to ensure a home victory. 'To win at this race would be immense, but we have to be realistic with our expectations,' he said. 'This is one race out of 17, and as with all the grands prix, I will do my best to win for the fans. But the most important thing for them is to enjoy the whole weekend, whatever the result will be.'

Lewis also went on to explain a little more about how he kept his feet on the ground; how he managed to keep things in perspective and how that ability to turn away from the track helped him when the time came for him to return to it. In a revealing interview with the talented freelance motoring journalist and author Rory Ross in the *Daily Telegraph* magazine, he would say: 'I think I am a fairly normal guy. I love very much being a family man, not just my immediate family, but aunties and uncles and cousins. Every year we meet up to have a big weekend together. I spend a lot of time with my brother, who is my best friend. I gain a lot of energy from my family and friends. I find it hard to trust people, and so I really feel trust needs to be earned. I can count my friends on one hand and I keep those closest to me.

Down to business, he was now camped out at Silverstone on the Thursday before the race; taking a look around the track and enjoying the pre-race laughter with family and the McLaren backroom boys before the serious business began with practice the next day. Jenson Button was asked about that Thursday's hype and what he thought about 'Lewis-mania'. He said, 'He deserves the amount of hype he's been getting. He's doing a great job, leading the Championship by 14 points in his first season. You can say that he's in the best car, which he has been for most of the year. But he's still beating his team-mate, so yeah, he has done a great job and he deserves the credit.'

As if Lewis did not have enough to cope with, there was also the small problem of the so-called 'spy scandal' that rocked the world of Formula One as he prepared to make his home debut. Motor racing's governing body, the FIA, announced they were to launch an investigation into the allegations that Ferrari engineer Nigel Stepney leaked design secrets to McLaren's chief designer Mike Coughlan. There were suggestions that Lewis could be one of the chief losers if the allegations proved true. Bernie Ecclestone was at pains to say he would be unaffected, although McLaren could be docked points: 'It is nothing to do with the driver. They [FIA] have got to prove that if any information was given by Ferrari, it was used. And if it was used, did it affect in any way the performance of the car, and if so where? In that case, they could take away Constructors' points from the team. But there is no way it would affect the driver.'

McLaren chief, Ron Dennis, was quick to defend his team's reputation. 'Personal integrity is important to me,' he said, 'and my company's integrity is more important. This matter does not involve our Company. I am absolutely confident, with the passing of time, that you will see how McLaren's position is one that is reflective of our statements.

'The team has never to my knowledge used other people's intellectual property. That is the key message. We are co-operating with the FIA and with Ferrari, and I have complete confidence in the outcome.'

Clearly he was affected by the revelations – he would even break down in tears as he defended himself and his team. But Lewis refused to allow the matter to affect him… on the surface, at least: 'I have managed to escape all that because of all the events I've been doing this week. I don't even know when it came out. I saw it on the Internet when I had half an hour at home, and I spoke to Ron [Dennis] about it.

'I'm not worried about it. Obviously it's not great, but McLaren have got a huge team so I don't think it's going to make a huge difference. And I don't think it has affected anyone in the team; they are still all completely focused. I think it was a small mistake that someone's made, and I don't really know them very well.

'I don't believe it will have an impact [on the Drivers' title points]. I don't think it will come to that. I've been so busy that I haven't had time to think about it, and it doesn't impact on my job. At the end of the day I have to come here and race the car, and try and win.'

It was a confident outward display, dismissing the issue as if irrelevant. But was there the possibility that it may have adversely affected Lewis during the race? That, as the talk continued about possible points deductions right up until the Sunday, it filtered through even subconsciously? One McLaren insider believes so, and told me: 'The boy had just too much going on by the Sunday; he would have had to be superhuman to have contended with it all and emerge unscathed. He was carrying the hopes of the nation, was expected to be the saviour of Silverstone's future, was expected to win, was expected to see off the challenge of a fired-up Raikkonen and Alonso... And then was also expected to put out of his mind 100 per cent any fears he had about the spy scandal. A scandal, I might add, that brought even the usually "nothing-will-ruffle-me" Ron [Dennis] to tears.

251

'Surely it had to have some effect on a young man like Lewis with everything else that was going on too? The fact he could suffer from no doings of his own?'

In the event, McLaren were cleared at a hearing in Paris a month later, but Lewis would hardly have been human had he not been subconsciously affected by the threat of losing points, or being banned in his debut season because of the scandal. No matter, on the Friday morning he got down to the first serious business of his Silverstone weekend: the first practice session in windy conditions, and it appeared that he had somehow put all the pressures of the week out of his mind. He stormed around the circuit in 1:21.100, the leader of the pack, with Raikkonen just a tenth of a second behind. But in the afternoon session he finished fourth behind Raikkonen, Massa and the surprisingly forgotten figure of the season, Ralf Schumacher.

After that disappointing second session, Lewis remained upbeat, saying: 'It is great to be here at my first home grand prix and to be driving a Vodafone McLaren Mercedes Formula One car in front of all the British supporters. Today has been really positive, and the work we have done seems to be taking us in the right direction. The car feels great to drive around this track, which is one of my favourites, and I am looking forward to the rest of the weekend, where I expect us to remain strong. We gathered a lot of useful data, which we will look at overnight and then continue our work tomorrow.'

He admitted it had been a thrill to roar around Silverstone for the first time in a Formula One car, that he was living the dream and that the reality had turned out to be just as good as he had hoped. Smiling, he almost purred: 'It is an awesome track – it really has always been one of my favourites. Turn one, the first sector, the high-speed corners, the history of the circuit and seeing how many people were there today, especially in the last sector. That's great to see and there are obviously a lot of British flags. So it's very exciting for me.

'I think it is a very physical circuit but extremely technical as well. Especially when it is so windy it makes it even harder to tune the set-up, even more so than on other circuits I have experienced. I go into qualifying with quite a bit of confidence in my car and I really do feel that at least on a single lap we will be quicker than the Ferrari.'

Saturday dawned and Lewis again appeared off the pace, finishing fourth behind Raikkonen, Alonso and Massa – but then the miracle. It seems to me that he works best when the chips are down, when he has something to prove and the pressure is at its most intense. Then, his natural instincts kick in – and so it was in qualifying at Silverstone, when he magically stole pole off Raikkonen, taking the top position on the very last lap of the day. His time of 1m 19.997s sent the crowd, and the nation, into raptures as he beat Raikkonen by 0.102 seconds, with Alonso, who was fastest in the earlier sessions, third on the grid. Massa was fourth.

Lewis knew he had put himself into prime position to win the British Grand Prix at the first attempt. He said: 'That was an intense qualifying session. The Ferraris were extremely quick, as was Fernando. I lost a bit of time on my first flying lap, so I really just had to pull it all out and thankfully I did a sweet job on that last lap. I really couldn't have done it without the team, who changed the tyres so quickly and got me out in time. I just can't wait for tomorrow now, and I am going to do the best job that I can. It is great to see so many supporters; today has been fantastic. I nearly lost my voice – when I came across the line I was screaming just as loud as all the fans. They gave me a real confidence boost with their support; they were great.

'Usually there are pockets of supporters, but here it's the whole grandstand. I can't believe how many people are here today and it's been fantastic.'

Raikkonen could not hide his disappointment at his own showing, but still issued an ominous warning that it would be a different story on race day: 'I made a mistake at the exit of the final corner on my second run in the last session. I finished up slightly on the grass and lost traction, which cost me a lot, cost me too much time. But it's not worth spending too long thinking about it. What's done is done and it cannot be changed. But it's not over yet. We will do our best to bring home the best result possible.'

Alonso also said he was confident he could still win the race despite starting third on the grid. 'I am quite happy with the car,' said the World Champion. 'Obviously I would rather be on pole position but third is the best I could do today and hopefully tomorrow it will pay off and we can overtake people in the race.

'On Friday we tried to work a little bit with the set-up in

terms of race pace to understand how the tyres perform in the long runs. I was not too happy with the car and our pace did not look too good. But overnight we did some changes and I found a completely different car. There's no reason why I now cannot be competitive.'

Both men were to finish ahead of Lewis as their predictions of dominance proved far from idle boasts. Raikkonen, in particular, appeared to be throwing down the gauntlet to Lewis with a drive that was not far off perfection. After winning the first race in Australia at the start of the season, and the one in France, a week before Silverstone, the super Finn became the first driver to notch three wins in the current season.

Lewis was unable to turn his pole position into a win, losing the lead at the first round of pit stops. But his one consolation was that Raikkonen's win meant Alonso ate less into his Drivers' Championship lead. He was now on 70 points: 12 points ahead of his team-mate and 18 in front of Kimi, with Massa fourth, a further point behind. At least he held off Raikkonen as they both hit the first corner, but he was destined to finish third after that disastrous pit stop on Lap 16.

Lewis tried to accelerate off before the crew had finished refuelling; he believed the lollipop was being lifted. It sort of summed up his day: after that he seemed resigned to *not* winning, almost embarking on a rather flat damage limitation exercise. Perhaps it had got to him – the full weight of the day and the expectation of the crowd and the nation for a new hero to cheer them. Then there was the almost-bullying driving of Raikkonen and Alonso in his slipstream prior to the pit stop and the clear fact that Kimi was in a faster car.

In the circumstances damage limitation would not be a bad option. He retained his lead in the fight for the title and finished just one place behind Alonso, who was closest to him. It also meant his podium record as a rookie continued: only Michael Schumacher and Alonso now had more consecutive podium finishes. Schumacher had 19 for Ferrari in 2001-2, while Alonso had 15 for Renault in 2005–6. Lewis joined several drivers on nine and was in position to move ahead of them at the next race: the European Grand Prix on 22 July 2007 at Nürburgring in Germany.

Luck was certainly on his side with Massa's misfortune. Starting from the pit lane after an engine problem, he managed a superb fifth place and, given the quickness of the Ferrari cars that weekend, would surely have beaten Lewis into fourth and ended his run of podium finishes had he had a clear run. Alonso would later make a point of saying that Lewis was 'a lucky boy', that Massa would *definitely* have beaten him into third. Yet that luck was also tempered by the skill of Hamilton in saving his day when he made the mistake in the pits. Although he tried to drive off while refuelling continued, at least he had the skill and guile to hit the brakes and avoid an even worse situation. Remember how his karting pal Nico Rosberg, son of former Formula One champion Keke Rosberg, had suffered when he had accelerated off with the fuel hose still in the petrol tank on the fortieth lap at Indianapolis on 17 June 2007? Lewis said: 'I selected first gear ready to go and thought I saw the lollipop move a little, so I let the clutch out, trying to anticipate it and I was too early.'

Raikkonen was first home in a time of 1:21:43.074 for his twelfth Formula One win of his career, 2.459 seconds ahead of Alonso and 39.373 seconds in front of Lewis. Hamilton saw the race like this: 'I got a good start and tried to pull out a gap, but Kimi was extremely quick. Unfortunately I made a mistake in the pit stop, which obviously lost me a few seconds of valuable time. I tried to push, but continued to struggle with the balance. I tried to drive round the issues, and although I was a bit more consistent towards the end, the team chose to save the engine for the Nürburgring and backed off for a safe third.

'I think that the tyre choice played a big role in the race, and ultimately starting with the harder tyre was not the best way to go as the softer tyre was clearly faster. However, we have come away with more points. I have to say the fans have been tremendous this weekend and the race would have been harder without their support.

'Being on pole I felt quite strongly that we could have had a better result. However, to come to your first home grand prix and still get a podium after difficulties on your second and last stint... I have to look on the bright side, you know. We still have nine podiums in a row and I don't know if that has ever been done, but I'm very happy with that.'

He gave a touching answer when asked if he was using a particular role model to stay cool at the head of the Championship race: 'I don't particularly have a role model anymore because I'm 22 years old. But my brother inspires me because he has always got a smile on his face, no matter what – I think you can learn a lot from that. As I always say, whatever he does – he can't play football like the rest of us, he can't play any type of sport like the rest of us – he still gives it 110 per cent even though it is that tough. I think you can learn so much from that, so he inspires me.'

Ron Dennis confirmed Lewis had been told to save revs and offered praise for Alonso: 'Fernando did a tremendous job making every effort to turn our short fuel middle stint into a race win. Ultimately, both he and Lewis were asked to turn their engines down in order to ensure that we had the best ability to attack again in Germany. We didn't quite have the pace, but both drivers did a great job, and we still went away with valuable points.'

Alonso was sanguine about losing out to Raikkonen: 'Yes, I think second place was the maximum today. I don't know, we lacked two or three tenths [of a second] a lap to Ferrari in the same conditions with the same fuel loads. All weekend it has been like that so there were no surprises in the race. I am happy with the second place.' The Spaniard led the race's middle stages after using a short-fill at his first refuelling stop to race ahead of both Lewis and Kimi, but the ploy did not pay off as Kimi capitalised on a longer second stint to get back in front.

Alonso gave the impression that he could not resist niggling Lewis for surrendering his pole advantage when, after the race, he was asked how McLaren could have held off the Ferrari. Fernando said: 'The only way to win that race was to go from pole – and put some distance between us and the Ferraris.' He added 'Sooner or later I will close up the gap on him [Lewis]. Since Canada I have been faster than him. At Indianapolis I couldn't overtake him, and at Magny-Cours I had that gearbox problem. Here, we had a normal race and I finished over 30 seconds in front of him.

'There are favourable races coming up now, like Germany and Hungary, and the target is to finish ahead of Hamilton and reduce the gap. I must be on the podium always one step higher than him. It's good that the Championship leader has more difficulties on track, and especially here in England and after starting from pole.'

To his credit, Lewis continued to rise above the jibes and the sniping from some press who believed he was 'now being found out'. He also refused to blame anyone but himself for his showing at Silverstone: 'I need to step up my game, which I intend to do. I'm still learning. I have to find time in myself through experience.' He then admitted he had got it wrong with his choice of chassis: 'Obviously we worked extremely hard this weekend. I think we made a wrong decision, or I made a wrong decision with the set-up. I chose a different rear end to Fernando and I think it really caused me problems during the race. Even in qualifying we didn't really have the pace that I should have had, but it was too late by then to change the car. It's a good lesson.' That attitude only served to endear him even more to the pit crew, especially after it was suggested that the man holding the lollipop may have been more to blame for the pit problem.

Alan Henry, writing in the *Guardian*, compared Lewis to Michael Schumacher in his refusal to blame his crew: 'The British Grand Prix was yet another indicator of Hamilton's remarkable maturity and composure. At his first refuelling stop, where he lost 2.5sec, it seemed to some observers that the McLaren mechanic holding the "lollipop" to signal when Lewis should rejoin the race was a little hesitant in warning him not to move prematurely. This may have been a trick of the light but Hamilton willingly took responsibility for the glitch.

'Similarly, when it came to assuming responsibility for the handling imbalance which slowed his car he took full responsibility for its set-up configuration, further strengthening his relationship with his mechanics who work around the clock fettling his machine.'

Alan Henry was spot-on. I spoke to one of the McLaren team and he told me that, yes, they felt a real allegiance to Lewis and that his willingness to take the flak only strengthened that bond: 'It's been one hell of a week, what with the Ferrari situation and Silverstone. If the same thing had happened to Fernando in the pit stop, he would be spitting fire, looking for someone to blame. Lewis took it on the chin as usual and accepted full responsibility. That makes the guys respect him all the more, if that's possible. He's the star of the show but he acts like he's just one of the team.'

Yes, Lewis may have suffered a setback at Silverstone but there was a silver lining... he had strengthened his bond with his crew and proved he could still get among the points even on a relatively bad day at the office. Two days later he proved he was back in business by blowing away the cobwebs of despondency at Spa in Belgium, ahead of Raikkonen and Massa.

The Lewis Hamilton debut season story in Formula One was far from over... on the contrary there were many twists and turns to come as the boy from nowhere battled to put his Silverstone disappointment behind him. Before we move on to the next stage of the season, with races in Germany and Hungary, let's examine another often-debated subject as we've been focusing on the British leg of his debut campaign... So how does Lewis rate among other British motor racing legends, and the man he himself maintains was the No. 1 driver of the modern era, the great Michael Schumacher?

CHAPTER 15

SCHUEY AND THE BRIT PARADE

The build-up to Silverstone led to many pundits being drawn into a debate about just how good a Formula One driver Lewis was, and how good he might become. Also, how, in the grand scheme of things, he compared with former British greats such as Jackie Stewart, Nigel Mansell, Mike Hawthorn, James Hunt, Jim Clark and Graham and Damon Hill. And just how did he measure up against his hero, the seven-times World Champion Michael Schumacher, who chalked up a string of wins at Silverstone during his remarkable career?

Even before his debut Formula One win in Canada Lewis had already made a case to be bracketed among the greats. After finishing second in Monaco, he notched up a total of 38 points in the Driver's Championship. At the same stage in his career, triple World Champion Jackie Stewart had amassed 19 points, Nigel Mansell had none, James Hunt eight, Graham Hill none, while his son Damon had 12, Jim Clark had eight and the first British World Champion, Mike Hawthorn, had 10.

In international terms, he also compared favourably: Michael Schumacher at that stage had four points, Ayrton Senna five, Niki Lauda zero, Alain Prost three, Jack Brabham zero, Alain Prost three and Juan Manuel Fangio had accrued 26. As for the British Grand Prix itself, Lewis would have to wait for that first Formula One win as he finished third on his debut at Silverstone. In comparison, Stirling Moss claimed his maiden victory in the British Grand Prix at Aintree in 1955, beating the great Argentine Fangio by two-tenths of a second. Jackie Stewart won at Silverstone in 1969 by more than a lap after a fascinating duel with Austrian Jochen Rindt and James Hunt triumphed at Brands Hatch in 1976, only to later be disqualified. A first-corner accident seriously damaged his car and, fearing a riot if the British hero was excluded from his home grand prix, he was allowed to participate with his illegally mended car. The race eventually went to Niki Lauda, who finished runner-up.

In 1987 Nigel Mansell was finally taken to the hearts of the British public when he won a mighty duel with team-mate Nelson Piquet. Mansell had been leading, but was forced to pit with 20 laps remaining because of a wheel vibration. When he rejoined the fray he was 20 seconds adrift of the Frenchman, but brilliantly closed the gap in 15 laps and won, after overtaking Piquet at 200mph on Hangar Straight. Seven years later, Damon Hill ended a family jinx by winning at Silverstone. His father Graham never won his home race, but Damon put that right in 1994.

In terms of achievement and winning their first ever grand prix the comparison between Lewis Hamilton and his British predecessors makes interesting reading. Mike Hawthorn won the hearts of the public by becoming the first Brit ever to reach the top of the sport. He started racing in 1950 and made his grand prix debut in 1952. While Lewis would win his first grand prix in his sixth race, Hawthorn would do it in nine while driving for Ferrari in France in 1953. He went on to win three races in 45 starts, earning four poles and six fastest laps along the way. In 1958 he won the world title in the Ferrari 246 Dino, but was tragically killed in a road accident near Guildford on 22 January 1959 just 3 days short of his 30th birthday.

Graham Hill won his first grand prix at the thirty-third attempt. A late starter, he competed in his first F3 race at Brands Hatch in 1953 at the age of 24, Nonetheless, he went on to win the world title in 1962 and 1968. In 176 grands prix he won five times at Monaco among a total of 14 triumphs. He earned 13 poles and 10 fastest laps. Hill was also the only man ever to have won the Triple Crown: the World Championship, the Indianapolis 500 and the Le Mans 24 Hour race. Tragically, he died on 29 November 1975, aged 45, in a plane crash in foggy conditions over Arkley Golf Course in north London. Five members of the Embassy Hill team, including up-and-coming driver Tony Brise, were also killed in the accident.

Jim Clark was another great British driver, winning two

world crowns and also triumphing at the Indy 500. The Scot spent most of his career driving for Lotus and lifted those world titles in 1963 and 1965. He was the best driver of his era with 25 grand prix wins and 33 poles from 72 races. Yet he too would not outpace Lewis in terms of that first grand prix win – it took him 17 races. Jim died at Hockenheim, aged 32, on 17 April 1968 when his Lotus left the track and hit a tree in a Formula Two race.

John Surtees won the Formula One world title in 1964 with Ferrari and he notched up his first grand prix win in his twenty-seventh race. Surtees also won seven World Championships on two wheels between 1956 and 1960, and he remains the only person ever to have won World Championships on both two and four wheels. In 1996, he was inducted into the International Motorsports Hall of Fame. The Federation of International Motorcycling (FIM) honoured him as a Grand Prix Legend in 2003 and he is still involved in single-seater racing cars as the chairman of A1 Team Great Britain. His son Henry competes in the Formula BMW UK series for Carlin Motorsport.

Jackie Stewart would push Lewis close for that quickest Formula One win, triumphing in his eighth grand prix. The triple World Champion (1969, 1971 and 1973) started racing in 1960 and would go on to win 27 of his 99 grands prix. Like Lewis, he had also previously won the F3 crown and raced in Formula Two. Stewart's Formula One record with Tyrrell also included 17 poles and 15 fastest laps. He retired in 1973, but returned with his own racing team, Stewart Grand Prix.

James Hunt won his first grand prix at the thirtieth attempt. He raced in 92 grands prix and won 10 of them, getting the pole in 13 and setting the fastest lap in eight. Initially he raced for Lord Hesketh's independent team, winning the 1975 Dutch Grand Prix at Zandvoort. He then joined McLaren in 1976 as Emerson Fittipaldi's successor, taking the world crown after Niki Lauda was sidelined following his horrific accident at the Nürburgring. Hunt retired and became a much-loved TV commentator, only to die prematurely from a heart attack at the age of 45 on 15 June 1993.

Nigel Mansell was to take an incredible 72 Formula One races in which to record his first win – at Brands Hatch. Yet in 187 starts he eventually claimed 31 wins, 32 poles and 30 fastest laps. Another late starter in the sport, it would also take time for the British public to take him to their hearts. Seemingly over-confident, he was really a rather introverted man. Mansell did not make his Formula One debut for Lotus until 1980, retiring in the Austrian and Dutch grands prix and failing to qualify for the Italian. Yet his 31 grands prix successes placed him behind only arch rivals Alain Prost and Ayrton Senna in the all-time rankings when he finally quit Formula One after winning the world title for Williams in 1992. Only Michael Schumacher has since eclipsed Mansell's number of grands prix wins.

The year after he turned his back on Formula One, Mansell went on to win the Indycar title and ended his racing career in 1998, finishing fourteenth and eleventh in the British Touring Car Championship at Silverstone.

Damon Hill followed his famous father Graham into Formula One, becoming the first son of a World Champion to win the title himself after his brilliant season with Williams in 1996. He won his first grand prix at the thirteenth attempt (in Hungary) and took part in 116 altogether. Out of these, he won 22, took pole in 20 and set 19 fastest laps. He joined Brabham in 1992 for his debut season in Formula One and then moved to Williams after Mansell fell out with Frank Williams at the end of 1992 over money and the prospect of Frenchman Alain Prost joining the Renault-powered team. Williams was reported to have neglected to tell Mansell that Prost had signed for 1993 at only the second race of the 1992 season, in Mexico. Mansell consequently left to join the Newman/Haas CART team in 1993.

Initially Hill played second fiddle to Alain Prost and then Senna. When Senna was killed at Imola, his chance had inadvertently come and he duly won the title. He then joined the Arrows team and finally moved to Jordan, bringing the latter their first grand prix win at Spa in Belgium in 1998. This was his last Formula One win and he retired a year later.

Recent Brits worthy of mention are David Coulthard, Johnny Herbert, Jenson Button and Eddie Irvine. Coulthard was the last Brit to win at Silverstone in 1999 and 2000, and won his first grand prix at the twenty-first attempt. Johnny Herbert – who won at Silverstone in 1995 – won his first grand prix at the seventy-first attempt, while Jenson Button achieved it at the one hundred and thirteenth attempt: in

Hungary in August 2006. Eddie Irvine succeeded at the eighty-second attempt.

Moving on to Lewis' living Formula One idol... Until Hamilton's arrival Michael Schumacher's first full season in Formula One had been deemed the best ever in the sport, with the young German garnering 53 points for Benetton in 1992. He also finished third in the Driver's Championship. 'Schuey' won his first grand prix at the eighteenth attempt; he also competed in part of the previous season. Similarly to Lewis, the young Schumacher grew up in karting, progressing through junior Formula races before making his name in Formula One.

I asked Formula One insider Darren Simpson to provide a rundown and full analysis on how Lewis is shaping up against his hero. His findings make intriguing reading: in some ways the two men have obvious similarities, in others there are striking differences linked to their personalities. Darren told me: 'Lewis Hamilton's performances in his first season are no fluke, and his honesty in the fight is already putting him apart from the greats that have gone before him ... especially Michael Schumacher. Comparisons between Hamilton's arrival and the early impact of Schumacher are now commonplace, but while he may match Schuey's skills, Lewis might have something the seven-times World Champion did not possess: an ability to fight in a less aggressive way and still win the day.

'Schumacher resorted to daring tactics that often led to collisions. His impregnable self-belief made it impossible for him to contemplate defeat, thus legitimising in his mind the use of any conceivable tactic. And by thus intimidating opponents he spread fear.

'Hopefully Hamilton can keep his enemies at bay without them going into the scenery. He has already displayed aggression. Whether Hamilton would buckle in the face of Schumacher's invincibility is, alas, unlikely to ever be put to the test in the cauldron of the Formula One Championship racing. But he would nonetheless relish the challenge.

'When asked which driver from the past he would most like to face, Hamilton replied: "The likes of Juan Manuel Fangio, Alain Prost, Ayrton Senna and Michael Schumacher because I have always wanted to race against him." He then joked, "The year I get here, he bales out – I don't know if I had something to do with that!"

'In the unpredictable world of Formula One, where hype can make or break a driver's career (just ask Jenson Button), is Lewis Hamilton the next truly great driver or a one-hit wonder? It is true that in Formula One, those who go on to achieve a higher level of success announce their arrival with verve rather than a slow build-up. Cast your mind back to Schumacher's first year, qualifying seventh on the grid in Spa on his debut, and generally showing his legendary team-mate Nelson Piquet that there was a new kid on the block and he was not willing to sit patiently and wait for his turn.

'The late, great Ayrton Senna and four-times World Champion Alain Prost also destroyed the competition in their first season before moving on to destroy each other. Hamilton has all the makings of a hero worthy of joining that elite group. He is calm, consistent and hardworking but also has an edge about him – for example, the way he chooses to drive so close to the wall, allowing him to maintain incredible speed coming out of corners. And the kind of tactics that he used in the US Grand Prix against his team-mate Alonso when he used a centre-to-right and then slight right-back to centre defensive overtaking manoeuvre that just about avoided punishment.

'Schumacher, however, was far more precise and rehearsed, using the stealth of a Ninja. His machine-like qualities were developed on the track over many years. Whereas Hamilton, although apparently bursting on the scene as a freshman, had been carefully crafted and tuned from an early age by one man – Ron Dennis – to be a monster the minute he hit the circuit in a tried-and-tested car.

'Comparing the two on their first season results is a bit of a non-starter because Schumacher started in the days when cars were much less computerised with no active suspension and no traction control by way of example, whereas Hamilton has started at a time when cars are almost radio-controlled. This, however, does not detract from his courage, or the natural aggression that all champions are made of.

'But there is an inescapable fact: Hamilton drives like a karter. He loves the edge of the track and takes a late turn in to the hairpin and clips a late apex. In fact, his driving does reflect that of Schuey's early in the German's career. Lots of sharp turn-ins, lots of brake lock-ups... Hamilton displays his lairy youth by pushing himself and his car to the very limit. Driving so close to the wall is a breathtaking tactic while it pays off, but will he, one day, end up in the wall like Senna? Of course, we pray not...

'Only once was the wall a problem for Schumacher, when he broke his leg in 1999 at Silverstone. The rest of the time Schumacher's ruthless "win at any cost" mentality, which on occasions resulted in Formula One driving becoming a contact sport, was the problem. Ask Damon Hill.

'One person I spoke to recently suggested that Lewis, because of his brilliance, is already in danger of becoming boring. He said: "The problem is he may be so successful with metronomic consistency that he may decide never to display the genius driving talents he may already have, or that he may develop in the future. If he wasn't English, we'd be saying he's boring like Sampras."

'Well, if metronomic wins races, then what's the problem? It is a very effective way of winning, especially if all around are being anything but metronomic and throwing their cars off the track. Comparisons to Schumacher are difficult – we really need to see how Lewis is doing in, say five seasons, and then look at them both again. Hamilton has got off to a flying start but he hasn't been a title contender in 12 out of 14 seasons and hasn't turned second-rate teams into World Champions.

'When you compare drivers, you have to take into account everything. How they drove/performed in different cars, different circuits, different situations, against different opponents... Hamilton may be awesome but we have only usually seen him sit coolly at the front of the field. Calm under pressure, yes, but would he be able to handle the rain like Schuey? Can he scythe through the field after a blundered pit stop or spin, or should he have to start from the back of the grid due to some technical issue or rule breach; would he still climb the podium at the end?

'Schuey proved he could do all of those things. We'll only be able to properly compare Hamilton to Schumacher in 10 years' time once all factors can be taken into consideration. The only way to settle the Formula One argument (don't even think about a true contest in the Race of the Champions) would be for them to go head to head in cloned cars on the same track – the young tiger versus the old lion. Sparks would fly and and set the entire Formula One paddock alight.' Indeed they would, but for now the idea of that happening remains a pipe dream, even though Schuey admitted during the 2007 season that he would love to take on the new young whippersnapper.

Let's now return to that thrilling debut season. Our next stop, ironically enough, is a wet weekend in Germany, where Lewis is tested to the extreme, with all the obstacles Darren Simpson has already suggested he might one day have to face and overcome, including a spin and having to start from the back of the grid...

CHAPTER 16

THE FEUD WITH ALONSO

Fernando Alonso would do well to heed that old showbiz maxim: never work with children or animals. Children, in particular... they would soon suss him out. One day I was talking with friends about the ever-developing feud between the Spaniard and his team-mate Lewis Hamilton when my 9-year-old son Frankie piped up: 'He's a bit like Dick Dastardly off *Wacky Races*, isn't he, Dad?'

Well, yes, I suppose he has similar intentions to win at all costs. Only while Dastardly manages to conceal his intent, at least until the end of each cartoon show, Alonso seems unable to do so. After Lewis' debut Formula One win in Montreal his face and body seemed awash with signs of discontent. Yet perhaps he could not see he was getting better treatment than his rookie co-driver, or so many of the British public thought, for although in public Big Ron

Dennis always appeared keen to talk about the parity meted out between his two drivers, that could have been merely to stop the British public getting restless.

If there was parity why did Dennis seem to tell Lewis to back off in Monaco? And why was he always so keen to talk up Alonso's performances? The fact of the matter was that for 25 years Ron had always run a team based on parity. Now he had signed up a double World Champion on break-the-bank wages. If you'd splashed out all that cash on the World Champion, wouldn't you be happy if he won again – and Lewis was runner-up? Wouldn't that be the ideal scenario?

Dennis' problem appeared to stem from an unusual flaw in assessing Lewis Hamilton. In my view, he knew better than anyone that the boy was a winner, but what he hadn't guessed was that he could have been a winner in his first season otherwise, why bring in Alonso to lift the title in the first place? Also, he hadn't counted on Lewis' determination to grab Alonso's crown; again he knew his personality better than most, but he had been left gasping at Hamilton's fierce desire to become World Champion rather than No. 2.

But could Alonso's problem have been altogether more serious: was Lewis Hamilton the better driver? Certainly the results suggested so as we headed towards the European Grand Prix in the Nürburgring on 22 July 2007. The public also seemed to agree and maybe it was that, more than anything, riling Alonso. Despite the outstanding achievement of being double World Champion, he was not receiving the public acclaim such an achievement would normally bring.

Before the Nürburgring, one British Formula One fan, Ade Johnson, succinctly summed it up: 'After heated outbursts from the two-times Formula One World Champion Fernando Alonso, McLaren have a choice to make. Do you keep him in the team, despite the fact that he may disrupt what is going on and the fact that he appears to be off the pace he was setting in 2005 and 2006, or do you sack one of the foremost drivers around? In my view, McLaren would probably be better off dropping Alonso from the team.'

If we study Alonso's behaviour more deeply, though, perhaps he deserves some sympathy for there he was, the outsider in a British team... a British team with a new boy who was not only British, but British and brilliant. Also, Alonso himself was racing under a dark cloud for much of the season and certainly from the French Grand Prix onwards. That weekend, returning from the Magny-Cours circuit to his hotel the night before the race, his preparation was unhinged when he was told that one of his closest friends, Emmanuel Longobardi, had been killed in a helicopter accident.

Naturally, an all-consuming melancholy appears to have swept over him. Certainly, from that weekend on, he seems to have lost a little of his love for the magic of Formula One. When told of the tragic news he admitted he had been left 'a little bit frozen'. Later, he would tell the Spanish newspaper *Diario As* – 'I was with him on Saturday afternoon. I have known him for years and we had a good friendship. He got on a helicopter to go to his hotel and we lost him. This sort of thing makes you think about what we do and what really matters. Really, the most important thing is to wake up every morning and be healthy.'

No doubt about it, Fernando Alonso Díaz is a complex character. Born on 29 July 1981 in Oviedo, north-east Spain, he has what many describe as a typical Latin temperament in that he is emotional and does not believe in keeping things in. Yet away from the circuit he also has a liking for the quiet life: he lives in England, in Oxford, and owns another house near the tranquil shores of Lake Geneva in Switzerland.

He won his first World Driver's Championship in September 2005, at the age of 24 years and 58 days, breaking Emerson Fittipaldi's record of being the youngest Formula One Champion and he is the youngest Double Champion. Yet he can also be a master of manipulation when it suits him. The previous season he played out a brilliant mind games campaign against his Renault backers before the penultimate race of the season in Japan. He spoke to the press about how he felt that Renault were not backing him well enough in his battle with Michael Schumacher for the title, which had the desired effect as the French team moved heaven and earth to help him in Suzuka in October 2006.

Alonso appears to have worked similarly against Lewis Hamilton as the season unfolded, with gentle trickles of complaints about favouritism from the British team for its British driver, building up to more specific allegations and an admission to the *Daily Telegraph* that he has 'never felt totally comfortable'. All this ended in anger by the time of the Hungarian Grand Prix on 5 August 2007 when his tactics saw him thrown five places down the grade from the pole position he had seemingly won.

His apparent discontent began in the build-up to the US Grand Prix. Clearly, he was rankled by Lewis' win in Montreal. McLaren's build-up was dominated by his public sniping on his favourite outlet, Spanish radio, about favouritism within the team. When it came to the crunch Ron Dennis brought both drivers home safely to preserve the points, but from Alonso's point of view the problem was that Hamilton had won again.

Lewis was asked if he was surprised by Alonso's jibes about favouritism. He said: 'I find it strange because I feel that ever since he joined the team, the team have been extremely motivated to push us both towards winning. Ron and the other guys on the team have been working very hard to make sure we have equal opportunity. It's probably always going to be difficult in a business, but obviously I've got a great relationship with all the guys in the team because I've been with them since I was 13. At the end of the day when Fernando came into the team, they were extremely excited and, I feel, built a very good relationship with him. So I don't see why he would say that. But I guess because he is Spanish and I am English, he might feel that way, but I don't agree with it personally.'

And did he think that Alonso had been taken by surprise at his results? 'I doubt very much that he was expecting me to do as well as I have,' Lewis admitted. 'But I don't know whether that's why he would be saying what he's saying. But definitely coming into the team he's the two-times World Champion and he's not really been challenged – well, I think he has [had] some challenges in the past, but not really had probably someone as close as me. So it's a very difficult situation.'

Alonso was also asked the same question. He admitted: 'Yes, and no. I think we knew from the winter tests that Lewis was very quick and was very close times comparing with Pedro [de la Rosa] and me. So no big difference between the three drivers of the team. So, you know, why not fighting for victories, podiums and Championship? But on the other hand, I think it has been a surprise for me, and a surprise for everybody, to see him doing so well and leading the Championship at this point.'

After Indianapolis even McLaren chief executive Martin Whitmarsh seemed to feel obliged to comment on the growing feud: 'Do I expect more speculation about our guys and their relationship? Yes. The reality is both our guys are winners, they want to win. If Fernando got out of the car and said he was delighted Lewis beat him today, I would be very worried. It can be a distraction, but at the moment it isn't. But when you have two competitive drivers they're always going to have a go at each other,' he added.

Lewis did not appear to be letting all these distractions – or the possibility that McLaren might found guilty at the spy scandal tribunal the following week – get to him as he hurtled around the German track for the first practice session on the Friday morning, 20 July. Indeed, although he admitted to suffering from a flu bug, he posted the fastest speed, 1:32:515. But that easy-going atmosphere all changed just 24 hours later as Hamilton crashed with only 5 minutes of qualifying left.

The accident happened just after Lewis set the fastest split time through the first of the track's three sectors. As he peeled into Turn 8 – a 160mph, left-right flick – his right front wheel buckled, and his McLaren MP4-22 darted over the gravel trap and into the tyre wall. For a dreaded moment, the whole of Formula One went quiet, memories of Senna's tragedy coming to mind. Then, as medical crews sped to the scene, Hamilton moved his legs in the cockpit and started to slowly pull himself from the car. He collapsed beside it and it was only when he finally gave a thumbs-up as he was carried away on a stretcher, drip in arm and wearing a neck brace, that everyone breathed a huge sigh of relief.

Later it was revealed that a faulty air gun was to blame for the crash. It failed to correctly locate a wheel nut when Lewis pitted for a fresh set of soft-compound Bridgestones. When he reached Turn 8, the tyre was cut, either by the rim – which could have been damaged through contact with the suspension – or else by a brake duct.

Ron Dennis explained: 'Our telemetry shows that the deflation was absolutely instantaneous. We are analysing the air gun to see which bit failed, but we know for sure that the problem was caused by mechanical rather than human error.' After the Brit's accident the session was stopped and Alonso returned to the pits, only to learn that he too had a loose right-front wheel nut, fitted by the same air gun.

Interviewed later, Lewis managed to put a brave face on it, but the damage was done. Although he would deny it, he must surely have suffered trauma and certainly he was badly shaken up. His crash meant that he was relegated to tenth for the start of the race on the following day. Optimistically, he said, 'I'm absolutely fine and we will see later if I am able to race tomorrow. Everybody has been looking after me really well. We know what caused the accident and I'm just pleased that everything is OK and I really hope I can race tomorrow.'

He would make the date on the Sunday at the Nürburgring after being cleared in a final check-up by FIA doctor Gary Hartstein on the morning of the race. Looking back, it might have been better if he had used the day to rest up and avoid a race it would have taken a miracle to win, or even finish on the podium.

Alonso went on to win an action-packed European Grand Prix, 8.1 seconds ahead of Massa in second, with Mark Webber 57.5 seconds further back in third. For Lewis, it was the end of his podium finishes run as he finished ninth and out of the points. Fernando was just two points behind in the race for the Drivers' title. In slapstick conditions, his third win of the season put him right back in contention to retain his title. Rain had been predicted early in the 60-lap race but it came on the first lap and left the track like a skating rink. Lewis suffered more than most; by the first corner he roared to sixth place and fourth by the second, but was then hit with his first crisis of the day: a puncture.

The monsoon meant race officials red-flagged the event until conditions improved and the drivers returned behind the safety car. Lewis then took a gamble, pulling into the pits to take on dry tyres on Lap 7. But the risk did not pay off, and he slid off the track.

The spin left him with a bank of other competitors on the dirt at the side of the track. To his credit, he was the only one of the beached drivers to keep his engine running. When a crane eventually appeared on the scene and lifted him back on to the track, he could legitimately continue in the race. He then proved just how good he was by trading fastest laps with Massa as he climbed up to eighth by the fifty-third lap. But as the rain returned he needed to go back into the pit for wet tyres, a move which dropped him back behind the Renaults and out of the points.

For Hamilton this had been an extraordinary weekend, one he would admit had been 'good for learning': 'Yes, this was a new experience for me – I made a good start and was sixth, then fourth when the two BMWs went off, then I picked up a puncture. The team took advantage of this and fitted rain tyres, but it just got too slippery and I went off. I managed to keep the engine running and a crane was able to get me free – thank you, Nürburgring marshals!

'After the restart I pushed as much as I could to catch up, but when you are almost a lap down you really have to rely on other people's misfortune. I was able to get ninth in the end, but no points.'

To give him his due, Alonso had driven brilliantly to take maximum points – his overtaking of Massa on Lap 54 was sheer genius and daring; the Spaniard keeping his nerve as his own and the Brazilian's cars touched. Alonso, who previously admitted he loved nothing more than racing in the rain, said: 'It was so exciting to drive, and also to watch, I hope. The first three laps were unbelievable. It was so wet, we were aquaplaning everywhere; it was impossible. Then in the dry the Ferrari was a little bit quicker than us. At one point when I was second I was saying to myself it is not the right time to rain. I was happy with second, Lewis was out of the points – 8 were enough for me. But I like rain – no doubt, I am always quite happy to go and have some fun in it.'

Big Ron was in a buoyant mood: 'This was motor racing at its best. Fernando did a fantastic job demonstrating why he is a double World Champion. First of all, he kept the car on the road during the first downpour. From that moment both him and the team made all the right decisions. However, his second stint following the switch to dry tyres was hampered by a wing adjustment tool failing and as a result he struggled with understeer, but fortunately in his third stop we were able to properly adjust the wing, and from there his pace was fantastic.'

With that, it was on to Hungary... but not without another of Fernando's 'distractions' along the way. This time he was asked to contribute to a magazine's bid to help a charity. *F1 Racing* asked all 22 current Formula One drivers to sketch a picture of their team-mate. Lewis' doodle was a nondescript, but pleasant image of Alonso, while Fernando's work was altogether more pointed. He drew

Lewis in his McLaren leathers and on the right-hand collar he had written the word 'McLaren' and on the left the word 'Boy'. The magazine's executives seemed surprised. In an accompanying caption, they wrote: 'Notice the word "Boy" scrawled by Alonso on Lewis' shoulder...'

The teams started to arrive in Hungary on the Wednesday before a meeting that would explode the notion that Lewis and Fernando were friends rather than mere co-drivers and that the rivalry was purely a figment of a feverish press pack's imagination. By the time the trucks were loaded up on the Sunday night, it was clear that all was far from well in the McLaren camp. Some pundits were even questioning whether Ron Dennis was to blame for the fallout. Shouldn't he have been harder on both drivers and have told them in no uncertain terms that they worked for McLaren, not the other way round?

Upbeat, Lewis arrived at the site of the hot and dusty Hungaroring – the eleventh race out of 17 in what was becoming a thrilling season, thanks in no large part to the warring. Traditionally, it had been a tough circuit for drivers and they would later complain that it was virtually impossible to overtake and that grabbing pole was key to the whole weekend. Given what would happen, those were prophetic words: grim for Alonso, but delightful for Lewis in the final analysis.

The week before the race Lewis and McLaren received a considerable boost when the team was cleared by the FIA, Formula One's governing body, in Paris of any wrongdoing in the espionage affair. An extraordinary hearing of the 25-

strong World Motor Sports Council (WMSC), the sport's highest body, ruled there was no evidence that the British team had benefited from the confidential Ferrari documents found in the possession of their chief designer, Mike Coughlan. On leaving the hearing at the FIA headquarters at the Place de la Concorde, a relieved Ron Dennis said: 'The punishment fits the crime.'

If they had been found guilty, it was feared Lewis faced having points deducted. There was an unpleasant rider on the verdict: the FIA warned that if McLaren was found to have used the information passed to their suspended designer by Ferrari's Nigel Stepney they could still be thrown out of the 2007 season and also banned from the following year's Championship.

For most Formula One observers this was all hard talk for the public domain. In reality they felt McLaren had merely been given a slap on the wrist and that was the end of the matter. Ferrrari, however, refused to see it that way. Fuming, they vowed to appeal and to continue their demand for their chief rivals to be docked points.

But Lewis and McLaren did not believe it would come to that. The spring was back in their collective step as they planned their latest assault on the World Championship at the Hungaroring. However, their problems would not come from outside the camp that weekend; instead they stemmed from tensions within that had been brewing for months and would now boil over with disastrous consequences.

As he met the press on the Thursday ahead of the weekend Lewis smiled. He said: 'I feel quite positive going into the race. I'm still leading the Championship, which I find quite amusing, considering Germany was such a bad weekend.'

The circuit was notoriously difficult to predict. McLaren had won six of the 21 Hungarian Grands Prix to be staged there since the event was added to the Formula One timetable in 1986. Kimi Raikkonen had been their last driver to win there, in 2005, but he was one of five different drivers to have triumphed at the circuit in as many years. Rubens Barrichello (Ferrari) won in 2002, Fernando Alonso (Renault) in 2003, Michael Schumacher (Ferrari) in 2004, Raikkonen in 2005 and Jenson Button (Honda) in 2006. It was into this cauldron of uncertainty that Lewis Hamilton made his Formula One debut on the track, a weekend he would never forget.

In the first practice sessions he was fifth, then started to come to terms with the nuances of the track, moving up to third fastest by Friday afternoon. Memories of the Nürburgring came flashing back as he ended the session by spinning off the track into the gravel. He said afterwards: 'Today went smoothly, apart from my spin towards the end of the second session, which meant that I missed out on my last run, so maybe I could have gone faster. The spin happened as I was catching [Sakon] Yamamoto on a flying lap and I was probably a little too fast going into the corner. Despite this we were able to make some positive steps and I am confident with our performance so far at this track.'

By the end of the third practice session on the Saturday morning Massa was fastest, with Alonso second and Lewis third. But it was to be the calm before a massive storm for

Vodafone McLaren Mercedes. The qualifying session that followed brought out the worst in Lewis and Alonso as both battled for the pole that would likely set either of them up for victory on the Sunday. And yes, in the interests of fair play, it must be said that Lewis was equally out of order on that extraordinary Saturday in Hungary.

At the end of the day, on paper at least, it appeared Alonso had edged out Lewis for pole position. But he had used dubious tactics to do so, remaining in the pits for too long as Lewis sat behind him. It meant he had enough time to complete his final lap, and claim pole, but thwarted his team-mate. Lewis arrived at the start line only to be greeted by the chequered flag. It was a mean trick, but it seemed to have paid off. He would most likely have outpaced Alonso on his final race around the track but it was Alonso who would now start in that all-important pole position. Or so it seemed...

Ron Dennis tried to defuse the tension by explaining that it had been Alonso's turn to benefit from 'the longer fuel burn' and saying Lewis should have slowed to allow him to pass him in the final qualifying session. Dennis said, 'He charged off. That was somewhat disappointing and caused some tensions on the pit wall.'

Certainly, Lewis' part in the events of the day was far from innocent; indeed he should have allowed Alonso past. Later he would admit this, saying: 'I made a mistake – I apologise, it won't happen again.' But equally Alonso should not have blocked him from his final attempt, and, turning to Ron Dennis: if he was quick enough to condemn his rookie driver for his wrong-doing, shouldn't he have been just as swift to deride his double World Champion who surely should have known better? Instead Dennis seemingly tried to defend the indefensible: 'He is under the control of that engineer; he determined when he goes. That's the sequence and if you think that was a deliberate thing, then you can think what you want.'

Yet Big Ron had not been slow in rushing to the engineer to give him a public blasting for not getting Alonso out on the track. Ron did admit, 'There are definite pressures in the team; we make no secret of that – they are very competitive. They both want to win and we are doing our very hardest to balance these pressures. We were part of a process that didn't work today.' Alonso himself claimed: 'The team held me back.'

The incident caused a temporary disagreement between Dennis and the young man he had trained for nine years to become a champion. In a heated post-qualifying exchange Dennis ended up throwing his headphones at the pitwall. Most pundits believed this was over his anger at Alonso impeding Lewis in the pit lane but subsequent analysis of the radio traffic between Dennis and his protégé came up with a different reason. Lewis, angered by the delay, had blamed it on Dennis, allegedly screaming over the team radio: 'Don't ever f****** do that to me again!' Dennis reportedly hit back, blasting: 'Don't ever f****** speak to me like that!' Lewis is said to have responded: 'Go f****** swivel!'

It was an undignified exchange that did neither any favours. Indeed, Dennis later denied it had taken place. But surely Dennis owed it to his team to come down heavily on Alonso for impeding his fellow driver? Instead, it was, rather unusually, left to the FIA to dispense justice. They ruled later on the Saturday, deciding Alonso should forfeit five places on the starting grid – he would start sixth with Lewis on pole. And for not bringing their own justice to the farce, McLaren would also be punished: they would not be allowed to score Constructors' points.

Alonso, Hamilton and Dennis were summoned to an FIA inquiry to explain why the Spaniard had stopped for such a long time. 'The commissioners decided that Alonso unnecessarily interfered with another competitor, Hamilton, and he has been penalised five places on the grid,' said an FIA statement. 'The attitude of the team at the end of qualification was considered prejudicial to the interests of competition and motor racing.'

But Lewis refused to criticise his opponent outright for his delaying tactics: 'There's not really much to say – you saw what happened.' When asked by how long he had missed out on what should have been his final lap, however, he said pointedly: 'About the same amount of time I was held up in the pit stop.'

The morning of the race McLaren released a statement that appeared to put the blame for the delay fairly onto Alonso's shoulders – a U-turn that again did not sit well with Ron Dennis' comments and attitude the previous afternoon. The statement said: 'The process of managing two such exceptional talents as Fernando and Lewis is made more challenging by having a race-winning car. We do not believe that the findings of the stewards and the severe penalty imposed on the team are appropriate. Every effort was made [in qualifying] by the team to maintain our policy of equality. However, in the heat of the battle there are occasions when the competitive nature of drivers sees them deviate from the agreed procedures.

'During this intense and frenetic period of qualifying, decisions are necessarily made in seconds to enable the drivers and the team to position their cars on the track at the optimal moment. We agree with the stewards that, when the team decided to hold Fernando for 20 seconds, there were four cars on the circuit. However, we do not understand the relevance of this observation as the team needed to estimate where all the remaining cars would be in the final minutes of the session.

'Similarly the team does not agree with the statement of the stewards that the 20-second hold caused Lewis to be impeded. Tensions were undeniably high and the problem at Fernando's first stop, the desire to enter a clear track and concerns expressed following the fitting of used tyres undoubtedly contributed to the delay in Fernando's ultimate departure.

'We do not believe that the findings of the stewards and the severe penalty imposed on the team are appropriate, and that our strenuous efforts to maintain the spirit of fair play and equality within the team have been misunderstood.'

Lewis meted out his own punishment to Alonso in the race: leading from start to finish and keeping the brilliant Kimi Raikkonen also at bay. The win meant that he increased his Championship lead over Alonso to seven points. So what looked like a nightmare scenario after final qualifying the previous day ended on a high note.

Lewis said, 'It's been an eventful weekend and quite emotional for all the team. With all the drama that has gone on over the weekend, it would have been easy to lose focus. It's been a bit of a downer for the team.

'It was one of the hardest races I've ever had. Just to get the points is so important for me and for the morale of the team. We've shown that we can beat anyone. We made a really good step forward with a great package but we still weren't sure whether we'd be ahead of the Ferraris. You could see in the race they had great pace. Kimi was on my tail for quite a long time – he drove a great race. But I know how to win races.'

But Alonso wasn't about to be silenced. He finished a credible fourth in the race. Asked if he would be at McLaren in three years' time, he said, enigmatically: 'I don't know.'

Kevin Garside of the *Daily Telegraph* summed up Alonso's comments in this way: 'Cleverly he has allowed questions about his future to hang in the air. If McLaren team principal Ron Dennis believes there is a real danger of the champion slipping through his fingers with two years of a contract still to run, might he not be minded to meet Alonso's demands from the team over the course of a tight run-in?'

When it was his turn to face the cameras, Dennis himself looked like an exhausted man. He seemed full of self-pity and could hardly drum up the enthusiasm to pay tribute to

Lewis for keeping his cool and winning the race. Without a hint of humour, he said: 'When you go through the period in your life from 30 to 60 you often get the expression "character building" but I can tell you at 60 years old I don't need my character building any more. This is extremely challenging for me, emotional and stressful. I'm not alone in having to carry that burden but nevertheless, we will continue to function as a grand prix team with specific values and if anybody does not want to be part of those values, irrespective of where they sit in the organisation, ultimately they all have a choice.'

Alonso did indeed have a choice, as did Lewis, as Ron wearily conceded: 'We have two drivers who are contracted for several years into the future. We will respect our part of that bargain and that part of the situation – we hope that the drivers respect theirs, because that's what a contract is about.'

However, Alonso swiftly responded with: 'What happened was something new for the team. Hamilton not listening, disobeying them, was something they hadn't experienced and I guess they wanted to make him see that. But anyway, in the next race I guess everything will be back to normal and we will both try to win the race.'

Remarkable comments. As much as the race wins it illustrated the power, belief and authority young Lewis Hamilton had brought to the sport. No doubt about it: his personality and success had opened Formula One up to the masses.

On the Monday after Hungary he revealed: 'He [Alonso]

doesn't seem to be speaking to me, so I don't know if he has a problem. If I walk in and I see him then I will speak to him, but I won't go looking for him and make him feel better.' Lewis added, 'I hope he still speaks to me. I'm easy to get on with, I don't hold grudges over anyone – but if he doesn't want to speak to me, then that's for him to decide. But I'm open.'

He also revealed that he and Big Ron were back in business: 'We sat down, we spoke about it and came to a mutual understanding and started with a clean slate. The relationship we have is very strong and something like this is not going to come between us, so we will move on to bigger and better things.'

As the summer break began, the surrogate father and his boy would live to fight another day, but how many more would Alonso survive? He himself could have done with a father figure such as Dennis to help him out. As Lewis took a deserved rest before the next race in Turkey, his double World Champion team-mate was looking more and more like the outsider.

CHAPTER 17

THE FINAL COUNTDOWN

As the final stages of one of the most significant, exciting and fascinating seasons of F1 ever loomed, one thing was clear above all else: that Lewis Hamilton – whether he won the title or not – had certainly come up with the greatest debut season ever in the championship's history, defying his critics and doubters. Everyone wanted a piece of the McLaren maestro: In September 2007, I was talking to an F1 insider who told me that it wasn't only Fernando Alonso who had been offered a way out of McLaren.

Every week during the summer a new angle on the Spaniard's future did the rounds: he might return to Renault, who were desperate to lure him back; he might take a year off; or he might see out his contract! But what of the future for Lewis? It is undeniable that both he and

Anthony had felt peeved at certain stages of the season by the controversy over Alonso – and what many viewed as the apparent lack of backing from Big Ron. But my trusty insider told me there had been another, behind-the-scenes development: that Ferrari had 'through sources' offered the Hamilton camp just over £20million to drive for them for three seasons if he tired of the rivalry which had been in the background – and increasingly in the foreground – since Melbourne in March. All he had to do was let them know…

Lewis at Ferrari: it was an unlikely scenario, but the very fact that it was even being discussed, albeit in whispers, would have done little to ease the pressure Ron Dennis might have felt as the season headed towards its climax. It had been arguably his greatest season for his protégé had come through as he had predicted; but the media's constant speculation over internal politics – and the effects of the dispute with Ferrari – had in some respects taken the shine off.

On the eve of the Turkish Grand Prix, Lewis added to the whispers about his future by admitting he was tempted to quit Britain and begin a new life in Switzerland. He said: 'Every time I go to London, cameras appear from God knows where. I'm definitely contemplating living outside the UK. I've always dreamt of living in London but it's becoming more and more difficult. My whole recent holiday [in the south of France] was in the papers. I was trying to relax, but I couldn't swim, because the cameras were waiting to get 10,000 for the pictures.

'If I can't live a normal life and enjoy my life without

being spread across the tabloids... we'll just have to wait and see. It's down to the media, really.'

In a way they weren't the wisest or best thought-out comments – and they brought the first real criticisms of the boy wonder from the press. The news boys saw it like this: OK, if you want to join Michael Schumacher and Kimi Raikkonen in Switzerland, go ahead and do it. But don't start moaning if you can't take the heat in the kitchen. Ever mindful of the public interest, the press always upbraid a 'star' for complaining of being photographed or asked questions, maintaining that press attention is part of the territory of being a public face.

On that holiday in the south of France, Lewis had been pictured in the sea with Sara Ojjeh, whose father is McLaren co-owner Mansour Ojjeh. Lewis denied that he was in a relationship with her, and it was this aspect of the press coverage that particularly infuriated him. He said 18-year-old Sara was engaged, eager to add: 'I'm not a playboy. I'm supposed to be dating one of the Ojjehs. I'm not. And the other day I went to the cinema with my best friend, his fiancee and my friend Mohammed. They said I was seeing this girl, meaning I'm cheating on someone else. I'm not. It's not me.'

But the talk of him and Sara did finally bring into the open what many had suspected for a while: that he had broken up with long-term girlfriend Jodia Ma. A spokesman for Lewis said: 'Yes, he has split with her, but they remain close.' My contacts in Hong Kong, however, said Jodia was devastated by the break-up. 'She was inconsolable – she really thought they had a future together,' my source said. The previous month, Lewis had been spotted with pop singer Natasha Bedingfield in the back of a taxi, and he was also linked with the glamour model and Celebrity Big Brother contestant Danielle Lloyd, though Lewis denied any romantic involvement with either.

It all seemed to be closing in on the boy who had taken motor racing by storm as he made his way to East Istanbul for the twelfth grand prix of the season. On the Thursday before the race, under a sweltering sun, Lewis took an early look at the 3.34-mile circuit designed by architect, Hermann Tilke – the man behind the new F1 tracks of Malaysia, Bahrain and China. He admitted he liked what he saw and felt he could increase his seven-point lead over Alonso in the title race. His optimism was founded upon his superb drive in GP2 in 2006. Back then, Lewis had sped through the field at the Istanbul Park circuit to take second spot with some daredevil manoeuvring through the field after he had spun off on the second lap.

Tellingly, at the press conference to mark the Turkish Grand Prix of 2007, Felipe Massa would also admit to a personal affection for the track. He said: 'It's a special circuit for me. I got my first pole position, my first victory here last year so it's very special. I like the place, the country, the city and especially the track. It's very challenging for the drivers, so hopefully I can have a great result here on Sunday.'

The brilliant young Brazilian had notched up his first ever GP win at the circuit 12 months earlier – and a similar result on the Sunday in 2007 would ensure him rocketing into contention for the drivers' championship. He was a dark horse who could yet upset the McLaren applecart of Hamilton and Alonso. A good friend of Lewis, probably his best on the F1 circuit, the Brazilian was in a similar boat: he too was seen as the number two to an established star (in his case Raikkonen), and he too was good enough to eclipse his more decorated senior co-driver, having possibly the best mentor in the business, Michael Schumacher. By the Sunday night in Istanbul, Lewis would know for certain that he had more to worry about than just Alonso as Massa once again lived up to expectations.

Talking of Alonso, Massa was asked at the same press conference if he thought the 'problems between the McLaren drivers' would ultimately prove beneficial to himself and Raikkonen at Ferrari. He said: 'I hope so. But I don't know. Actually we don't know exactly what's happened. We know that there's a big competition between the McLaren drivers but there's also a big competition between every driver.'

Certainly, prior to pitching up in Istanbul, McLaren had – at the insistence of Big Ron – held clear-the-air talks between Alonso and Lewis. Lewis explained: 'We're extremely competitive. We can't be best friends. I apologised, he apologised and we said, "Let's just get it over with and get on with the rest of the year." After the last race, everything looked as bad as it could be. But we were not in a war. We met up had a good conversation. Lewis said it was a really constructive meeting, with each driver saying they had no problems with each other.

When questioned about the meeting, Alonso simply said: 'I have a long-term contract with McLaren and at the moment I am not in any hurry to move.'

Ron did not attend the meeting, but said: 'We are leading both championships, and it's tough to have such a difficult situation – albeit such a positive one – but we just have to do our job. The important thing is everybody recognised what their contribution was to the difficult circumstances we had after Hungary and were committed not to allow those things to repeat themselves in the future races.'

The McLaren owner is the first to admit they are very competitive individuals, and their competitiveness will stay on the circuit. From the team perspective he was adamant they would rigidly stick to equality, crossing any further bridges as and when issues arose.

David Coulthard, who spent nine seasons at McLaren, said in public that he was convinced if anyone could keep the two at arm's length it was Ron Dennis, saying: 'Ron is as experienced as any team principal to deal with what happened. I remember watching Prost and Senna, and I am sure [feuds] happened with other McLaren drivers before them.'

Triple World Champion Niki Lauda criticised Alonso. Lauda told BBC Radio 5 Live that the Spaniard should 'stop complaining', adding: 'Alonso is using all kinds of excuses. Instead of complaining, moaning and bitching, Alonso needs to concentrate on driving quicker. My worry is if he continues to find the reasons somewhere else, and not in his right foot, he will lose out because Hamilton is doing a perfect job, simply concentrating on his driving and he's quick. It's what Alonso should do.'

In the first practice session in Istanbul a day later, Alonso seemed to have heeded those words. He finished third, a place ahead of Lewis, but behind Massa and the early pace setter Raikkonen. Lewis had brilliantly turned the tables in the steaming heat at the end of the second session that afternoon – finishing first ahead of Raikkonen, with Massa third fastest and Alonso down to sixth. Alonso said: 'Track conditions were a bit of a problem today. It was slippery this morning when we first went out, but we made some adjustments and that seemed to make a difference. Then this afternoon it was very windy, and we started to suffer a little from understeer, which we will work on overnight. We are definitely among the strongest here, but as expected it will be a tough fight with Kimi and Felipe.'

Lewis added: 'I am happy with the performance so far, especially as the conditions today were not ideal. It is a shame that both sessions were interrupted, however the work we did was productive and we made some good progress.'

The boy from Stevenage was still out in front at the end of practice on Saturday morning, with Massa, Raikkonen and Alonso behind him in that order. Lewis set the fastest time of 1:27.325, bettering Massa by 0.041 seconds and a tenth faster than Kimi Raikkonen, with Alonso four-tenths off the blistering pace.

By the end of qualifying that day, Massa, ominously, had pinched a possible pole off Lewis, clocking the best time of 1:27.329. Lewis would take second place on the grid after notching up a time of 1:27.373, with Raikkonen and Alonso behind him, respectively in third and fourth.

Significantly, during qualifying McLaren had given Lewis and Alonso each a separate pit area, with a separate pit crew, no doubt to avoid any repetition of the problems they had encountered in Hungary when Alonso's car had blocked Lewis in the pit lane. Lewis said: 'They decided it was easier to have two pit crews and it worked out quite well.' That was one of the benefits of racing at a modern circuit like Istanbul – the pitlane and garages are much larger than at older tracks, and thus able to accommodate two sets of mechanics per team if required.

After securing pole, Massa said: 'We have had many tight qualifying sessions this year. Pole position is always difficult. I was pretty competitive for the whole weekend. The balance was right and I just managed to put it together when it counted. It is very difficult to be concentrated and do everything right. We have a good race car but they [McLaren] are going to be very competitive as well.'

Lewis was also pleased with his own outcome: 'Going into qualifying I knew I had the pace. I was quite confident. It is also obviously a positive to finish ahead of

Fernando. He has been improving all the way through.' Though he seemed to lack pace at the beginning, Lewis was very pleased that he was able to pull out the pace and get ahead of Alonso. His GP2 experience and knowing where and how to overtake definitely eased his mind. 'At some tracks you cannot get close enough, here is still tricky but it is possible. We have a good car, a good strategy and I am looking forward to having a good race with these guys.' As ever, Lewis credited his hardworking team, some of whom hadn't taken holidays in order to prepare the car for Turkey.

Alonso was also content despite ending up fourth on the grid. He said: 'I am happy with my qualifying today. I made the decision to go out on prime Bridgestone Potenzas for my final flying lap, but I do not think this was the wrong decision. That final lap was actually quite stressful as our planned timing was for me to run at the very end of the session with only a couple of seconds left to cross the line.'

He got stuck in traffic, so these factors probably played a role in not improving his lap time and coming fourth. No doubt he was also in a fairly good mood after receiving a special gift from Big Ron in recognition of the fact that the race in Istanbul represented his one hundredth grand prix. The Spaniard was given a huge metal scale-model of a 1954 Mercedes-Benz F1 car and smiled when Dennis quipped: 'It's something heavy for him to throw at us!'

The joking stopped the following morning. The tension

was as high as the scorching trackside temperatures. By the end of a tough day for Lewis his lead in the drivers' championship over Alonso had been cut to five points. Lewis had driven well and was on course for a creditable third place finish before suffering a puncture on lap 43, with 15 remaining. It was a cruel blow, especially as Alonso soared past him as he led the McLaren back to the pits for remedial work on his right-front tyre. Credit where it's due: Lewis did well to get the car back to the pits as he still had a third of a lap to manoeuvre it around the circuit. Unfortunately, there was also damage to the aerodynamics at the front of the McLaren. He finished fifth, with Alonso third and Nicklaus Heidfeld fourth.

Alonso trailed in 26.1 seconds behind race winner Massa, who led a Ferrari 1-2 ahead of Kimi Raikkonen – the Iceman finishing 2.2 seconds behind. It was the Brazilian's third win of the season and fifth overall of his career, and it moved him up to third in the standings, ahead of Raikkonen. The result also meant Ferrari had closed the McLaren lead in the constructors' championship to 11 points.

Lewis was defiant afterwards, saying: 'It was just a little bit of a problem. You always have setbacks. I'm still leading by five points. It is not over.' Of the tyre blow-out, he added: 'The team was fantastic all weekend. We had the pace of the Ferraris, but when you are behind you lose a little bit of downforce; we were just matching them for most of the race. I saw some bits fly off the tyre and then it just blew on braking into Turn Nine. It was lucky that I didn't put the car in the gravel and managed to control it back to the pits, as this meant that in the end I only lost two places.'

Norbert Haug, Mercedes Motorsport Director, made a telling point in his analysis of the race: 'It's a shame – the puncture on Lewis' car prevented him from finishing on the podium...however, Lewis saved four important points under very difficult conditions. These points could be decisive in the end.'

Alonso had got lucky – and he knew it. Until the tyre problem, Lewis had once again outdriven the double world champion. Alonso admitted: 'To be overtaken by two cars and find yourself sixth going into the first corner is not great. You just have to wait for the miracle and it only happened with Hamilton. If someone had told me on lap two that I would have been on the podium it would not have been easy to believe.'

It was later pointed out to Lewis that Nigel Mansell's world championship bid was wrecked by a blown tyre in Adelaide in 1986 – with his rival Alain Prost benefiting as Alonso had in Turkey. Did that send shivers down Lewis's spine? No, not at all...'I don't remember it; I was only one at the time!'

The boy who had taken F1 by storm in his debut season was made of sterner stuff. He still had much to do if he were to crown his remarkable feats by winning the championship, but he had changed dramatically as a person. He was tougher and stronger and now had begun to believe himself he could triumph – after months of playing down his hopes. He knew he had his work cut out after Alonso reduced his points deficit from five to three after the Spaniard finished first and Lewis second in Monza. And he admitted he was wary of the final three races in Japan, China and Brazil as he had never raced at any of those circuits, but still felt he could do it, saying: 'It is possible it could go to the final race in Brazil, but I hope not. I hope I get it earlier but at the end of the day it doesn't matter if I get the title earlier or the last race.'

The wonder boy from Stevenage had come of age; the era of Lewis Hamilton was truly upon us. Now just watch him complete the fairytale by dominating F1 for the next 10 years...